TOKUGAWA JAPAN

TOKUGAWA JAPAN

The Social and Economic Antecedents of Modern Japan

Edited by

Chie Nakane and Shinzaburō Ōishi

Translation edited by

Conrad Totman

UNIVERSITY OF TOKYO PRESS

Translation supported by grants from IBM Japan and the Japan Foundation.

99 98 97   6 5 4

Contents

Foreword

CONRAD TOTMAN

This volume brings to readers of English some of the recent scholarly work of several distinguished Japanese scholars. The essays were originally prepared in Japanese for a symposium that explored Tokugawa antecedents of modern Japan, and Chie Nakane's Introduction adumbrates the ways in which the essays, as translated here, highlight aspects of Tokugawa society that helped shape the character of modern Japan. As the book's title implies, however, the essays do more than simply identify facets of the early modern experience that relate to recent developments. They also give readers access to aspects of Tokugawa society that have not hitherto been available in English.

Shinzaburō Ōishi's overview of the political system's formation conveys nicely a sense of the diverse considerations and piecemeal moves that step by step ended domestic turmoil and gave the early modern polity its stabilized form.

Tsuneo Satō, in a tour de force that is remarkable for both conciseness and breadth of coverage, describes how rural society was organized, how villagers worked and lived, and how the conditions of their existence changed as the generations passed.

Satoru Nakamura examines the evolution of the cotton industry, using it to illustrate long-term patterns of change that characterized the rural economy as a whole.

Katsuhisa Moriya offers a lively introduction to the variegated urban world of the Tokugawa period, the dynamic messenger systems that linked cities and towns, and the vital publishing industry that produced the myriad written materials demanded by an omnivorous reading public.

Hidenobu Jinnai takes readers on an elegant tour of Edo, from the bustling waterfronts and waterways so crucial to the urban hoi polloi to the gracious mansions and disciplined neighborhoods occupied by the ruling samurai class.

Yōtarō Sakudō examines the rise and evolution of early modern merchant families and describes the business organization and ideology of such great business families as the Mitsui and Sumitomo.

Tatsurō Akai examines the popular treatment of religious paintings and the character and uses of ukiyo art to illustrate the lively public interest and the decisive role of commoners in paintings of the Tokugawa period.

Masakatsu Gunji provides a remarkably rich and revealing picture of the world of kabuki and of its development and vicissitudes from the early seventeenth to late nineteenth centuries, finding in that experience reflections of the changing times and of Tokugawa society's gradual decay.

In a closing essay, Chie Nakane skillfully casts a wide net to outline concisely and boldly the essential characteristics of Tokugawa social structure and to indicate their enduring influence on modern Japan.

Many people deserve thanks for the publication of this volume. The authors were patiently understanding of the need for flexibility in translation so that materials originally addressed to a Japanese audience could be refashioned enough to reach a foreign readership. The several scholars who prepared the original translations, each identified at the end of the essay he or she translated, handled their tasks in a thoroughly professional manner and still made deadlines as requested. And finally, the professional staff at the University of Tokyo Press was patient in dealing with solving numerous problems as they arose.

TOKUGAWA JAPAN

Introduction

CHIE NAKANE

In sharp contrast to the medieval period which preceded it, the nearly three-hundred-year Tokugawa period, referred to as the Kinsei or early modern period, was marked by a highly organized administrative system and economic development based on an unprecedented level of agricultural productivity. This is the period in which Japan's distinctive culture attained its apex. The abundance of surviving historical records, right down to the local level, makes this one of the periods most studied by Japanese historians. It is of interest not only for its own sake, but because it provides valuable insights into the country's modernization and why Japan is what it is today. The process of development since the Meiji period is cited to explain Japan's global economic stature today, and it also is considered an experience relevant to modernizing societies, but it is important to realize that the groundwork for this process was laid in the Tokugawa period.

Three times, in 1983, 1984, and 1985, the contributors to this volume held symposia sponsored by IBM Japan, on the theme "The Tokugawa Period and Modernization," and a comprehensive record of the sessions, including the papers presented and the discussions that followed, was published as *Edo jidai to kindaika* [The Tokugawa Period and Modernization] (Tokyo: Chikuma Shobō, 1986). Our aim with the present publication is to share our findings with readers overseas. Unlike the original Japanese version, however, this book does not take the form of a symposium proceedings, but has been edited with the intent of presenting the fundamental character and specific features of the Tokugawa period as they relate to Japan's modernization.

The immense volume of research on the Tokugawa period is

dominated by publications and dissertations of finely detailed historical inquiry that are nearly inaccessible to the nonspecialist. Furthermore, polity, economy, and culture are normally treated as separate and isolated foci of study, making it difficult to acquire a comprehensive grasp of the period's fundamental character. Not being a specialist in the period myself, I have long wished for a full-scale presentation of the period that would be useful in making comparative studies. Through the series of symposia in which I happened to be one of the organizers, I have been able to gain a vivid picture of the period as would never have been possible by reading books limited to overviews. Anxious to impart this image to as many readers as possible in other countries, we have sought in this book to present a coherent introduction to the Tokugawa period based on the symposium proceedings.

The contributors to this book, selected from among the symposia participants, are all historians specializing in the Tokugawa period. They were asked to write on their particular areas of expertise, based on the findings of the symposia and their long years of research and accumulation of reference materials. I believe this has resulted in something much more than a simple overview, offering a lively account of the Tokugawa period replete with specific examples and highlights of its major aspects.

The first chapter on the Tokugawa political structure (bakuhan taisei), which more than anything else shaped the period, was prepared by the foremost scholar of Tokugawa history, Ōishi Shinzaburō. His description of the process by which the bakuhan structure was formed and the features to which it gave rise is buttressed by concrete detail.

Chapters two and three focus on the peasantry, which accounted for 80 percent of the population and are the subject of the bulk of Tokugawa research. Basing his explanation on village-level historical records, Tsuneo Satō analyzes the farming village in terms of the bakuhan structure's control of the peasantry, rural administration, and agricultural techniques.

In the Tokugawa occupational stratification of society into the four status groups of samurai, peasant, artisan, and merchant, the peasants in the villages were set apart from the others who resided in town. It is easy to suppose, therefore, that the agricultural population lived in a world quite unlike that of artisans and merchants, but in actuality, the period saw pronounced developments in village industry as well as urban growth due to the emergence of a nation-wide network of commerce. In his discussion of village industry, Tetsu Nakamura suggests that at the beginning of the eighteenth century, the low wages that could be paid in farming villages attracted industry, and by the late eighteenth and early nineteenth centuries, village industries had reached an early stage of capitalism. This, in his view, was one of the historical prerequisites to Japan's development as a capitalist nation after it opened its doors to the world.

Chapters four through eight deal with the economic, social, and cultural features of Tokugawa urban life. Katsuhisa Moriya notes the existence of more than two hundred castle towns, forty large port towns, and many communities clustered around famous temples and shrines in addition to the three great cities of Kyoto, Osaka, and Edo—respectively, the period's cultural, economic, and political centers—and stresses their function as interconnecting points in a remarkable nationwide transportation and information network. He sees this network as the foundation of modern Japan.

Hidenobu Jinnai, whose essay furnishes a detailed examination of Edo, a city of one million residents, reveals the distinctive features of the early modern political center.

Yōtarō Sakudō deals with merchant house management, analyzing the three major Tokugawa merchant houses of Kōnoike, Sumitomo, and Mitsui. He perceives the roots of contemporary Japanese management practices in the organization and concepts of these houses, particularly noting that in Mitsui's case, a prototype of the zaibatsu had already formed in the Tokugawa period.

It hardly needs to be mentioned that kabuki and ukiyo-e, two well-known examples of traditional Japanese culture, are products of the Tokugawa period. Masakatsu Gunji's chapter on kabuki and Tatsurō Akai's on painting describe the social context within which these arts developed and how they were received by people of the day. These papers reveal clearly that kabuki and ukiyo-e belonged to the world of the townspeople and the common masses more generally, with the samurai, in contrast, playing only a passive role in their development. Indeed, samurai authorities issued a constant stream of regulations limiting, and sometimes prohibiting, the activities of the kabuki theater and its actors. At one point, the Edo magistrates issued a ban directed at the print sellers guild, forbidding it to market prints of actors, prostitutes, and geisha as a corrupting influence on public morals. According to the Confucian ethics of the ruling samurai, these cultural pursuits were to be discouraged.

Despite this government stance, however, kabuki and ukiyo-e remained popular among the common people, whose fun-loving vitality comes alive in Gunji and Akai's writings. Moriya, in his essay, refers to the high literacy rate among Tokugawa commoners and reports that during the course of the eighteenth century, bookstores (which were also publishing houses) numbered 536 in Kyoto, 564 in Osaka, and 493 in Edo. With this active publishing of prints and novels, according to Akai, by the middle of the century nearly all the common people in Edo owned copies of ukiyo-e prints and popular novels.

Even some among the samurai purported to enjoy the popular culture. "Manners are normally something learned from above, but these days it is the manners of the common people that are being transferred to the elite," is a quote from a Tokugawa-period document selected by Akai. Thus, in early modern Japan, these elements representative of traditional culture were developed almost entirely by the common people rather than under the patronage of a wealthy upper class, as was the case in European societies of the time. A wealthy upper class, such as that of Western Europe, India, or China, did not form in Tokugawa Japan despite its affluent economy. The samurai class, while ranked at the top of the social hierarchy, was by no means wealthy. Most samurai possessed no land of their own and depended on stipends measured in *koku* of rice. Rather, wealth rested in the hands of the larger merchant houses. By the late Tokugawa period, the number of poor, low-ranking samurai had increased, and even the regional barons, or daimyo, were forced to borrow money from merchants. This legacy surely fostered the tendency in modern Japan in which no single class controls both wealth and power.

In the chapter on social structure, I discuss key structural features of the society as a whole, drawing on the preceding chapters and bearing in mind the situation of other Asian societies. That basic social organization persists even today, so one can claim that the major political and institutional changes that took place in the Meiji period had no vital effect on the underlying social base. This is most evident in the village community, which, at least until around 1960, remained essentially unchanged from the Tokugawa period. In fact, it is easy in villages where records remain intact to trace histories back to Tokugawa times using data collected in fieldwork conducted around 1960. The description of a Tokugawa farming village in my chapter is based on sociological research and is corroborated in part by Satō's historical examination in Chapter Two.

All in all, it is clear that the almost-three-hundred-year Tokugawa era was by no means a static "feudal" period in Japanese history. Rather, it was a time of remarkably active development and preparation for the subsequent era of modernization. The political stability that followed consolidation of political and administrative systems in the first half of the eighteenth century, together with concurrent economic growth marked by conspicuous advances in commerce and village industry, underlay the maturing of the society. In government, bureaucracy emerged, and in the village, the institution of the *ie* (household) as the basic social unit. The village functioned as a clearly defined organizational body, and the structure and doctrine of the merchant house was codified into the prototype of present-day Japanese management. Finally, the traditional performing arts that are still practiced today made rapid advances in the nurturing medium of popular Tokugawa culture. In all these aspects of the period, we can see the formation of Japanese values and social structures that continue to exist today. It is thus evident that, despite the major upheaval of the Meiji Restoration and the modernization process that followed, society has experienced no fundamental structural change.

What were the factors contributing to the maturation of society in the Tokugawa period, and why are the values and social structure of this period still evident today? Certainly, Japan's limited natural resources and homogeneous society have something to do with this. For one thing, the nation as a whole had reached, by the latter half of Tokugawa, the limits of growth possible with the technology of the day. Because it was an insular nation, and one completely covered by a single administrative system, Tokugawa Japan experienced such rapid technological advancement that there were no more frontiers left in either agriculture or commerce and the nation became bottled up within itself.

A look at other societies of the same period shows that in southeast Asia, the rate of population increase was very low, and development of technology and commerce insignificant. In China and India, where technology was further along and population increase rapid, the fact of their being continental societies ensured that there were always new frontiers to be explored in agriculture and commerce. Although the societies of Europe no longer had frontiers for expansion, their peoples could emigrate to other countries. The Tokugawa policy of forbidding Japanese to go abroad did not make this an option for the people. Elsewhere it was not uncommon for merchants to transcend political boundaries in their activities, but in Tokugawa Japan where administrative control was thorough and far-reaching, merchants, with very few exceptions, were compelled to conduct their business within the boundaries imposed by the government.

Given these conditions, the possibilities for expansion in any field were extremely limited. The size of the pie was essentially fixed and in most circumstances the only way to enlarge one's portion was to lessen another's. Thus, emphasis was placed on vested interests, competition was severe, and not surprisingly a value system emerged in which hard work was deemed a virtue. Mechanisms for ranking and categorizing, which ensure stability, proved to be highly effective in preventing unprofitable confusion and strife. The principle of succession by the eldest son—that is, by birth order rather than personal qualifications—whether in the shogunal line or a common household, is one example of how this mechanism worked. Ōishi's essay refers to the establishment of succession by the first-born as a means of stabilizing Tokugawa rule and also notes as another feature supporting the Tokugawa system the organizational principle by which the level of one's official position in government corresponded to one's household status.

Household status was predetermined, and only those from households with the proper status could aspire to certain positions. Talent and good fortune were secondary considerations. The same principle was followed in farming villages, as noted in the last chapter, where only those from households with appropriate status were allowed to become village officials. Household status was important among merchants as well. Gunji points out that even among actors there was a system of ranking, and after the eighteenth century,

household status was especially emphasized, making it difficult
even for those with talent to get very far without the proper background. Over time, the appellations of rank used by actors were
widely adopted by artists, scholars, and others in a variety of fields
to emphasize distinctions, similar to the *honbyakushō* and *mizunomi*
classifications of peasants referred to in chapters two and four.

The stable hierarchy of status in every field created by this system compromised possibilities for the development of a merit system. The propensity to rank, which is a consciousness of differences
in status, is still evident today in various areas of Japanese society.
Businesses within a single industry are ranked, schools are ranked,
and within various organizations, members are ranked according to
when they joined the group (for employees this means seniority
determined by date of hire). These systems of ranking have not
determined everything since Tokugawa, but they have been given
priority in principle. Still, they have served as a stabilizing element
in society, preventing it from becoming overly competitive.

The Tokugawa period was thus a time of social as well as political
institutionalization. Rather than being the result of specific administrative policies, however, this institutionalization was based on factors present from much earlier times which emerged to take distinct
form in the Tokugawa period when conditions were favorable. Elements characteristic of the period that are still evident today are
thus features that have been adapted to meet current conditions
rather than simply remnants of Tokugawa institutions. Unlike in the
Tokugawa period, Japan today is open to the rest of the world and
has made marked advances in technology. Yet Japanese society still
consists of a homogeneous people sharing a long history and common culture. The continuity of the society is compelling testimony
to all that has been discussed thus far.

The Tokugawa period laid the groundwork for Japan's modernization. It is, as well, a period in history from which much can be
learned about Japanese values and social structures.

(Translation by Susan Murata)

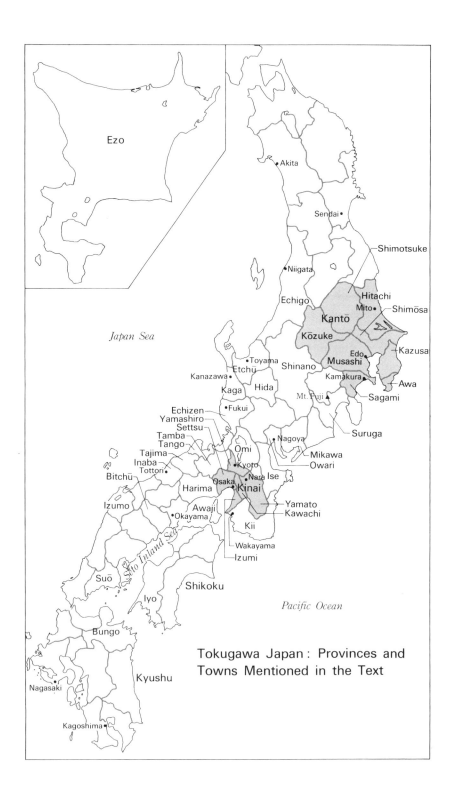

Ezo

•Akita

Sendai•

Shimotsuke

•Niigata

Echigo

Hitachi
Mito•
Shimōsa
Kantō
Kōzuke
Kazusa
Edo•
Musashi
•Toyama
Etchū Shinano
Kanazawa•
Kamakura•
Awa
Kaga Hida
Mt. Fuji▲
Sagami
Echizen
Yamashiro
Settsu
Suruga
Tamba
Tango
•Nagoya
Tajima
Omi
Mikawa
Inaba
•Fukui
Owari
•Tottori
•Kyoto
Bitchū
Nara Ise
Harima
Osaka•
Kinai
Izumo
Awaji
Yamato
•Okayama
Kawachi
Kii
Suō
Wakayama
Izumi
Iyo
Shikoku
Japan Sea
Pacific Ocean
Bungo
Seto Inland Sea
Tokugawa Japan : Provinces and
Towns Mentioned in the Text
Kyushu
Nagasaki•
Kagoshima•

Chapter One

The Bakuhan System

SHINZABURŌ ŌISHI

The epoch known as early modern society is one stage in a general historical periodization that divides Japanese history into ancient, medieval, early modern, and modern eras. It covers the three hundred years from 1568 when Oda Nobunaga, aspiring to unify the country, entered Kyoto, home of the emperor and the Ashikaga shogun, to 1867 when the Tokugawa bakufu fell. Specifically, the 265 years after 1603, when Tokugawa Ieyasu established the bakufu, or military government, in Edo, are referred to as the Tokugawa or Edo period. In other words, early modern society encompasses the thirty-five years when Oda Nobunaga and Toyotomi Hideyoshi wielded political power and the subsequent 265 years of Tokugawa rule. In the political system of periodization, the period is also known as Edo, which like the Nara, Heian, Kamakura, and Muromachi periods derives from the practice of distinguishing historical eras in terms of the geographical location of the ruling authorities.

1. The Historical Roles Played by Nobunaga, Hideyoshi, and Ieyasu

The Muromachi period is so called because the Ashikaga shogun, wielder of political authority, resided in the Muromachi section of Kyoto. During this period, members of the Ashikaga family struggled over succession to the shogunal title, and in 1467 the powerful barons (known as *shugo*, or constable daimyo) who served as pillars of the political system split into two factions and launched a divisive power struggle. The massive civil strife fragmented political control, drastically weakening the authority of both shogunate and constable daimyo. Soon the country was plunged into the era of warring states in which regional feudal lords contended for power. This period lasted for approximately one hundred years, with regional lords repeatedly rising and falling. By the mid-sixteenth century, only a small number of constable daimyo, such as the Gohōjō, Uesugi, Takeda, Imagawa, Oda, Mōri, Ōtomo, and Shimazu, survived on domains scattered from the northeast to southern Kyūshū, and they ceaselessly struggled with each other, hoping to bring the nation under their own control.

The regional lord who moved ahead of the pack was Oda Nobunaga. The Oda family served as deputy constable under the Shiba, constable of Owari province. Shiba, like almost all of the constable daimyo, resided in Kyoto, while the deputy constable remained in the domain and served as executive officer on the spot. As a result, Oda Nobunaga began to strengthen his control over Owari. After he defeated Imagawa Yoshimoto, the major regional lord of the Tōkaidō area, in the battle of Okehazama in 1560, he rapidly expanded his power. Proclaiming his loyalty to the shogun, Ashikaga Yoshiaki, Nobunaga soon entered Kyoto. In 1576, he constructed a mighty castle at Azuchi and launched his campaign to unify the country, hoisting a banner emblazoned with the words *Tenka fubu*, "Extension of Military Rule throughout the Land." But in 1582 he was slain by his vassal, Akechi Mitsuhide, at Honnōji temple.

Although death ended Nobunaga's plan for national unification, his achievements were many, adding up to the complete destruction of the social order that had been in existence from the Nara and Heian periods. At the core of this process was his head-on confrontation with Buddhist temple forces that were not only spiritual leaders but also secular overlords. Among the actions he took against Buddhist forces were the destruction by fire of the venerable temple, Enryakuji, on Mt. Hiei just northeast of Kyoto, and an all-out campaign against uprisings by the religious orders of the Ikkō sect, which had extended their influence widely among villages throughout the land. Earlier, he had welcomed the arrival of Christianity, not only because he saw the religion as the bearer of new objects like the musket, but also because he believed it could help him suppress Buddhist forces.

Another of Nobunaga's accomplishments was the elimination of guilds (*za*), which had been used by such traditional wielders of power as temples, shrines, and aristocrats to maintain their monopolistic control over commerce. In their place, he supported open-market arrangements (*raku-ichi, rakuza*) that enabled people to engage freely in the production and sale of goods. He also abolished in many areas the checkpoints (*sekisho*) that had hindered free flow of goods, thus establishing the early modern commercial marketplace.

In Nobunaga's time, the commodities that had the widest commercial circulation were grains, such as rice and wheat. In transactions they were measured with measuring boxes (*masu*), but the size of the boxes was not uniform. Boxes that nominally held one *shō* of grain actually differed greatly in capacity. For example, the *masu* used by a feudal lord to calculate the rice tax he received from peasants (known as the tax collection *masu*) differed significantly from the *masu* he used to calculate his own payments (known as payment *masu*).

Without a uniform system of grain measurement, the extent of economic growth could not be calculated accurately. Nobunaga sought to achieve uniformity by designating the *masu* then used by merchants in the Kyoto vicinity as a standard grain measure, the *kyō-masu*. Toyotomi Hideyoshi completed the process of standardizing by making the *kyō-masu* the official unit for measuring rice throughout the land. With the adoption of a uniform measure, the system of calculating rice production in terms of the *koku* was introduced nationwide. By this system (the *kokudaka* system), a daimyo who is referred to as a 100,000-*koku* lord is one who rules a domain that produces 100,000 *koku* of rice, as measured by the *kyō-masu* standard. Needless to say, Tokugawa Ieyasu retained this system.

Compared to Nobunaga and Ieyasu, Hideyoshi came from an extremely humble social background. The common view that he was a child of a lowly peasant in the village of Nakamura in Owari is probably stretching the truth a bit. That he came from the lowest rank of the samurai class is probably closer to the truth. He could not get along with his stepfather and left home as a youngster and experienced much hardship. He thus became streetwise about human nature and acquired a unique ability to win over the hearts of people. He rose rapidly as Nobunaga's follower. When Nobunaga

was killed by Akechi Mitsuhide in 1582, Hideyoshi returned from
his campaign in the Chūgoku region (western Honshū), engaged
Mitsuhide in battle at Yamasaki in Kyoto, and slew him. He then
defeated his rivals, Oda Nobutaka and Shibata Katsuie, in the
struggle for supremacy after Nobunaga's death.

At this time, Nobunaga's ally, Tokugawa Ieyasu, was extending
his power from his home base in Mikawa into neighboring regions.
In 1584, however, he came up against Hideyoshi at the indecisive
battles of Komaki and Nagakute and, after some negotiations,
agreed to submit to his authority. Hideyoshi then went on to defeat
the Chōsokabe in Shikoku in 1585, the Shimazu in Kyushu two
years later, and in 1590 the Gohōjō of Odawara, thus completing
the task of national unification. One would have expected him at
that point to concentrate on strengthening the internal political
order, but almost before taking up this task he sought to realize his
dream of building an empire that would encompass all of continental China. He launched two reckless invasions of the Korean penin-
sula and in 1598 died at the age of sixty-three amidst reports of
military defeats in the Korean campaign.

Besides completing Nobunaga's policy of unifying the country,
Hideyoshi also adopted his economic policies, refining them and
applying them throughout the land. Among these policies were the
extension of open-market arrangements, the minting of a currency
for use throughout the land (the large and small gold coins of the
Tenshō era), and the systematizing of foreign trade (the licensing of
vessels engaged in foreign trade with documents stamped with red
seals).

The most significant of Hideyoshi's policies was the nationwide
cadastral survey (known as the Taikō Kenchi) that he conducted
using a uniform standard of measurement. The survey not only
shaped the foundation of feudal landholding but also facilitated the
separation of military and peasant classes, thus expediting the formation of feudal class distinctions. Needless to say, the *kyō-masu* was
used nationwide as the standard measure in implementing the land
survey.

A popular ditty goes, "Oda pounds the national rice cake,
Hideyoshi kneads it, and in the end Ieyasu sits down and eats it." It
was Tokugawa Ieyasu who inherited and made peaceful the land
that Nobunaga and Hideyoshi had unified. Ieyasu was born heir to

the lord of Okazaki Castle, a military chief who, as head of the Matsudaira family, wielded power in the heart of Mikawa province. To the east were the Imagawa of Suruga; to the west, the Oda of Owari. Hemmed in by these two powerful daimyo, the Matsudaira were subject to constant pressure from them, with the consequence that Ieyasu served as a child hostage first to the Oda and then to the Imagawa. He also experienced domestic misfortune: he lost his mother early in life, and when he was seven, his father was slain by a vassal during an internal family conflict.

Even as a youngster, then, Ieyasu had to worry about how to sustain the Matsudaira family and strengthen its position. From his youth, therefore, he concentrated his thoughts on the problem of how to maintain and expand the political system. In this respect, the difficulties that confronted him differed greatly from Toyotomi Hideyoshi's troubles, which had to do with sustaining his daily existence and dealing in general with human relationships. Hideyoshi's daily experience had little to do with theories of political organization, such as how to establish tranquillity in the land over which he had gained control. This truly was Ieyasu's primary concern. It was Tokugawa Ieyasu, then, who succeeded as the ruler of the land unified by Nobunaga and Hideyoshi. He consolidated order throughout the land, thereby inaugurating the Tokugawa period and its 265 years of peace. And the organization of the baku-han system, with the bakufu as the central government of a federation of over 270 daimyo domains (*han*), provided the political and administrative framework with which the Tokugawa shogunate held power.

2. Why the Forces for National Unification Emerged from Owari and Mikawa

Of the three leaders who created the early modern society of Japan, Nobunaga and Hideyoshi emerged from the central region of Owari, while Ieyasu emerged from the heartland of Mikawa. One might ask why early modern Japanese society emerged from the Owari-Mikawa region. There is no simple answer, but one might address the issue in the following way.

History does not progress in a linear fashion. Nor do changes in

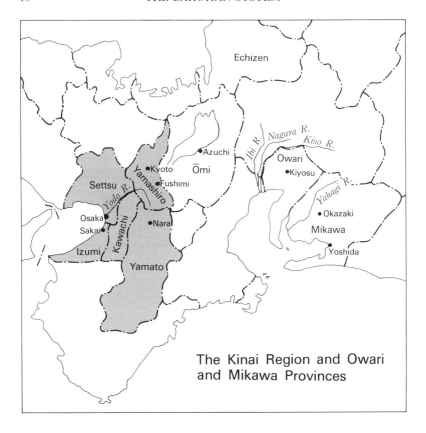

The Kinai Region and Owari and Mikawa Provinces

the seat of political authority. For example, the ancient government, with its former capital at Heijō in Nara, was revived following the transference of the capital to Heian. The *bushi* (samurai), who emerged as private soldiers organized to defend the *shōen* (estates) of the Heian aristocracy in Kyoto, extended their authority, consolidated their position under the leadership of Minamoto no Yoritomo, and in 1192 established the Kamakura bakufu with its capital at Kamakura in the Kantō region. During the 1330s, however, this government was destroyed by Ashikaga forces. The Ashikaga shunned the city of Kamakura and established their bakufu in the Muromachi district of Kyoto. Thus, with successive changes in political authority, the political center shifted from Nara to Kyoto to Kamakura and back to Kyoto. The reason the seat of political power changed in this fashion was that even though the old political authority had weakened, its influence remained strong near its seat of government, making it difficult for the new regime to develop there. This could be said of the new political force that emerged in place of the Muromachi bakufu. It did not rise from that regime's power base, the Kinai region (the provinces of Yamato, Yamashiro, Kawachi, Izumi, and Settsu), but from along its outer rim in the Owari-Mikawa region.

But why did the new political forces arise in Owari and Mikawa rather than some other part of the Kinai rim? Although it may not be a wholly satisfactory explanation, the key surely lies in the great agricultural richness of those provinces, as the following reasoning suggests. The *bushi* who built the new era were not yet sharply distinguished from farmers. In time of peace they worked on the land as farmers, and in time of conflict they traded their farm tools for weapons and went into the battlefield. If we examine carefully the battles fought in the era of warring states, we find that, except under extraordinary circumstances, fighting was avoided during busy seasons such as planting and harvesting.

Because battles interfere with farm work, before class divisions between warriors and farmers were established, *bushi* could not engage in warfare whenever they chose. The policy of separating military men from farmers was designed to distinguish those who were indispensable for warfare from those who were essential for farming. Under this system, while peasants engaged full time in farm work, *bushi* could concentrate fully on military training and warfare. Naturally, the feudal lord who commanded an army of full-time *bushi* would have a military advantage over the lord whose *bushi* lived under a system in which the duties of warrior and farmer were not separated.

What circumstances determined whether class divisions between warriors and farmers could be instituted? The deciding factor was the productive capacity of the land held by a given lord, because only rich lands could support nonproductive armies. The area where Nobunaga and Hideyoshi emerged was the rich alluvial plain in the lower reaches of the Kiso, Nagara, and Ibi rivers. And Ieyasu came out of the broad coastal region of Mikawa, which was watered by the Yahagi River and other streams. In those years these areas had extremely high levels of agricultural production and could support such standing armies. Moreover, the muskets that were being imported from Europe were phenomenally expensive compared to the bows and arrows that had been basic weapons till then. But these regions had such enormous productive capacity that their lords were able to purchase large quantities of these expensive weapons.

3. Constructing the Tokugawa System: Ieyasu's Role

In August 1598, Toyotomi Hideyoshi died. He had launched his reckless campaign in Korea before completing the task of establishing a solid socio-political system, and as a result his political structure began to disintegrate promptly upon his death. One power center formed around Tokugawa Ieyasu and another around Ishida Mitsunari.

The task confronting Ieyasu after Hideyoshi's death was to wipe out the rival faction and unify the nation under his own authority. This opportunity arrived sooner than expected, and he achieved his objective in the battle of Sekigahara in 1600. Three years later, he was designated shogun, that is, *seii taishōgun* (barbarian-subduing generalissimo) by the imperial court, which title gave him a status that no daimyo could challenge, and he established his headquarters, the bakufu, at Edo, the heart of his own vast Kantō domain. Of the tasks remaining for Ieyasu, one was to dispose of Toyotomi Hideyori, Hideyoshi's heir, who was ensconced in Osaka. Another was solidifying the Tokugawa grip on the shogunate by making it the Tokugawa family's hereditary office.

It appears that Ieyasu initially attempted to integrate Toyotomi Hideyori into the Tokugawa political system as one of the daimyo. But ensuing events led to the Osaka campaigns of the winter of 1614 and summer of 1615, which resulted in Hideyori's death and the liquidation of the Toyotomi family. In the outcome, all the forces that might have posed a military threat to the Tokugawa family were completely eliminated.

The remaining task was to make the position of shogun, lord of the realm, the hereditary possession of the Tokugawa family. Oda Nobunaga had heirs, but his vassal Toyotomi Hideyoshi succeeded him. And when Hideyoshi died, even though Hideyori was alive, his vassal Tokugawa Ieyasu had followed as wielder of supreme political power. In light of these precedents, Ieyasu had to consider ways to ensure that the shogunate would become the Tokugawa family's hereditary office. In less than three years after being appointed shogun, Ieyasu passed the office to his son Hidetada. He then retired to the background but managed political affairs from behind the scenes. This practice of ruling from retirement was referred to as *ōgosho* government. Ieyasu had transferred the title of shogun to Hidetada and put him in nominal charge of affairs at Edo to let all Japan know that the shogunate was the hereditary possession of the Tokugawa family.

Ieyasu had established the principle of a hereditary Tokugawa right to the shogunal title, but he still had to decide how a choice was to be made among several children. He had eleven sons, and it was his third son, Hidetada, who became the second Tokugawa shogun. His eldest, Nobuyasu, had married Nobunaga's daughter, but Nobunaga later suspected him of being secretly in league with the enemy Takeda and ordered him to commit suicide in 1579. Ieyasu's second son Hideyasu was adopted by Hideyoshi and became the heir of the Yuki family, a prominent family in the Kantō region. In 1600, he resumed the Tokugawa family name and became the lord of Fukui in Echizen with a holding of 670,000 *koku*. He was alive in 1605, when Hidetada became shogun, and it would not have been out of line if he had been appointed shogun instead of Hidetada.

At this time succession within military families was moving toward the practice of primogeniture, but the memories of the era of warring states, when ferocious power struggles continued unceasingly, were still strong. Consequently, the practice of passing on the family leadership to the most able and suitable son was still prevalent. It is said that Ieyasu chose Hidetada as successor because he was the most obedient and docile of the sons; he was most acceptable to Ieyasu, who planned to exercise power while retired. Thus, Ieyasu's choice of Hidetada appears to have been a logical move. But if this way of choosing the shogun's successor were continued, internal strife over succession could divide the family, as the example of the Ashikaga shogunate—as well as many other lordly family disputes—clearly demonstrated. Should that occur, the Tokugawa family's control over the shogunate would be endangered.

Ieyasu settled this last dynastic problem, the principle of succession, when the question of Hidetada's heir came up. Hidetada had three sons: the eldest, Iemitsu; the second, Tadanaga; and the third, Masayuki. Of the three, Iemitsu and Tadanaga were sons of Hidetada's primary wife, Oeyo (the youngest sister of Yodogimi, Hideyoshi's favorite consort). Masayuki was borne of Hidetada's concubine, and at birth he was turned over to the Hoshina family as their adopted son.

The choice for third shogun thus lay between Iemitsu and Tadanaga. Iemitsu, the older, lacked promise from early childhood, appearing listless and even dimwitted. By contrast, Tadanaga showed quick intelligence and comported himself properly in all respects. His mother showered him with affection, and because of her ardent support, both his father, the shogun, and high Tokugawa officials inclined toward selecting him as the third shogun. This turn of events upset Iemitsu's wet nurse Kasuga no Tsubone, and late in 1611 she appealed directly to Ieyasu. He came to Edo from his retirement home in Sumpu and chose Iemitsu as Hidetada's heir.

Thus the practice of primogeniture was established for the Tokugawa shogunate. Ieyasu had decided that rather than choose a successor on the basis of personal characteristics by weighing the intelligence and physical condition of potential heirs, the goal of sustaining the Tokugawa polity would be better served if the order of birth was made the deciding factor. This would ensure the continuity of the Tokugawa regime.

Besides instituting the practice of primogeniture, Ieyasu attempted to endow future shoguns with absolute authority over their brothers. Immediately after deciding on Iemitsu, he wrote a letter of admonition to Oeyo: "Daimyo view the eldest son with special regard. Younger sons are considered to be akin to servants.... For the second son to have greater influence than the oldest is the root cause of family troubles." Ieyasu was well aware that in watching developments in the daimyo families, as well as his own, one must be especially alert to the relationship between brothers.

This awareness is seen in the way Ieyasu and Hidetada dealt with Hidetada's brothers. The older brother Hideyasu died in 1607 at the age of thirty-four, and he was succeeded as the lord of Fukui by his son Tadanao. Tadanao collided with Hidetada soon after Ieyasu's death, and in 1623 his domain was confiscated, and he was exiled to

Bungo. Misconduct was given as the reason for his punishment, but soon afterward the shogun's office was passed from Hidetada to Iemitsu. It is likely that Hidetada considered the presence of his older brother's family line a worrisome matter, and one can imagine that Hideyasu, had he not died so soon, might also have challenged the second shogun, perhaps following Ieyasu's death.

Ieyasu's fourth and fifth sons posed no problems, dying respectively in 1608 and 1602. In 1610 the sixth son, Tadateru, became a leading lord in north-central Japan as the daimyo of Takada in Echigo, where he held a 600,000 *koku* domain. It is said that he had a fiery temper and committed many intemperate acts, and in 1615 Ieyasu became angry at him following an incident in which Tadateru's men slew one of the shogun's liege vassals (*hatamoto*). In 1616 Tadateru was exiled to Asama in Ise; later he was sent to Hida, and in 1626 he was put under the custody of the daimyo of Suwa in Shinshū.

Although he submitted thoughtfully formulated petitions for clemency, he was never forgiven. He remained under house arrest for fifty-eight years until he died in 1683 at the age of ninety-two. Of course the basic problem was Tadateru's violent temper, but his treatment by the bakufu must have been based on the judgment that the presence of such a hot-tempered person in the shogun's family circle would be inimical to the Tokugawa polity's stability.

Ieyasu's seventh and eighth sons both died in childhood. The ninth, Yoshinao, was enfeoffed at Nagoya in Owari, the tenth at Wakayama in Kishū, and the eleventh at Mito in Hitachi. These three sons became the founders of the *gosanke*, the major collateral houses of the Tokugawa bakufu. Of the three sons, Yoshinao was closest to Hidetada in age, but there was over a twenty-year age difference between the two.

Iemitsu's younger brother, Tadanaga, who early in youth had been a rival for the shogunal succession, was made the daimyo of a 500,000 *koku* domain headquartered at Fuchū in Suruga province. He became known as the grand councillor of Suruga, but within months of his father's death in 1632, Iemitsu confiscated his domain and ordered him to commit suicide. The founder's policy of ruthlessly eliminating anyone who might possibly threaten the security of the shogunate was continued in this way by Iemitsu, who ruled until his death in 1651.

4. Perfecting the Tokugawa System

One can say that the task of establishing the Tokugawa polity, the
bakuhan system, on a firm basis was completed during the reign of
Iemitsu, who consolidated policies begun by his predecessors. The
key policies were manipulating daimyo, managing the imperial
court, controlling foreign relations, and sacralizing the Tokugawa
legacy.

The essential characteristic of the Tokugawa bakuhan system is
that it placed daimyo, who formerly were peers of the Tokugawa,
under their absolute authority. To this end the results of the battle
of Sekigahara were utilized as fully as possible. Ieyasu abolished the
military houses of Ukita Hideie, Chōsokabe Morichika, and others
who opposed him at Sekigahara, ninety-one in all, and confiscated
their holdings, which totaled over 4,200,000 *koku*. In addition, four
families, including Mōri Hidenari and Uesugi Kagekatsu, saw more
than 2,210,000 *koku* of their holdings confiscated. By these measures, Ieyasu succeeded in gaining control over domains worth over
6,420,000 *koku*, which he used to strengthen his political authority.
That is, he distributed the confiscated land to the lords who sided
with him at Sekigahara and to his own retainers. In distributing it,
he used the pretext of increasing their holdings to relocate many of
the daimyo. This policy of "transplanting" daimyo to new land
removed them from the power base they had established in their
former domains and served to weaken their position.

These measures of abolishing daimyo houses or transferring
them to other domains, carried out by the first three shogun, were
put into effect not only in wartime but also in time of peace. Iemitsu
was particularly aggressive in transferring daimyo, resulting in a
decrease in the number of *tozama* lords, meaning those whose
ancestors had not been vassals of Ieyasu in 1600, and an increase in
daimyo whose families had been in Ieyasu's service, the *fudai*
daimyo.

A lord could lose part or all of his domain in peacetime by failing
to maintain order, but the most common occasion for such a loss
was the absence of an heir in the daimyo's family. In principle, the
domain assigned to the daimyo was given by the shogun to a specific person. If the daimyo had no heir, his land escheated to the
giver. There were many instances in which daimyo houses expired

because they lacked an heir. This is seen even in Ieyasu's sons' cases. His fourth son Tadayoshi and fifth son Nobuyoshi were daimyo of Kiyosu in Owari and Mito in Hitachi, respectively, but they both died without heirs at an early age, and their holdings were abolished. In such instances, the deceased lord's surviving family members and vassals found themselves turned out homeless or unemployed into a cold world. This was one cause of the emergence of *rōnin* (masterless samurai) and the problems that accompanied them.

Even if a daimyo had an heir, succession was not automatic because the heir had to receive formal bakufu approval before he could inherit the domain. An adopted son could gain recognition as heir, but again it was necessary to have the bakufu's approval before the daimyo's death. Initially, the bakufu refused to recognize an heir adopted hastily after the unexpected death of a daimyo. But because so many heirless daimyo houses were being abolished, the *rōnin* problem became exacerbated. Consequently, the bakufu decided in 1651 to recognize heirs adopted at the last minute, which practice came to be known as "deathbed adoption" or "emergency adoption."

The most important measure for keeping daimyo under control was adoption of the *buke sho-hatto* (laws pertaining to the military houses). In 1615, within weeks of destroying Toyotomi Hideyori, Ieyasu convened the daimyo at Fushimi Castle and issued a thirteen-article directive to them. It consisted of restrictions on repairing castles, a requirement to obtain permission for marital arrangements, and so on. This was the origin of the *buke sho-hatto*. In 1635, the third shogun, Iemitsu, revised and expanded the thirteen articles, issuing a total of nineteen. These constituted the basis for subsequent laws pertaining to the daimyo. The central mechanism of bakufu control over daimyo consisted of these laws, regulations requiring their wives and children to remain in Edo, and the system of *sankin kōtai* (alternate attendance) that was instituted in 1634 and 1635.

The custom of daimyo visiting the shogun's castle in Edo had begun decades earlier. Many of them traveled the Tōkaidō route to visit the shogun, and it was customary for him to greet and send them off at Shinagawa, the first rest station south of Edo. In the documents of the Myōkokuji Temple near the Shinagawa rest sta-

tion is a record titled "The Third Shogun's Visits," and its last entry
is that of November 11, 1635, Iemitsu's forty-fourth visit. Thereafter, with the alternate attendance system institutionalized as a
daimyo's duty, it was no longer necessary for the shogun to proceed
to Shinagawa to greet or send them off.

Next in importance to dealing with the daimyo was arranging the
bakufu's relationship with the imperial court. Toyotomi Hideyoshi
gained control of the land, but he governed the country as imperial
regent and grand chancellor, an official status obtained from the
imperial court. Hence, when he conducted the national cadastral
survey, he submitted some of the cadastres (land survey ledgers) to
the emperor, who was the most prominent landholder, for approval.
In contrast, Tokugawa rulers took the position that the imperial
court and all its lands were under the jurisdiction of the bakufu.
They asserted this in practice as well as in their formal relationship
with the court, first of all by issuing the "laws pertaining to the
imperial court and court nobles" (*kinchū narabi ni kuge sho-hatto*) as
the courtly equivalent of the *buke*'s *sho-hatto*. Like the latter, Ieyasu
issued this set of directives soon after Hideyori and his mother
Yodogimi perished in Osaka Castle in 1615.

These directives combined the provisions in the "laws on court
nobles" (*kuge sho-hatto*) and the "laws on imperial awards of purple
gowns" (*chokkyo shii hatto*) that were issued in the previous year, and
added regulations on the conduct of the emperor himself. Among
the provisions of the *kuge sho-hatto* were these: (1) court nobles must
devote themselves to scholarship in accordance with imperial tradition; (2) those who violate the rules of proper conduct will be sent
into exile; (3) one must not neglect one's daily duties; (4) one must
not roam idly about the city; (5) servants who indulge in gambling
and games, and those who engage in improper conduct must not be
employed. It concludes by stating that the right to punish courtiers
who violate these provisions resides with the military authorities.
"The laws on imperial awards of purple gowns" had to do with presentation of purple gowns of office to those being promoted to the
highest rank of the Buddhist priesthood. Prior to this, the imperial
court had controlled such awards, but the *chokkyo shii hatto* stipulated that henceforth bakufu approval must be obtained before any
such award was made.

The *kinchū narabi ni kuge sho-hatto* of 1615 consists of seventeen articles. To get a flavor of the document, Article I stipulated that the primary duty of the emperor was scholarship. The distinction in functions of court and bakufu was clear: political affairs were the bakufu's responsibility while the emperor's function was to engage in scholarship. Articles II and III dealt with the court ranks of imperial princes, high court nobles, and retired court officials. Articles IV and V stipulated that in making court appointments one should give greater weight to ability than family background. Article VII held that official ranking of the military class was unrelated to court ranking and was to be decided entirely by the bakufu.

If all seventeen articles were followed strictly as stipulated, the court and nobility would be under complete bakufu control. However, the court-bakufu relationship did not go as smoothly as Edo wished. In 1615, Ieyasu's plan to have Emperor Gomizuno'o marry Hidetada's daughter, Kazuko, was realized, but the high-handed measures that Edo employed to accomplish this caused resentment among Gomizuno'o and his attendants and contributed finally to the purple-gown incident and Gomizuno'o's abdication in 1629. The purple-gown incident had to do with the defrocking of some seventy Buddhist prelates who had been awarded purple gowns by the emperor. The bakufu held that awarding the gowns violated the provisions of the "laws pertaining to the imperial court and court nobles." Four monks, including the priest of Daitokuji temple, Takuan, protested the defrocking and were sent into exile.

Under these strained conditions, Tokugawa Iemitsu visited Kyoto three times: in 1623, 1626, and 1634. On each occasion he entered Kyoto with a large army. On his third visit in 1634 he proceeded with an immense force of 307,000 men. To convey a sense of this army's size, if we estimate the space between each warrior as one meter, the first group of warriors would have reached the castle town of Yoshida in Mikawa before the tail of the retinue had left Edo. Iemitsu's aim was to intimidate the court with his huge army and thus solidify bakufu supremacy.

Among the important policies adopted by Iemitsu was that of national seclusion. Because the bakufu had managed only with great difficulty to subdue the Shimabara Rebellion a year before this policy was put in its final form in 1639, the policy of seclusion is usually linked to the bakufu's policy of banning Christianity.

Christianity entered Japan in 1549 when Francis Xavier arrived in Kagoshima and began his missionary work. The new religion was accepted by daimyo in western Japan and spread very rapidly not only because it was new but also because it was accompanied by muskets and other new items. Nobunaga actively supported the missionaries' work because he saw it as an instrument to help him suppress deeply entrenched Buddhist forces, and also because of the new products that the missionaries brought with them. Consequently, the religion took root swiftly in many areas.

Hideyoshi continued Nobunaga's policy of supporting Christian missionaries, and harmonious relations between his regime and Christianity continued for a while. Christian chapels were built in the castle towns of western daimyo and in Kyoto and Azuchi. And Christian converts emerged among the daimyo, including Ōtomo Yoshishige, Ōmura Sumitada, Konishi Yukinaga, and Takayama Ukon. However, when Hideyoshi entered Kyushu to launch his campaign against the Shimazu, he was disturbed by the large number of Christian converts. Understanding that converts believed Christ to be superior to all things, higher even than the national conqueror Hideyoshi himself, he concluded that Christianity was incompatible with his plan to establish his own political hegemony. Accordingly, he issued a decree to expel the missionaries in 1587. However, the decree stipulated that foreign trade was not included in the order, and in fact no serious effort was made to deport the missionaries, so the decree proved ineffective.

Ieyasu was aware of the profits foreign trade would bring to Japan and actively fostered it after 1600. At that time, the trade was mainly handled by Portuguese (Catholic) merchants who had close ties with the Toyotomi family and daimyo in western Japan. To compete with these groups, Ieyasu sought trade through English and Dutch (Protestant) merchants and therefore employed an Englishman, William Adams, and a Dutchman, Jan Joosten van Lodensteijn, as advisers. Japanese themselves also were actively engaged in overseas trade, and Ieyasu issued Red Seal permits to license their ventures. Among the initial recipients of these permits were such great daimyo as Shimazu, Matsuura, Arima, and Nabeshima, all of Kyūshū. Gradually, however, Ieyasu limited Red Seal permits to merchants with ties to the Tokugawa family.

Initially trade was carried on at many places, including Hirado, the castle town of the Matsuura clan, but by 1635, when Iemitsu was in control, it was limited to one port, Nagasaki, which was under the bakufu's direct control. At the same time, Iemitsu prohibited overseas trade and travel by Japanese. Meanwhile, foreigners came under closer control: in 1624 the Spanish were prohibited from coming to Japan, and in 1639 Iemitsu extended the ban to the Portuguese. The English had already withdrawn voluntarily, so the Dutch survived as the only Europeans permitted in Japan.

This situation is referred to as national seclusion, or *sakoku*, but as is clear from this account, it did not mean that the entire nation was sealed off from the outside. It meant that: (1) foreign trade—with Europe and China—was restricted to the single port of Nagasaki where the bakufu had direct jurisdiction and (2) the only foreigners allowed to come and trade at Nagasaki were the Dutch and Chinese. In effect, the bakufu had instituted a policy of monopolizing foreign trade, and in fact, compared to earlier years, the volume of foreign trade increased after the policy of seclusion was adopted. In return for receiving the exclusive European right to trade with Japan, the Dutch provided the bakufu with an annual report about significant world developments. In light of this, we can say that the policy of national seclusion was a policy designed to give the bakufu a monopoly in foreign trade and on information from abroad.

How then are the policy of seclusion and the ban on Christianity related? In 1587, Hideyoshi issued a decree expelling Christian missionaries, but because he valued foreign trade, he did not enforce the ban rigorously. Ieyasu continued to place foreign trade above concern about Christianity. However, there were an estimated 700,000 Christian converts at the beginning of the seventeenth century, and he began to worry that if this situation were allowed to continue, a second epidemic of Ikkō-like uprisings might break out. So in 1612 he issued a decree banning Christianity and set out to eradicate the religion from the country. He started by first destroying the chapels in Kyoto, ordering the Christian daimyo Arima Harunobu to commit *seppuku* (harakiri), and exiling Takayama Ukon. He then had ordinary Christian converts arrested and pressured into apostatizing. Those who refused were executed. There were many Christians among those who fought on the losing Toyotomi side in the winter and summer campaigns at Osaka Castle, and Hidetada broadened the persecution substantially, continuing it aggressively through the 1620s. Then in 1637 a peasant uprising broke out in Shimabara and Amakusa in Kyushu. Among the insurgents were many Christians, so the uprising took on the cast of a Christian uprising. After the uprising was crushed, the policy of hunting down and rigorously suppressing Christians was renewed. But it was not till 1671, more than thirty years after Shimabara, that the policy of establishing *shūmon aratame-chō* (registry of religious affiliation) was instituted nationwide. As a means of uncovering Christians and preventing the propagation of Christianity, this policy required every household to affiliate with a Buddhist sect and register annually with the local temple.

Finally, to complete the consolidation of Tokugawa authority, Iemitsu set out to sacralize Ieyasu. He regarded his grandfather with a respect akin to religious worship because it was Ieyasu who had ensured his succession to the shogunal position. As an expression of his sentiments, Iemitsu rebuilt the small shrine in Nikkō which his father Hidetada had built to enshrine Ieyasu. The result was the sumptuous edifice that we see today. For this reconstruction Iemitsu expended 570,000 *ryō* of gold, 100 *kan* of silver and 1,000 *koku* of rice. The labor devoted to the construction, it is estimated, came to 4,543,000 man-days. In 1645, upon Iemitsu's request, the imperial court upgraded Ieyasu's shrine in Nikkō, and it has thereafter been called Nikkō Tōshōgū. From the following year, the court commenced dispatching imperial pilgrimages to Nikkō.

5. The Administrative System

The history of the Tokugawa bakufu can be divided into three periods in terms of its administrative structure: (1) from 1603 to 1632; (2) from 1633 to 1854; and (3) from 1855 to 1867. The first period extends from Ieyasu's founding of the bakufu to the death of Hidetada. This was the period in which governmental affairs were conducted under the personal direction of extraordinarily talented administrators who were in the inner circle of Ieyasu and Hidetada's regimes. Among them were the father-and-son team of Honda Masanobu and Masazumi and the Buddhist priests Tenkai and Konji'in Sūden. There was also the merchant Chaya Shirōjirō who had supported Ieyasu from the days when he was a daimyo of

Mikawa. Even the English navigator William Adams (Miura Anjin), who served for a time in a capacity that might be called Ieyasu's foreign policy adviser, can be included in this circle.

The person who changed these administrative arrangements to a more regularly structured system, that of period two, was the third shogun, Iemitsu. He became shogun in 1623 but his father was still alive and was exercising authority as retired shogun, so he was unable to formulate his own policies. Iemitsu's own preferences began to surface following his father's death early in 1632.

At the top of the administrative structure were the *rōjū* (senior councillors) and immediately below them the *wakadoshiyori* (junior councillors). In 1634, the bakufu defined the limits of their authority and functions, with ten articles pertaining to the senior councillors and seven to the junior councillors. According to these regulations, the latter were to oversee affairs relating to *hatamoto* and *gokenin* (shogunal retainers with stipends of less than 10,000 *koku*), while the senior councillors' duties concerned daimyo (those lords with holdings of over 10,000 *koku*), foreign affairs, and financial matters. The office of *tairō* (great councillor) was not a standing position, and its functions were first defined in 1638 in the charge issued to senior councillors Doi Toshikatsu and Sakai Tadakatsu. It stated, "You are excused from concerning yourselves with minor administrative matters. You need attend the shogun's castle only on the first and fifteenth of the month. However, if matters of grave political importance should arise, you must attend the castle and confer with the senior councillors."

The officials who performed day-to-day administrative duties under *rōjū* authority were the "three magistrates" (*sanbugyō*); that is, the superintendents of temples and shrines, the city magistrates, and the superintendents of finance. As for the superintendents of temples and shrines, the first appointments were made in 1635 when Andō Shigenaga, Matsudaira Katsuoka, and Hori Toshishige were ordered to adjudicate legal disputes involving temples and shrines and areas beyond Edo. Several cities and towns under bakufu control, such as Osaka, Nara, and Yamada, were administered by magistrates (*machi bugyō*), and the magistrate of Edo was first appointed in 1631 when Kaganouri Tadasumi and Hori Naoyuki were placed in charge of the northern and southern districts of the city.

The chief duties of superintendents of finance were collection of taxes and management of expenditures. Those tasks were being performed from the early years of the bakufu by such men as Ina Tadatsugu and Ōkubo Chōan. Not until after 1633, it appears, were these tasks organized as a regular office of finances within the bakufu.

The important office of *ōmetsuke* (inspector general), which investigated a person's loyalty to the Tokugawa family and evaluated the performance of bakufu officials, was first filled in 1632 when Yagyū Munetsune, the shogun's instructor of swordsmanship, and two others were appointed to the position. The three magistrates constituted the chief members of the *hyōjōsho*, the Tribunal, which was instituted in 1635. When assembled as the Tribunal, these officials served as the bakufu's highest judicial body, and also studied and formulated plans concerning important legal and administrative affairs.

Besides this official governmental organization, there were arrangements in the interior of the shogun's household that concerned his personal life. The organizing of the inner court (*Ōoku*, the "great interior") occurred during this period, and the architect of the system was Kasuga no Tsubone, the wet nurse who had taken care of Iemitsu since his childhood.

The construction of this administrative system that buttressed the Tokugawa bakufu for 220 years until 1854 was accomplished by Iemitsu during the decade or so following his father's death. The third and final phase of bakufu organizational history started with the breakdown of the "seclusionist system," which had come to be regarded as the law of the founding fathers. This breakdown was precipitated by the policy of opening Japanese ports to the outside world, which was adopted in the 1850s because of the pressures coming from foreign powers. Prior to that time, the bakufu had not had to meet internal or external threats by resort to military force. As a result, it scarcely had a military system. Nor did it have a government agency that dealt exclusively with foreign affairs. Following the opening of Japanese ports, the bakufu attempted to cope with its rapidly changing circumstances by adding new government offices and positions to deal with military affairs and foreign relations. These included the superintendents of military education, warships, and foreign relations; general superintendent of foreign relations; and chancellors of the army, navy, and foreign affairs. Despite this flurry of institutional reform, the bakufu failed to meet the challenges of the swiftly changing times and collapsed in less than fifteen years.

6. The Capacity of the Tokugawa System to Cope with Problems

The administrative system that took shape under Iemitsu and sustained the Tokugawa polity thereafter had a number of special features. Most notably the rank order of official positions and the social status of their occupants dovetailed. In addition, most government positions were staffed by more than one official.

In modern society, a person's occupation and income are theoretically dependent on each individual's preferences and ability, but in the status-based order of the Tokugawa-period samurai, occupation and income were determined not by one's personal ability, but by the standing of one's *ie* (household). This term *ie* does not refer simply to a family's dwelling place or members but also to its pedigree. That is, the standing of a family was determined by how well its ancestors had served the Tokugawa government. For example, whether an individual was qualified to serve as a city magistrate or superintendent of finance depended first of all on whether he was born in a *hatamoto* family with a stipend equivalent to 3,000 *koku* or more. Being talented or lucky was of lesser importance.

Inevitably a status-based social system is subject to numerous criticisms, but one also must acknowledge that the bakufu-centered social structure of the bakuhan system contributed to the stability and order of the time. Can we say, then, that the Tokugawa system succeeded in maintaining general social stability for 250 years because it managed to preserve the class linkage of social rank and government office? No, not at all. Rather, revisions and adjustments were made whenever necessary.

If we construct a chart of bakufu retainers, we find, quite naturally, that the higher one moves up the ladder of family standing, the fewer the number of families. This means that the higher the official position, the fewer the families from which the position could be filled. Viewing this situation in simple terms of probability, the higher the official position, the fewer men of talent there were to fill it. This was a major worry for the bakufu and it was overcome by invoking the shogun's absolutist authority to promote and employ men of ability. However low a person's family standing, as long as he had the shogun's confidence and backing, he could acquire authority superior to that of the senior and junior councillors. This practice served as a relief valve that compensated for the administrative ossification produced by the basic system of status differentiation. It was Tsunayoshi, the fifth shogun, who incorporated this practice into the political system.

Iemitsu's third son, Tsunayoshi, was born in 1646 and died in 1709. His older brother Ietsuna became the fourth shogun in 1651, but he had no offspring, and when he died in 1680 , Tsunayoshi succeeded. When the question of succession arose, a serious controversy allegedly broke out in the bakufu's inner circle. It was during Ietsuna's reign that Iemitsu's recently organized status-based administrative system functioned most smoothly, with the government controlled by Sakai Tadakiyo and others who served as great councillor or senior councillor. These were men whose families enjoyed, as *fudai* daimyo, the highest pedigrees among shogunal retainers. It has been said that they wished to solidify the status-based administrative system and bring real control of the bakufu into *fudai* daimyo hands by making a young imperial prince the successor to Ietsuna. Hotta Masatoshi, who had just been appointed senior councillor the previous year, was the only one who insisted adamantly that Tsunayoshi should become shogun because he was a mainline descendant of the Tokugawa family. The councillors failed to resolve their differences, however, and Tsunayoshi succeeded to the shogunate in accordance with a stipulation in Ietsuna's will. There is some question about the authenticity of this story, but in any case Tsunayoshi does not appear to have been bound very much by the political arrangements established during prior administrations.

First of all, Tsunayoshi established a new position called senior councillor in charge of fiscal affairs (*katte-gakari rōjū*). Strictly speaking, *katte* means kitchen and, by extension, it refers to practical financial matters. So *katte-gakari rōjū* meant a senior councillor in charge of financial affairs. The usual number of senior councillors was four, and hitherto the four had managed the bakufu's political affairs by deliberating together. Tsunayoshi, believing that financial management should be based on long-term considerations, and that one official should assume full responsibility for them, established the new post of *katte-gakari rōjū* and placed its holder in complete charge of economic and fiscal affairs. He then assigned the duty to Hotta Masatoshi, who had earlier helped him win appointment as shogun. But in 1684 Hotta was slain in the castle by a junior councillor, and Tsunayoshi transferred the duty to his *soba-yōnin* (grand chamberlain). The *soba-yōnin* was a variation of the personal attendants (*sobashū*) who took care of the shogun's personal needs and served as his confidants. These *sobashū* did not have any authority to deal with political matters, but the *soba-yōnin*, being at the shogun's side, acted as a messenger, conveying the shogun's political views to the senior councillors and bearing councillor's reports to the shogun.

After Hotta's death, Makino Narisada and then Yanagisawa Yoshiyasu served in this capacity and ran affairs for Tsunayoshi. Yanagisawa was the son of a minor finance officer who served Tsunayoshi when the latter was still daimyo of Tatebayashi in Kōzuke province. In terms of pedigree, this ancestry utterly failed to qualify Yoshiyasu for high-ranking position, but his personal connection to the shogun overcame that disability.

This arrangement—in which a person such as Yanagisawa, who lacked proper pedigree but enjoyed complete shogunal confidence, required sufficient power to surpass the high-born senior and junior councillors and direct political affairs—is referred to as *soba-yōnin seiji*, or government by grand chamberlain. This pattern of control continued during the brief reigns of the sixth and seventh shoguns, Ienobu and Ietsugu, when Manabe Akifusa and Arai Hakuseki served as influential attendants. During Yoshimune's rule, Arima Ujinori and Kanō Hisamichi served in that capacity, and under his successors Ieshige and Ieharu, Ōoka Tadamitsu and Tanuma Ogitsugu did so. Of these men Manabe was formerly a Noh actor, and Arai a Confucian scholar. Arima and Kanō had been Yoshimune's vassals when he was still the lord of Kishū. Ōoka Tadamitsu came from a branch of the liege-vassal Ōoka family, and Tanuma was the son of a foot soldier (*ashigaru*) of Kishū.

The officials who actually managed bakufu finances under the direction of senior councillors, *katte-gakari rōjū*, and grand chamberlains, were the superintendents of finance, normally four officials who were appointed from among the shogun's *hatamoto* with stipends of 3,000 *koku* or so. There were some 5,200 *hatamoto* families, but only about 250 had stipends of 3,000 *koku* or more. So the superintendents of finance were chosen from a fairly small pool, meaning the probability of able people filling that position was fairly low. Since the *katte-gakari rōjū* served as a general director of finances, he did not need great practical ability in the subject. But the superintendents of finance did handle details, so they had to be well-versed in economics and computation. Because only about 5 percent of the *hatamoto* could serve in this capacity, inevitably there was a paucity of qualified men to fill the post.

Tsunayoshi solved this problem by asserting that in filling the superintendent of finance position, ability rather than pedigree was to be the deciding factor. The first person to emerge as a superintendent of finance under this guideline was Ogiwara Shigehide. He, in cooperation with Yanagisawa, managed bakufu finances during the Genroku period (roughly the years of Tsunayoshi's shogunate), an era generally seen as a turning point in Tokugawa history. With a family stipend of about 100 *koku*, he came from the lowest ranks of the 5,200 *hatamoto* families.

Ogiwara was the first of three famous superintendents of finance during the Tokugawa period. His currency policies, notably reminting of coinage, are regarded as the birth of modern monetary policy in Japan. The second most famous superintendent of finance was Kamio Harunaka, who managed bakufu financial affairs during the latter half of the eighth shogun Yoshimune's reign. He is credited with the haughty assertion that "with peasants and sesame seeds, the more you squeeze them the more you get from them." He thus symbolizes the ruthlessly exploitative superintendent of finance, but in reality he was an extremely able financial officer who did much to shore up the bakufu's finances. The third superintendent of finance who contributed greatly to the fiscal revitalization of the bakufu was Matsumoto Hidemochi who, as assistant to Tanuma Okitsugu, conducted a survey of Hokkaido, among other important measures. Kamio and Matsumoto both came from families that were even lower than Ogiwara's in status, being from *gokenin* (housemen) families, the lowest category of liege vassals.

Nearly one hundred years passed between the founding of the

Tokugawa bakufu and Tsunayoshi's heyday. The economy, which had grown at a phenomenal pace during that century had more or less reached its zenith. The abundant financial resources of the bakufu were just about depleted, and the regime was entering an era when budget deficits were to plague it. No longer could the bakufu spend its money freely on whatever project seemed worthy; instead, expenditures had to be weighed carefully against revenues. Hence, it no longer sufficed to select financial officers on the basis of family standing. It was necessary to search broadly and recruit capable men, and Tsunayoshi's policy of employing men of ability in his financial office was a response to that situation.

The bakufu employed investigative officials such as inspectors general (*ōmetsuke*) and inspectors (*metsuke*) from its early years. Tsunayoshi established an additional supervisory position to deal only with financial affairs, the *kanjō gimmi-yaku* (budget examination office), which was similar to a present-day board of audit. Ogiwara Shigehide started his career as a minor official in the finance office, later became budget examiner, and subsequently moved up to become the superintendent of finance.

Most of the bakufu's administrative positions employed more than one official per position. For example, there were four senior councillors, two (at one time, three) city magistrates, and four superintendents of finance. Unlike today's administrative arrangement, in bakufu offices judicial and administrative functions were not separated. For example, in their management of bakufu funds, the superintendents of finance handled legal disputes, tax collection, and management of expenditures. Yoshimune improved the efficiency of the office by separating these matters into judicial and financial affairs. He assigned legal and judicial matters to two superintendents of finance who were responsible for judicial affairs, and all fiscal matters to two superintendents of finance in charge of financial affairs.

In this fashion, even though the Tokugawa bakufu was constructed around a system of status differentiation, it invoked the shogun's authority, as necessary, and adapted to the movement of history by boldly employing men of talent regardless of their social status. This is what enabled the Tokugawa system to survive for 265 years in the midst of violent shifts in the historical current as the mode of production was changing from feudalistic to capitalistic. However, this practice in which men of talent were employed regardless of social status under the shogunal system changed as political authority shifted from Tanuma Ogitsugu to Matsudaira Sadanobu after the rule of the eleventh shogun Ienari from 1787. A conservative reaction unfolded as men of high pedigree recaptured political power. This hampered the bakufu's ability to cope with the rapidly changing historical tide, and as a result, it ended up treading the path of decline and disintegration.

(Translation by Mikiso Hane)

Chapter Two

Tokugawa Villages and Agriculture

TSUNEO SATŌ

The Tokugawa period constituted Japan's final stage as an agriculture-based society. The population at the end of the seventeenth century was approximately thirty million, and it remained stable until the later years of the nineteenth century, which encompassed the Meiji Restoration and the advent of modern Japan. Approximately 80 percent of this population consisted of peasants. It can be said, therefore, that the historical character of Tokugawa society was deeply shaped by the nature of agriculture, farm villages, and the peasantry.

1. Specific Features of Agricultural Villages

Most people in Tokugawa Japan were villagers, and most villagers were engaged in agriculture. It should be noted, however, that besides agricultural villages (*nōson*), which will hold our attention, there were mountain villages (*sanson*), whose members relied heavily on upland and forest production, and fishing villages (*gyoson*), whose residents worked the sea as well as the land. Throughout the period, farm work remained the foundation of rural society and determined village structure, but as time passed, agriculture experienced substantial commercial and technological advances.

Cadastral Surveys and Updating of Temple Registrations

The transition from medieval to Tokugawa society took place during the violent years of the era of warring states, when "those below challenged those above" and lower-level members of society forcefully overthrew their superiors. The social transformation that took

37

place in this period entailed the rejection of the common form of medieval social control, wherein the overlord lived in the community, and the adoption instead of the policy of segregating the warrior class and peasantry. This separation of warrior class and peasantry was brought about through policies adopted by Toyotomi Hideyoshi, who implemented such measures as a general cadastral survey, confiscation of the peasants' swords, forced relocation of the populace, and transference of domainal lords. The Tokugawa bakufu, which succeeded Hideyoshi's rule, inherited and brought this social reorganization to completion.

Warriors of the era of warring states engaged in farm work during peacetime and took up arms in time of war. In other words they were peasant-warriors. When the classes were separated, men had to choose between being classified as warriors or peasants. At the same time, peasants were prevented from moving up into the class of domainal lords. The warriors were required to leave villages and congregate in castle towns. Hence the segregation of warriors and peasants also entailed the geographical separation of the two. Moreover, merchants and artisans also were compelled to live in castle towns so that the separation of merchants and artisans from peasants was also effected. Farm villages then became purely communities of agricultural producers.

The most decisive factor bringing about this separation of warriors and peasants was Hideyoshi's cadastral survey. The survey was conducted nationwide under a uniform method of land surveying and a common standard of weights and measures. Moreover, the overlapping rights to land that diverse interests had enjoyed until then were eliminated. The policy of identifying a specific peasant with each plot of farmland was applied to all arable lands, and landholding rights became a simple arrangement between domainal lords and peasants. At the same time, village boundaries were delineated, and a cadastral record was compiled as the official land register for each village. Hideyoshi's cadastral survey was not conducted with the individual tillers as the unit of survey but rather with the village, that is, the agricultural producers' community as a whole, as the unit of survey.

The Tokugawa bakufu retained the surveying practice introduced by Hideyoshi's cadastres as a way to strengthen the economic foundation of its political hegemony. By the end of the seventeenth century it had conducted several cadastral surveys in its demesnes, which were scattered throughout the country. For villages under the bakufu's immediate jurisdiction, the cadastral records that were compiled at the end of the seventeenth century, which became the most authoritative land registers of Tokugawa society, constitute the most revealing source of information on all aspects of village economic and social relationships. Many daimyo also undertook cadastral surveys like those of the bakufu in the domains they controlled. Thus, all farmland was recorded in land registries with villages as the units of survey.

Paddy fields, upland fields, and residential plots were the three categories of land surveyed by the cadastres, but in practice uplands that were not rice fields and homesteads were assessed as if they were producing rice. At the end of each land register the total annual production of the village was recorded in terms of an estimated rice yield, the village's *kokudaka* (the rice yield measured in *koku*). In Tokugawa society, *kokudaka* became the yardstick to indicate the size of villages and the scope of agricultural production. The amount of rice that peasants were required to turn over to the bakufu and daimyo as feudal tax was based on the village's *kokudaka*. Moreover, *kokudaka* figures were used to indicate the size of the domains controlled by the bakufu and daimyo as well as the stipends of the retainers. The *kokudaka* fixed by cadastral surveys thus served as the yardstick to measure the social standing and wealth of the members of society. In other words, Tokugawa society was a feudal society integrated through a common denominator, the production figure of a single crop, rice.

In 1644, the bakufu ordered the administrators of its own domains to submit ledgers entitled "Numerical records of residential buildings, people, and horses." This practice, commonly referred to as the "updating of population records" (*ninbetsu aratame*), was repeated periodically and served the same purpose as the censuses that daimyo of the era of the warring states conducted in their domains to strengthen and enrich their territories. These earlier censuses enabled lords to keep the peasantry under their control so that in time of war peasants could be conscripted for corvée and compelled to pay land taxes. In the later "Numerical records," bakufu administrators detailed the peasants' names, statuses, and ages, as well as records of their houses, domestic animals, and landholding. This updating of population records was not undertaken annually but was a census of family records conducted irregularly and on a regional basis.

In 1614, the bakufu banned Christianity and conducted surveys of religious affiliation (*shūmon aratame*) to establish that peasants and townspeople were not adherents of Christianity or other forbidden religions. The surveys assigned people to designated Buddhist temples, so this policy of the bakufu is referred to as a "system of temple surety" (*terauke seido*). The registers that were compiled under this system of temple surety, the *shūmon aratame-chō*, were prepared annually by all villages.

During the early Tokugawa period, the compilation of population registers, which served primarily to facilitate the conscription of laborers for corvée duty, and the updating of temple registers, which was conducted to ensure strict enforcement of the ban on Christianity, were undertaken separately. However, from the middle of the Tokugawa period, the updating of census figures, which originally had been a simple survey of households without religious significance, came to be absorbed into the temple registers that were the backbone of the temple surety system. These became the *shūmon ninbetsu aratamechō*, "emended temple and population registers," which villages compiled every spring. The temple registers listed for each household the name of the household head, names of household members, their ages, relationships to the household head, the *kokudaka* of the household, the numbers of horses and cattle in the household, and so on. At the end of each register the total number of households and population in the village, population size compared to the previous year, etc., were recorded. The entire population of the country, regardless of age or sex, was thus recorded in the temple registers.

Peasant Control and Peasant Obligations

The bakufu and daimyo's ultimate purpose in registering the population was to extract the land tax from the peasants year after year. For this purpose the most important policy decision concerned the best way to link peasants to the land. The first decree issued by the bakufu to control peasants, the Proclamation of Seven Articles, issued in 1603 immediately after Ieyasu took office as shogun, reveals the basic policy of peasant control that was to prevail thereafter. This decree assumed that villagers were obligated to pay taxes from their assigned plots of land and tried to protect them from excessive exploitation by giving them the right to leave the village if they had a legitimate grievance against the overlord and if they followed procedures established by the authorities. It also prohibited the warrior class from executing peasants without legitimate cause.

The most authoritative decree issued by the bakufu to control the peasantry was the Keian Proclamation of thirty-two articles, promulgated in 1649. It enjoined peasants to obey bakufu decrees, consider the payment of land tax as their primary responsibility, work diligently at their farming, rise early in the morning to cut grass, cultivate fields during the day, and make straw ropes and sacks at night. Except when sleeping they were to devote all their time to farm work, and neither they nor their wives and children were to drink sake or tea. They were to plant bamboo and trees around their houses for use as firewood, and from the first of the year they were to repair farm equipment to have them ready for use in the spring. Toilets had to be built near houses and ample provisions made to store human waste, which was to be turned into fertilizer by mixing with grass and water. They were to apply as much fertilizer as possible to paddy and upland fields.

Regarding their diet, peasants were instructed not to consume all the rice and other cereals after the fall harvest; instead, as their normal staple they were to eat barley, millet, cabbage, and *daikon*. During years of poor harvest, they were to use the leaves and stems of soybeans, peas, and other plants as food supplements. The husband was to work in the fields and the wife at the loom. Both husband and wife were admonished to labor diligently at their respective tasks. Goodlooking wives who neglected their husbands had to be divorced. A man was to marry a woman who would produce many children and work hard.

The proclamation also dealt with such matters as proper methods for taking care of horses and cattle, clothing, supplementary work, servants, filial piety, and health care. In this manner the Keian Proclamation concentrated on binding peasants tightly to the land and listed in detail rules and admonitions concerning every aspect of the peasants' daily life and farm work.

The Keian Proclamation was, however, in some respects meant to be an instrument of edification for the peasants who, as subjects of the ruling authorities, were expected to embrace it as a set of ideals befitting their place in the social hierarchy, even though they did not fully abide by it in practice. It was the public face, the official ideal, not a delineation of how Tokugawa peasants actually behaved. Because of the rural economic growth that occurred from the mid-Tokugawa period, peasant behavior came to diverge appreciably from the ideals embodied in the decrees that the bakufu and *han* authorities issued to regulate it. Specific causes of this divergence can be found in shifts in landownership, the rise of commercial production, an increase in peasant combativeness, and the outflow of rural population to urban centers.

The obligations imposed on the peasantry for land use consisted of a regular land tax (*nengu*) and miscellaneous dues. The land tax constituted a basic usage fee imposed on paddy fields, upland fields, and residential plots. The villagers who had to pay the levy were those peasants recorded in the cadastral registers. However, the tax was imposed on the village as a whole on the basis of the *kokudaka* determined by the cadastral surveys, and the peasants did not pay taxes to their feudal lords individually. Rather, payment was the joint responsibility of the village as a whole. If a peasant failed to contribute his share of the tax, the village as a whole had to make up the deficit. This system of communal responsibility for the land tax is a distinguishing characteristic of Tokugawa taxation.

Every fall the bakufu and daimyo dispatched a notice of the land tax rate (*nengu waritsuke jō*) to each village in their respective jurisdictions. That rate, when applied to the village *kokudaka* specified in a cadastral survey register, determined the village's land tax obligation for the year. Village leaders then assigned individual peasants their share of the year's tax on the basis of that rate.

As time passed, however, using the register to determine individual tax levies became more difficult for several reasons. First, a register listed each plot of paddy land, upland, and homestead, not by the name of the tiller or user, but by its geographical location. Moreover cadastral surveys were undertaken only a few times during the Tokugawa period, mostly during the seventeenth century. In addition, land usufruct began to change as villagers divided land among themselves, passed it on to heirs, mortgaged it, and so on. As a result, it became increasingly difficult to assign each villager his share of the tax on the basis of the register. This situation led each village to compile its own record book listing paddy fields, upland, and homesteads with estimated yields for each villager. Although based on the register, as a working registry it recorded the name of the tillers of land. When the village completed its payment of the year's taxes the collector issued the village a receipt indicating that payment had been made in full.

The amount of taxes extracted from the peasants depended basically on the power relationship between the rulers and peasants. This relationship, however, did not remain consistent throughout the Tokugawa period. For example, if we treat the income received by the bakufu and daimyo on the basis of the *kokudaka* fixed by the cadastral survey as the gross tax rate, and trace its changes over time, we can discern a long-term decline in the land-tax rate. In the first half of Tokugawa, the extraction of surplus value, that is the amount above that required by peasants to sustain themselves, was stringent and thorough. In this stage of exploitation, peasants were to be so taxed, as the saying went that they "could not live but would not die," and the tax rate reached a high of 60 percent. But from the end of the seventeenth century, peasant uprisings increased, commercial production grew, and the living standard of the common people rose. Under these circumstances, another party of exploiters, landlords, merchants, and others, wedged themselves between the rulers and the actual tillers of the soil. This led to a decline in the exploitative capacity of government, and during the eighteenth century the bakufu's tax rate dropped to about 33 percent.

The *kokudaka* based on cadastral surveys represented the annual income of the villagers, although their actual earnings, needless to say, varied from year to year. These village *kokudaka* figures remained unchanged during the centuries after the surveys were made in the latter part of the seventeenth century, but the real income of villagers increased because of additional work that they undertook, such as handicrafts, forest work, and fishing. Because of these developments, the tax rate decreased further during the latter half of the Tokugawa period, with the actual rate of extraction declining to about 20 percent.

There was also a change in the way governments calculated the tax rates. During the early Tokugawa period, rates were fixed annually by examining the quantity of the harvest, but from the eighteenth century a fixed rate was imposed regardless of whether the harvest was bountiful or meager. Under the former system, it was necessary to undertake an annual assessment of crops in the field, and that required a considerable outlay of labor, time, and funds. It was also a taxation system that permitted local officials to engage in dishonest practices. As a result, the bakufu and *han* adopted the practice of imposing fixed rates of taxation as part of broader financial reforms.

In Tokugawa society, the basic principle of paying tax with rice prevailed. But under the cadastral system the taxes on areas that did not produce rice were also assessed in terms of rice, so mountain villages, fishing villages, and farming villages with upland fields found it impossible to make the required payments. Instead, they had to make tax payments in money. In the first half of the eighteenth century, about 50 percent of bakufu receipts were in rice, but later the proportion of payment made in currency gradually increased. This occurred against the background of increasing commercial production and use of money in villages. Moreover, from the middle of the Tokugawa period, bakufu taxation began to shift its emphasis from the peasantry to other sources of revenue, namely donations and forced loans extracted from merchants and the growing commercial economy.

The regular tax (*nengu*) included supplemental taxes known as "lost rice," (*kake-mai*), "deficient rice," (*komi-mai*), and a surcharge called *kuchi-mai.* "Lost rice" was designed to replace whatever rice may have been lost during shipments; "deficient rice" was collected to make good any shortage that occurred when the rice was being measured; and the surcharge was imposed as a fee for handling the rice. These supplements amounted to about 10 percent of the regular tax. In addition there was the "five *ri* transportation fee," which required peasants to pay for up to five *ri* of the rice's overland journey to the port of shipment. Beyond five *ri* the bakufu and daimyo were required to pay, with the transit fee being determined by the number of rice sacks and the distance they had to travel.

As for miscellaneous dues, there were four categories: "produce fees" (*komono-nari*), "special levies" (*takagari-mono*), "country service" (*kuniyaku*), and "labor service" (*buyaku*). Produce fees were imposts on the yield from woods, brushland, and land adjoining lakes, ponds, rivers, and seas that were not subject to regular taxes. They also included fees on small commercial and industrial activities, in effect constituting a form of business tax. The labels, kinds, and amounts of produce fees varied greatly depending on time and place, but compared to the regular land tax these levies were low-level imposts on the peasantry. Special levies were collected to pay for highway repair, culinary expenses for Edo Castle, costs of rice storage, and so on. Country service was occasional levies collected by the bakufu to defray the cost of repairing rivers, roads, levees, damage from natural disasters, entertainment of foreign envoys, etc. Labor service was corvée demanded of the peasantry. In the early years of Tokugawa rule, the burden of corvée was heavy because of labor services required for military purposes. But as social conditions became more stable, these duties decreased, and the only regular service demanded of villagers was to provide labor and horses for the depots along main highways. In any case, compared to the land tax, these levies were relatively minor burdens on the peasantry.

Organization of Agricultural Villages

The bakufu and daimyo placed villages at the bottom of the social structure to keep the peasantry under control. However, the basic function of villages was to enable peasants to cooperate in the processes of economic production and daily living. In the latter half of the Tokugawa period, there were about 63,000 villages whose sizes differed considerably. According to the cadastral surveys, the average village had an estimated yield of about 400 *koku* and a peasant population of a little over 400. Of course, there were large villages with estimated yields of over 1,000 *koku* as well as small ones with yields of barely 50 *koku*. As for residential patterns, generally houses were grouped together in a cluster pattern, but in rare instances dwellings were dispersed.

Basically villages consisted of peasants who were roughly equal in economic resources and social standing. When we examine the economic condition of a village's core members (*honbyakushō*), the following pattern emerges:

1. A typical peasant household was a nuclear family with husband, wife, and children as the core, possibly with the addition of parents.

2. It had a residential plot, a house, and a work shed.
3. It possessed about one *chō* of farmland.
4. It owned the tools necessary for farming.

These four conditions would be found in a typical farm family. Although the peasants were subject to the authority of the bakufu and daimyo and were compelled to pay land taxes to them, they were, at the same time, economically autonomous entities who on their own and their family members' initiative engaged in agricultural production. Needless to say, there were different levels of agricultural undertakings in the villages.

Honbyakushō were registered in the cadastral register and possessed enough paddy land, upland, and homestead to be independent farmers. The bakufu and daimyo regarded them as the villagers who were responsible for payment of basic land taxes. Within the village they were allowed to attend village assemblies and had the right to voice their opinions on village affairs. In contrast, peasants known as *mizunomi* held only minimal strips of land and were not allowed to take part in deciding village affairs.

This class distinction within the village between *honbyakushō* and *mizunomi* came about from late in the seventeenth century as the process of opening up new farmland peaked and villages reached the maximum number of people they could support. This development limited the number of people who could be admitted to the status of *honbyakushō*, which meant restricting fresh entry into the status by peasants who emigrated from other villages, by second and third sons of influential families who had established new households, and by upwardly mobile semi-indentured peasants. However, the emergence of a restricted *honbyakushō* status did not guarantee the perpetuation of consanguineous households. If the village assembly approved, families not related to current *honbyakushō* and peasants who had moved to the villages from other communities could buy or be granted *honbyakushō* status. Also, changes in the status of *honbyakushō* families could result from problems that beset individual families, such as natural calamities, sickness, accidents, and other unforeseen developments. The *mizunomi*, however, remained a class of peasants who were excluded from *honbyakushō* status.

There were, besides *honbyakushō* and *mizunomi*, indentured peasants known by various names. Their class standing was lower than the *mizunomi*'s. They were allowed to reside in the village under the auspices of specific *honbyakushō* and worked in their fields. These class divisions of *honbyakushō, mizunomi*, and indentured peasants did not mean, however, that family status endured over a long period. Changes in the economic and social conditions of individual peasants resulted in shifts in relative class standing.

In principle, *honbyakushō* possessed the attributes necessary to exist as independent farmers, but individual farm households did not manage to survive through succeeding generations by themselves. A number of community organizations reinforced their ability to perpetuate their existence as independent farmers. Typical of these communal organizations were the *suiri kumiai* (association on water usage) and *iriai* (association on community woods and fields).

Rice growing was the backbone of Tokugawa agriculture. Needless to say, the most important condition for the production of rice was maintaining the water supply for paddy fields. Individual peasants could not possibly ensure the supply of water or regulate its use. It was necessary to form a special local association or a communal organization to administer water usage. Groups known as *igumi* (well association) and *mizugumi* (water association) were such organizations. These village-based organizations were established in all localities.

The associations that regulated water usage might involve only a single village, but often several villages cooperated to build irrigation facilities. In some instances, large organizations managed water usage of areas encompassing as many as fifty villages. The associations, which were managed by consultation among representatives from participating villages, dealt with such matters as collection and distribution of water, maintenance of the water supply system, selection of paddy fields to be abandoned in time of drought, and allocation of manpower and financial obligations.

Normally, running streams were used to water the paddy fields, and where dams were built to regulate the flow of water for irrigation, allocation to villages upstream and downstream constituted a major problem. The allocation often depended on the power relationship among villages, but in principle downstream villages were given prior rights, although in some instances village *kokudaka* figures determined allotments. As for the method of regulating water usage, in some cases the allocation was regulated by the hour, while in other cases special facilities were devised to regulate it.

When rainfall was scarce and damaging drought followed, serious conflicts often broke out over the allocation of water among contending villages in an association. These disputes among rival villagers frequently became violent, even ending in bloodshed, and it was not uncommon for many people to be killed and injured during such fights. To prevent the unfair diversion of water, representatives of the association were positioned day and night as watchmen at points where water was distributed. Moreover, within the village itself there was a fixed order of water usage in irrigating the paddies, and paddy fields owned by individual farm households were dispersed about the village so the householders could not irrigate their paddies as freely as they pleased. Rice production was thus controlled closely by the system of irrigation managed by the association on water usage.

Iriai refers to community usage of forest and wasteland by specific groups. The woods and waste can be divided into three categories according to usage. There were forest preserves (*otomeyama*) whose timber was reserved by bakufu and daimyo for construction of castles and for public works. Then there was *iriai* woodland for common usage by the peasants. Third were household woodlands open to use by the individual householder.

As for the types of *iriai*, some were restricted to a single village. Others involved several villages, or in some cases scores of villages, and they regulated the use of mountains that transcended the boundaries of any one village. In the former, villagers used in common the wood and wasteland not under tillage. In the latter, villages likely to compete for the use of woods and waste that encompassed a large area attempted to cooperate to utilize the resources in common. Despite such efforts, however, disputes often broke out among member villages over usage rights.

The products from *iriai* land were used in a host of ways for the peasants' productive work and daily living. They included vegetation that could be used as fertilizer, fodder for horses and cattle, construction material for irrigation facilities, public works, and housing, wood to make farm tools, firewood, miscanthus thatch for roofing, and edible products like fruits, nuts, and mushrooms. There were strict rules governing the use of *iriai* privileges. These related to when the resources could be extracted, the methods and tools for extracting them, the products that could be collected, the persons allowed to utilize the area, and so on. It should be added that in regulating the use of rivers, marshes, and the sea, the principles that governed *iriai* were adopted to regulate communal use by people engaged in fishery.

Village disputes consisted of three main types: disputes over water rights involving the association on water usage, disputes over usage of *iriai* resources among villages in multiple-village *iriai*, and boundary disputes. In settling these disputes, the ultimate authorities to which villagers could appeal for final decisions were the bakufu and the *han*, but ordinarily disputes were settled among the contending villagers themselves by talking things over. If at all possible, they avoided appealing to the bakufu and *han*, preferring to have an influential third party act as mediator. The rulers themselves preferred not to invoke their judicial authority in civil disputes among the common people and encouraged the disputants to settle their differences among themselves. The same policy was adopted in respect to civil disputes among peasants in the village.

At a lower level of village organization, we find the *gonin-gumi* (five-man group) system. The *gonin-gumi* system was introduced by the bakufu together with the practice of attaching everyone to Buddhist temples in implementing its policy of banning Christianity. It was a neighborhood self-policing system established to preserve peace and order in the villages. Depending on time and place, there were some variations, and three-man, four-man, and six-man groups were established, but usually five adjoining households were organized to form one unit. The five-man group thus formed on the basis of household proximity was the lowest-level organization that the bakufu and daimyo used to control the peasantry. Each *gonin-gumi* selected a head who represented the group to higher authority and took care of its business.

Villages were responsible for compiling new *gonin-gumi* registers annually. These consisted of two parts: an introduction and an agreement. The former consisted of rules and regulations issued to the peasantry by the bakufu or daimyo. It listed all the injunctions relating to farm work and daily life. The latter was a pledge by the *gonin-gumi* to be responsible for the enforcement of the injunctions listed in the introduction. All male members of a village had to affix their seals to the register in pledging to abide by the injunctions.

The functions of the *gonin-gumi* included the obligation of members to make up any shortage caused by delinquent taxpayers in their group; to prevent criminal activity by policing each other's daily behavior; to cooperate with one another in farm work; to serve as guarantors in civil suits and in contractual agreements; and so on. In other words, the smallest organization in the village served as the upholder of the village's system of joint responsibility.

Villagers were also categorized by age group, and each age group was assigned certain village functions. Among these organizations was the young men's group (*wakamono-gumi*). It consisted of young men who had reached adulthood but had not yet married. The group had its own building and belongings, and for set periods of time its members lived there in a communal fashion. Young men's groups were strongly independent organizations unencumbered by consideration of their parents' social standing or economic status. In some villages, a young women's group (*musume-gumi*) was organized for unmarried young women. The tasks undertaken by these young people's groups included performance of certain functions in village festivals and religious affairs, service as night watchmen and firefighters, and so on. By participating in their group's activities, the members of the young men's and women's groups acquired the skills and knowledge needed for farming, village politics, and the daily activities of the village. The organizations thus served as training grounds for future members of the village, giving them the experience necessary to function as qualified village adults.

Village Codes and Village Officials

In governing the peasantry, the bakufu and daimyo did not interfere directly in village affairs and regulate their lives on the spot. Rather, they adhered to the principle of holding the entire village or *gonin-gumi* jointly responsible, thus delegating to the villagers responsibility for upholding the laws of the domain. This delegation of responsibility emerged during the process that split the warriors and peasantry into separate classes during the years of the warring states and the beginning of the Tokugawa period. The spatial separation of warriors and peasants transformed villages into communities of agriculturalists. In the early part of the period, control of the peasantry was backed up by force, but from the midpoint of Tokugawa rule, authority over the peasantry was exercised through improved mechanisms of control, and the practice of delegating authority to the villages became increasingly common.

Typical of this delegating of authority was the practice discussed above of making villagers responsible for tax collection. Beyond the obligation to pay land taxes, this system of joint responsibility included responsibility to maintain law and order and regulate all aspects of daily life in the villages. It can be said that the villages were peasant communities with autonomous organizations at their core in which all problems that affected them were to be resolved by the villagers on their own responsibility.

The villages, then, were autonomous organizations in which the *honbyakushō* shared governing responsibility through their village assemblies. All problems of the village, internal and external, were discussed in the assembly meetings, which were held regularly several times a year. The New Year's meeting was especially important because general village policy for the coming year was decided then. Besides regular sessions, emergency meetings were called to deal with internal matters of special importance or disputes with other villages over water, mountain resources, or boundaries.

The items agreed upon by *honbyakushō* in the village assembly became the regulations governing village life. They included not only written regulations but unwritten laws based on customary practices of the village. Whereas the decrees issued by bakufu and *han* to regulate the lives of peasants represent the vertical power relationship between overlord and peasant, the village regulations signify the horizontal mutual relationship among *honbyakushō*. Among these regulations, however, there were instances in which decrees of the bakufu and *han* were adopted in toto as well as cases in which the introductory section of the *gonin-gumi* register was adopted as the village code. Village codes of this kind are clearly different in character from the self-regulating rules adopted by villagers themselves.

The code adopted in 1792 by Naka-shinden village in Shinano province is a perfect model of the self-governing regulations of Tokugawa villages. The code opens with an explanation of the procedures required for instituting civil suits in internal disputes. This is followed by twenty articles that constitute the body of the document.

   1. Young people are forbidden to congregate in great numbers.

2. Entertainments unsuited to peasants, such as playing the samisen or reciting ballad dramas, are forbidden.
3. Staging sumo matches is forbidden for the next five years.
4. The edict on frugality issued by the *han* at the end of last year must be observed.
5. Social relations in the village must be conducted harmoniously.
6. If a person has to leave the village for business or pleasure, that person must return by ten at night.
7. Father and son are forbidden to stay overnight at another person's house. An exception is to be made if it is to nurse a sick person.
8. Corvée assigned by the *han* must be performed faithfully.
9. Children who practice filial piety must be rewarded.
10. One must never get drunk and cause trouble for others.
11. Peasants who farm especially diligently must be rewarded.
12. Peasants who neglect farm work and cultivate their paddies and upland fields in a slovenly and careless fashion must be punished.
13. The boundary lines of paddy and upland fields must not be changed arbitrarily.
14. Recognition must be accorded to peasants who contribute greatly to village political affairs.
15. Fights and quarrels are forbidden in the village.
16. The deteriorating customs and morals of the village must be rectified.
17. Peasants who are suffering from poverty must be identified and helped.
18. This village has a proud history compared to other villages, but in recent years bad times have come upon us. Everyone must rise at six in the morning, cut grass, and work hard to revitalize the village.
19. The punishments to be meted out to violators of the village code and gifts to be awarded the deserving are to be decided during the last assembly meeting of the year.
20. Gifts to the honorees will be awarded during the New Year meeting.

In the following year, the same village adopted eight more articles.

1. Agricultural holidays will be the same as in other years.

2. Overgrown branches of trees that shade paddy and upland fields must be pruned.
3. Crops must not be harvested at night.
4. Crops in the fields must not be stolen.
5. The start of the season for using *iriai* land will be the same as in other years.
6. The products that may be gathered from household woods must be limited to those permitted in the past.
7. Fertilizer, ashes, miscanthus, etc., must not be sold to other villages.
8. The usual procedures must be followed in gathering fallen leaves and grass in the woods of the windbreak.

Other articles were subsequently added to the Naka-shinden village code. They dealt with such matters as taxes, water usage, *iriai*, security of the village, festivals and religious affairs, thrift, and frugality.

Violators of village codes were punished according to established practice. The severest punishments were exile from the village and ostracism (*mura-hachibu*). When a person was ostracized, villagers were to have nothing to do with him except in special circumstances, such as a funeral or fire. Exile and ostracism were held in reserve as punishments of last resort and were seldom invoked. The most common forms of punishment prescribed by village codes included specific monetary fines, a requirement to donate rice or sake, and punitive service as water guard, night watchman, storage house guard, and so on.

It was the village officials who actually applied the codes in managing village affairs. There were three types of officials: the headman (*nanushi* or *shōya*), group leader (*kumi-gashira, toshiyori*, or *otona-byakushō*), and peasant deputy (*hyakushōdai*). Known as the three village officials (*murakata san'yaku*), they represented the interests of villagers to the overlord while also serving as the administrators who controlled the peasantry on behalf of the bakufu or *han*. In other words, in managing the affairs of the village, they stood at the midpoint between rulers and subjects. Because of the crucial dual role these officials played, they occupy a significant place in any analysis of the historical character of Tokugawa villages.

The positions of the three village officials were established at different times, and they fulfilled different functions. The position of headman, or *nanushi*, was the only one present from the beginning of the period. In principle, there was only one *nanushi* in each village, and as the most responsible person in the village, he had the biggest voice in village politics. The position of group leader, or *kumi-gashira*, was established later. Originally the head of every *gonin-gumi* assisted the headman as group leader, but eventually it became common for only a few selected heads of *gonin-gumi* to provide this assistance. The position of *hyakushōdai*, which was created much later, differed in function from those of the headman and group leader. It was established to deal with such village conflicts as those that arose from accusations of misconduct leveled against *nanushi* or *kumi-gashira* or that led to demands for reforms in village government. As representatives of ordinary peasants, the *hyakushōdai* came to serve as watchdogs of village government. The holders of these three official positions became formally responsible for village governance only from the middle of the Tokugawa period. From about then, whenever formal documents or important papers were submitted to the bakufu or *han* by a village, the "three seals," that is, the seals of the *nanushi, kumi-gashira,* and *hyakushōdai* were affixed to them.

In principle, village officials were selected by the village assembly, and the bakufu and daimyo refrained from interfering and merely ratified the choice. The official most responsible for village affairs, the *nanushi*, was selected in one of the following three ways:

1. The position was a hereditary one retained by an upper-level family or by a family that had been prominent in the village since its founding.

2. The position was rotated every year or once in several years among the *kumi-gashira* who had served as the *nanushi*'s assistant.

3. The position was filled through election by the *honbyakushō*. The method of selection differed in time and place, of course, but generally speaking the hereditary system prevailed during the early Tokugawa. After the middle years, the rotating and elective systems became more common. In less advanced regions, the hereditary system persisted in many villages.

Needless to say, a person had to be a *honbyakushō* to become a village official. But officials also had to be educated enough to read, write, and work the abacus. They required knowledge about the economic and social affairs of the village and had to enjoy the support and respect of the villagers. Not everyone in the village could serve as a village official.

There were significant differences between hereditary *nanushi* and rotating or elected *nanushi* in terms of the administrative structure of the village and the character of the *nanushi*'s position. Where the hereditary system prevailed, the *nanushi* position was monopolized by one particular family and village governance was conducted by a handful of people. Where the rotating or elective system prevailed, there had to be a number of people capable of performing the duties of village officials and their ability to deal with numbers and their literacy level had to be high. In such villages, political affairs were conducted by the *honbyakushō*, who got together to discuss things as a body.

The duties of village officials were complex and varied. Their most important task was to make sure that the village's taxes were paid in full every year without a single case of delinquency. To perform this function, the *nanushi* and *kumi-gashira* had to assure that all villagers were aware of decrees issued by the bakufu or *han*. They had to observe carefully the condition of the year's crops, guide villagers in their farming techniques, make an accurate estimate of the yield each peasant was likely to produce, record it in the roster of villagers, and make an equitable allocation of the tax burden among the peasants.

They also had to ensure that peace and order prevailed in the village, so they served as mediators when conflicts of interest arose among the villagers. When disputes with other villages broke out, they had to take the lead in upholding their village's cause. They had to serve as guarantors when villagers concluded agreements about farmland, and they were responsible for the maintenance and repair of village shrines and temples. Also, they had to draft many documents. In other words, Tokugawa village officials performed all the administrative functions that town and village officials perform today. In general, the headman's house served as the village office, and village officials performed their duties without financial remuneration, though in some villages they were paid a nominal fee from the village treasury.

Village Finances and Social Security

The Tokugawa village functioned as a self-governing system of collaborating *honbyakushō* who assembled at village meetings where
they adopted regulations regarding village life and agricultural production. Village officials, as key figures in its government, actually
administered affairs. For this arrangement to work, a regular financial system had to be established. Village finances were generally
called *mura-nyūyō*, or village necessities, meaning the expenses
needed to manage village affairs. They are akin to the expenditures
covered by local taxes today.

The expenditures that came under *mura-nyūyō* were many. They
included expenses incurred in collecting taxes for the lord, in enter-
taining the lord's regional officials, and in organizing shrine and
temple festivals and services. They also included the costs of maintaining roads, rivers, bridges, and canals; purchasing paper, ink,
brushes, and other articles needed for conducting village business;
and defraying the travel expenses of village officials. Moreover,
when there were disputes with other villages, additional amounts
were consumed by the costs of litigation.

In managing village finances, officials made payments as necessary, and at year's end calculated their expenditures for the year
and collected that amount from the villagers. The most common
method of allocating expenditures among the villagers was to
divide the costs on the basis of each household's *kokudaka*. Other
methods involved assigning an equal share to each household, calculating each household's obligation in proportion to the number of
people in the household, or calculating each household's obligation
by the length of residential plot facing the road. Sometimes a combination of these methods was adopted. There also were cases
where village officials estimated the economic resources of every
household, ranked them in a hundred or more classifications, and
assessed each household according to its classification. As a general
principle, the assessments for defraying village expenditures were
designed to be fair and equitable.

The *nanushi* and *kumi-gashira* were required to create a *mura-nyūyō*
ledger as a record of the village's financial state. At year end, when
expenditures for the year were calculated and imposts on the peasants allocated, the *hyakushōdai* always attended the meeting to wit-
ness the proceedings and audit the accounting. The *mura-nyūyō*

ledger then had to be submitted to the bakufu or daimyo for inspection. This requirement came about because village controversies broke out over charges that the *nanushi* and *kumi-gashira* had embezzled village funds or allocated taxes unfairly. Indeed, the main source of conflict between village officials and ordinary peasants was the management of village expenditures. Nevertheless, from the middle of the Tokugawa period it became common practice for the bakufu and daimyo simply to affix their seals of approval to village financial ledgers as long as there were no errors in calculation, leaving to village officials and participants in the village assembly responsibility for calculating and auditing village expenditures. In this respect, the creation of the post of *hyakushōdai* had great value for the development of village government as a system of self-rule by collaborating *honbyakushō*.

The economic activities of *honbyakushō* were constantly endangered by unexpected occurrences; personal problems such as sickness or indolence; and natural calamities such as earthquakes, rainstorms, and drastic fluctuations in temperature. The rulers, seeking to preserve the *honbyakushō* system that sustained their own political authority, instituted relief measures to rehabilitate farm villages when disaster struck. These measures included the operation of relief shelters for the needy in time of crop failure and famine, emergency provision of rice or money to the needy, and provision of health care centers and child care to ensure the future supply of farm laborers. However, these measures to ensure the preservation and stability of the *honbyakushō* system were not integral components of the basic administrative policies of the bakufu and *han*, and as a general rule relief measures were regarded as matters to be handled by the villagers themselves.

In the grain storage system, rice, barley, millet, etc., were stored in normal times in anticipation of natural calamities, at which time the grain would be distributed to the victims of crop failure and famine. Although this was one of the village rehabilitation programs promoted by the bakufu and *han*, in practice the villagers themselves were responsible for its implementation. Every year, village officials exacted a certain amount of grain from the peasants at harvest time and stored it in the village's community storehouse, keeping an annual record of the amount stored.

Rice or money for peasant relief was financial assistance that the bakufu and daimyo loaned to villagers in times of natural calamity to help them pay for food, seeds, and farm tools. The funds were in reality a part of the land tax that the peasants had paid, and the lords charged 30-percent interest on the loans, which had to be repaid within a fixed period. Of course, the funds did provide temporary relief to needy peasants and aided their survival, but they also served to reinforce the exploitation of the peasantry. However, within the village the manner in which stored grain and money for peasant relief were distributed indicates that the economic condition of the impoverished peasants was given careful consideration.

In times of crop failure and famine, village officials and wealthier peasants donated to the village, without compensation, an amount of grain and money appropriate to their resources. Needy peasants received portions of the grain or money and attempted to rehabilitate their lives as farmers. Alternatively, assets of the *mura-nyūyō* might be tapped for rice or money to aid the needy, or village officials or heads of *gonin-gumi* might pay their debts, and on occasion members of the *gonin-gumi* paid the land tax or *mura-nyūyō* dues of those in trouble. These forms of communal assistance in village economic life reflect the principle of mutuality that prevailed within the peasantry.

The *kō*, or mutual aid society, was a noteworthy village association that provided aid to its members. The *mujin* (literally, unending) and *tanomoshikō* (literally, association which mothers and children can count on) were *kō* that provided financial services to the common people. They were local organizations whose members were bound together by geographical proximity. Their purpose was to assist those in distress or to cover the costs of house construction, roof repair, the purchase of horses and cattle, and so on. These then were financial institutions run cooperatively by the peasants who deposited funds in them.

A typical function of these associations was to serve as a kind of insurance system. The peasants contributed grain or money to the association according to their economic ability. Village officials or wealthy villagers then served as trustees, paying a fixed interest to the association for use of its funds. Then when famine, unanticipated crisis, or tax payment delinquencies occurred, villagers used the funds in the association to deal with the difficulty. There also were *kō* created to set aside funds for religious and recreational purposes. Such *kō* might accumulate funds so people could travel to worship at celebrated shrines and temples, and every year several members were selected to represent the *kō* in such pilgrimages. Diverse other religious *kō* were created to serve followers of popular cults.

Despite the elaborate measures developed to succor distressed villagers, peasant unrest was common. The number and kind of peasant conflicts that occurred in the Tokugawa period varied in time and place, but they can be classified in terms of three broad categories: *hyakushō ikki, yonaoshi ikki*, and *murakata sōdō. Hyakushō ikki* were peasant uprisings directed against the rulers most commonly to get taxes reduced. *Yonaoshi ikki* were uprisings demanding social reforms to eliminate extreme disparities in wealth. *Murakata sōdō* were protests directed against village officials, condemning them for unjust actions or demanding their recall.

Of the three types of conflict, peasant uprisings had the strongest characteristics of class struggle. However, these *hyakushō ikki*, or peasant uprisings, were not class struggles in which peasants demanded fundamental changes in the power structure of the bakufu and *han*. Most were merely economic struggles dealing with tax rates, with protesters calling for temporary reductions in taxes. The other two types of peasant conflict accompanied changes in village life. From the mid-Tokugawa period, a type of rich farmer, the so-called *gōnō*, began to emerge. These *gōnō* acquired a great deal of land, served as village officials, dealt in grain and fertilizer, lent money, gradually drifted away from agricultural production, and began to behave like merchants. The targets of *yonaoshi ikki* and *murakata sōdō* were primarily these profit-seeking, rich farmer-merchants; and the purpose was to obstruct their economic activities, which were undermining the *honbyakushō* system. As a whole, Tokugawa peasant conflicts can be regarded as economic struggles to correct growing disparities of wealth and equalize the distribution of income within the existing class system of samurai, peasants, artisans, and merchants.

Information and Documents in the Villages

As discussed above, the Tokugawa farm village was virtually a closed communal system. The system was designed to prevent the exacerbation of peasant class divisions by sustaining the core peasant group. However, villages were not completely sealed off from one another or from other domains and urban centers. Villagers had contact with other people, and material goods and information flowed in from the outside. In fact, villagers encouraged the inflow and utilized it constructively. Thus, the villages were communities of producers open to the outside world.

Village officials traveled frequently to the castle town on village or *han* business and brought back whatever sorts of information they had acquired there. The peasants themselves traveled to castle towns, towns along the highways, and port towns to sell their surplus products or buy daily necessities. These urban centers were not only distribution centers for consumer goods; they also served as cultural and information centers for the outlying regions. Peasants who went on sightseeing junkets and pilgrimages to distant temples and shrines brought back with them the latest urban fashions as well as new information.

In Tokugawa society, goods were transported mainly by water. Inland villages received their goods and information via boat stops located along rivers. For villages in mountainous areas, people and goods came directly over mountain passes. These arrangements enabled villages to maintain fairly swift communication with one another. Seafood and salt traveled from fishing villages along the seacoast, up river valleys, and over mountain passes to highland villages. Many routes were opened to mountainous areas to facilitate delivery of salt. Also, village officials tended to establish marital ties with officials in other communities, and their networks of information overlapped the web of marital ties. Thus, Tokugawa villages were not communities isolated from other areas.

Even today in Japan a huge quantity of village documents is stored in farmhouses, museums, and archives. A farm family whose ancestors served as village officials in the Tokugawa period and continued into the modern period as a prominent, wealthy family might have more than 30,000 documents from the period in its possession. There is a story about a farm family that hired people to help it burn its documents right after the defeat in World War II. It took them three days and three nights to finish the job. One can imagine that the number of Tokugawa village documents must have been astronomical. Rarely in world history have the subject people of a premodern era composed with their own hands and passed on to the present such huge amounts of documents which attest to the history of their own lives.

All official documents were written in a standard style, and for all social classes the forms of documents were uniform regardless of whether they were official or private in nature. Despite differences in dialect from one province or domain to another, through the medium of written materials one's intentions were easily communicated regardless of the status or the distance that separated communicants. What made this situation possible was the high literacy rate of the common people, not to mention the warrior class.

Village officials were fully capable of drafting formal documents in the official style. They submitted administrative documents to the bakufu and the *han* and issued the papers necessary to conduct their business. As an example, for a young woman from village A to move into village B to marry, papers concerning her family record had to be prepared. The *nanushi* of village A had to check the temple registration and census record where the woman was registered and also look into her background. He then prepared a certificate called *ninbetsu okurijō* (certificate of transference of a person) and sent it to the *nanushi* of village B, whereupon the latter recorded the young woman's name in his village's temple register as a new resident. He then dispatched to the *nanushi* of village A a document called *hikitorijō* (certificate of acceptance) certifying that the young woman had indeed moved to his village. After receiving that document, the *nanushi* of village A removed the young woman's name from her former temple register. In other words, when a single person moved to another village, at least two documents had to be prepared. The officials of village A and village B took care of the business of registration by exchanging documents. A similar procedure was followed in marriages where the groom joined the bride's family, in cases of divorce, and when a family or person moved from one village to another. Similar procedures were used in transactions involving material goods.

Decrees issued by the bakufu or the *han* circulated from village to village according to a fixed schedule, with a single copy circulating among several or even scores of villages. Village officials copied the information in the village record book and passed the document on to the next village. The last village to receive it had to report to the bakufu or *han* that its circulation had been completed. There are instances in which peasant uprisings and riots broke out because village officials made mistakes in reporting the content of the decrees or kept information to themselves, leaving the villagers uninformed. Village officials were expected to convey decrees and reports to their villagers accurately and quickly. In this area, also, the *hyakushōdai* who served as watchdogs for the villagers performed an important function.

2. Advances in Agriculture

During the centuries of Tokugawa rule, many changes and advances occurred in agriculture. There was a great expansion in arable acreage, and much of this expansion was accompanied by improvements in irrigation technique. There were advances in the organization of farm work, the technology of agronomy, and the use of fertilizers and crop varieties. There was a marked growth in production for the commercial market and in regional specialization. Finally, these changes in agronomy were recorded in a rich variety of horticultural writings that contributed greatly to the diffusion of the new agronomic practices.

Expansion of Arable Land

From the time rice culture became established in Japan in the Yayoi period, an active policy of increasing the arable land has been pursued, but the area under cultivation has not seen a steady linear increase. The period from the years of warring states to the early Tokugawa period constituted the greatest age of land reclamation because unparalleled acreages were brought under cultivation then.

Precise figures on the increase of arable land are hard to come by, but general estimates can be made. Around A.D. 930 arable acreage totalled about 860,000 hectares; around 1450, it was 950,000 hectares; around 1600, 1,640,000 hectares; around 1720, 2,970,000 hectares; and in 1874 it was 3,050,000 hectares (or about 7.5 million acres). These figures suggest the grand scale of the land reclamation that was undertaken between the fifteenth and eighteenth centuries. For rulers of that age, reclamation meant an expansion in the area of productive land under their control. This expansion was essential to their policy of increasing their wealth and strengthening their military power (*fukoku kyōhei*), so naturally they fostered land reclamation projects.

The large-scale land reclamation projects of the warring states to early Tokugawa period were made possible by rapid improvements in engineering. Warring states daimyo utilized military technology extensively in the construction of fortresses, opening of mines, and land reclamation. In particular, advances in hydraulic engineering proved to be the most significant factor affecting the economic productivity that stimulated the social transformation which unfolded from the medieval to Tokugawa period. Agriculture was based on paddy culture that required irrigation, so advances in its productivity depended utterly on the assurance and upkeep of a reliable water supply. Reclamation of farmland did not entail merely the expansion of arable acreage but depended on the combination of land and water.

The irrigation system mostly relied on water drawn from rivers, which differed from the practice of using water stored in reservoirs that was typical of the ancient and medieval eras. In the Tokugawa period, levees, dams, and water inlets had to be constructed in the rivers, and lengthy canals were built to carry the water to the fields. These measures increased tremendously the water available for agriculture, which made possible comparable increases in the land under irrigation. Japan is a volcanic archipelago whose topography is dominated by extremely precipitous north-south running ranges that make the rivers short and swift compared to those of other countries. In consequence, to use river water for irrigation, which was necessary if agricultural production was to be increased, it was absolutely essential to devise measures for preventing rivers from flooding or rampaging wildly.

A representative warring states daimyo, Takeda Shingen, developed the Kōshū-style water-control system to regulate the Kamanashi River which rampaged through his domain. Instead of constructing continuous dikes running parallel to the river, he had discontinuous levees built that projected into the river at optimal angles for guiding the river's flow. He reinforced the levees by planting trees and bamboo on them. Kōshū-style water control thus used the natural flow of the river to regulate the wild currents of the flood season.

The Tokugawa bakufu employed the Kōshū-style system in its

land development programs, not only to prevent flooding of farm-lands but also to make water for agriculture and daily usage available in a stable and reliable fashion. It also helped to improve water transportation, which was the primary mode of transporting goods. In these several ways, the Kōshū style improved dramatically the utilization of river water.

The basic principles adopted by the Tokugawa rulers in river control were to leave the meanders of a river untouched, as much as possible, to broaden the riverbed, and in place of high dikes running along the river, to construct dikes low enough to let the river spill over during flood seasons. To handle the overflowing river water either double embankments or wide catchment basins might be built. Along the reaches of big rivers, additional channels were dredged to prevent flooding of farmlands and urban centers by diverting water from the main river. Thus, from the era of warring states to the early Tokugawa period, the bakufu and daimyo transformed the principal rivers into artificial waterways by mobilizing large numbers of peasants to work on water-control projects in their domains.

These riparian projects enabled peasants living along the middle and lower reaches of large rivers to engage in farming. Large areas of alluvial soil and low swamp land could be brought under cultivation for the first time. Prior to this, the land opened up for irrigation consisted mainly of thin strips located in narrow valleys among low hills or in mountainous regions. Rice cultivation could not be increased significantly under these circumstances. Now not only were lands in the middle and lower reaches of large rivers reclaimed for cultivation, but long canals were built to draw water into hitherto unproductive land and foothills. Drainage projects were initiated to remove water from swamplands. Thus, in the transition from medieval to Tokugawa agriculture, the acreage of arable land increased greatly. Also, it must be noted, there occurred a substantial geographical shift of farm villages from the highlands to the plains.

Reclamation of arable land in the Tokugawa period is generally referred to as *shinden kaihatsu*, or development of new rice fields. The projects usually entailed reclaiming land for new paddy fields that would suffice to create one or more new villages. But the term *shinden kaihatsu* is also used more broadly to refer to the opening of small strips of land by individual peasants who used their own labor and resources to add to their farm plots. In the landholding system, the terms *honden* and *shinden* identified respectively those rice fields of a given locality that were brought under cultivation before and after the cadastral survey of that area had been conducted. For a certain number of years, the newly reclaimed rice fields were exempt from taxation. And after they were placed on the tax rolls, the tax rate was fixed at a level lower than that of *honden*. The development of *shinden* thus expanded a lord's productive lands while benefiting the people at large. For the peasants, it allowed more profitable husbandry, and for the townspeople, places to spend their unused capital by purchasing rural land and investing in land development. Even today we find on maps many villages from the Tokugawa period that have the term *shinden* affixed to the names of places, people, temples, and shrines.

The reclamation projects had limits, however, requiring adequate resources and proper social conditions. These limits caused reclamation projects to peak and level off from the second half of the seventeenth century. The woodlands and wetlands that had been the targets of reclamation had been fully exploited, and the opening of new land began contributing to the deterioration of existing farmland. The careless reclamation of hillsides, in particular, caused frequent floods in many areas. Moreover, it became difficult to provide sufficient manpower for the increased farm acreage, which led to labor shortages, higher wages, and slovenly husbandry.

To cope with careless reclamation, in 1666 the bakufu issued a three-article decree entitled "Regulations on Mountains and Rivers." The three articles stated:

1. In recent years people have been digging out the roots of grass and trees so that when it rains the soil quickly washes into rivers and streams. This has caused riverbeds to rise and floods to occur frequently. Henceforth, people are forbidden to dig out grass and tree roots.
2. Trees must be replanted in the upper reaches of rivers that have been denuded.
3. People are forbidden to turn the areas between river and river bank into farmland or to build any structures that might obstruct water flow. They are also forbidden to create slash-and-burn fields where such practices may cause soil erosion.

Figure 1. Tilling and harvesting scenes. Prints by Maruyama
Ōkyo. Eighteenth century. Cabinet Library Collection; repro-
duction courtesy of Nohsan Gyoson Bunka Kyokai Corporation.

The object of this decree was to curb excessive reclamation and
protect the land by adopting policies of river and forest management. In other words, the bakufu had decided to curtail the previous
agrarian policy of emphasizing land reclamation, and was turning to
a policy of efficient husbandry that would increase output of existing farmland.

Agricultural Technology

Tokugawa agriculture was based on production of the major grains:
rice, barley, and wheat, and most especially rice grown in paddy
fields. In line with the social hierarchy, the rice produced in paddy
land was to be used for tax payments to the rulers, while the products of upland were mostly to be used by the peasants for their own
sustenance. These upland products included wheat, barley, beans
such as soy and red beans, miscellaneous grain crops like millet,
barnyard millet, buckwheat, and common millet, and vegetables
like *daikon* and turnip.

The core of the farm labor force was the nuclear family. The husband and wife were the principal workers, but the elderly and children did what they could. During the busy season when the work such as rice planting or harvesting could not be handled by a single family, villagers formed mutual assistance groups called *yui* (knitting together) with members of their *gonin-gumi*, with other fellow villagers, or with people from nearby villages.

The goal of the household labor force was to make effective use of family workers without hiring outside help. In more commercialized areas, however, villagers employed day laborers, workers hired by the year, and household servants, whereas in some of the more backward areas, large-scale landholders farmed with indentured workers.

Another important form that village work took was when the entire village worked together in a communal fashion. For example, to keep large irrigation ditches in good order, villagers worked together during slack seasons every year to remove the accumulated mud and weeds. This maintenance work was patterned on the cooperative water usage established by the riparian association. The same kind of community cooperation is seen in the maintenance and operation of such community facilities as dikes, roads, bridges, and warehouses. Agriculture was thus founded on the dual labor system of individual household labor and communal village labor.

The most essential farm instruments were the hoe and sickle, which were crucial to the peasant's manual work (Figure 2). They functioned simply as extensions of the human hand, but they were light and easy to use and could be obtained fairly cheaply. The diffusion of such iron farm instruments among the peasants contributed greatly to increasing the productive capacity of Tokugawa agriculture . On the other hand, there was no close linkage between crop cultivation and animal husbandry because Japanese farming was peculiarly lacking in the latter. The extent of draft animal husbandry varied regionally, but fewer than 10 percent of all farm families engaged in it. Only the few upper-class farmers used draft animals in their field work.

The hoe was used not just to turn over the soil but also to break up clods and level paddy fields before planting, weed them after planting, and so on. The hoe that was most commonly used, a flat hoe, consisted of a wooden handle that was inserted into a wooden

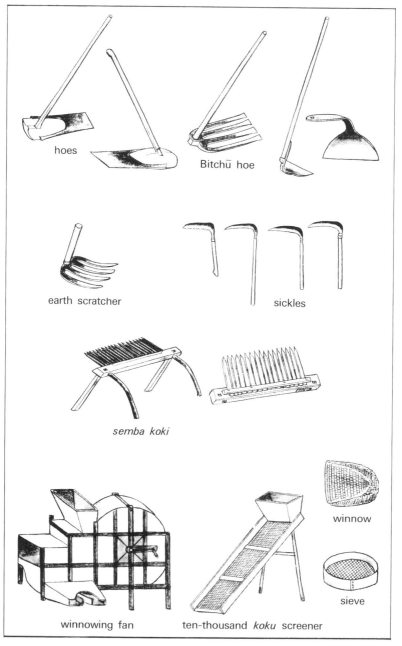

Figure 2. Farming tools. From *Nihon rekishi taikei: Kinsei* (Yama-kawa shuppansha, 1988).

base to which an iron blade was attached. Peasants chose the best quality iron they could obtain for the blade, taking old pots and pans to the blacksmith in the village or castle town to have him beat them into hoe blades. From the mid-Tokugawa period, specialized hoes were developed for diverse uses as well as for particular soil conditions. For instance there was the Bitchū hoe in which the flat hoe was transformed into an instrument with three or four prongs to be used exclusively for turning over the soil. The Bitchū hoe was especially valuable in the initial stage of soil preparation because it permitted deeper tilling. With the invention of the Bitchū hoe, the traditional hoe came to be used for light surface work, such as forming dirt partitions in the rice paddies and hilling around plants. For mid-season weeding, small rakes and earth scratchers came to be used, and at harvest time the sickle was the chief instrument for cutting off the stalks of grain. The stalks were cut to the root because they were used to make various straw products and served as fuel. The sickle, like the hoe, came to be modified for specialized use.

Improvements in farm tools were not limited to hoes and sickles: better methods of threshing were also devised. The thresher that was initially used to separate grain from the ear, the *koki hashi*, consisted of two sticks of bamboo across which the ears were drawn. It was very inefficient, however, and as wages rose, hiring temporary hands to do the work with *koki hashi* became too costly. Then the *semba koki*, a thresher with a "thousand teeth," was invented. It was nicknamed the "bankrupter of widows" because whereas women had done the threshing when the older, double-prong thresher was used, with the new device, threshing opportunities for widows virtually disappeared. The new thresher, which was constructed by attaching a series of iron teeth to a wooden plank, could handle ten times more ears than the *koki hashi*, and its diffusion reduced drastically the amount of labor required in threshing, thereby changing the annual pattern of farm work as well as the techniques of agronomy.

Other threshing tools also improved. The wooden mortars used in hulling the rice were replaced by earthenware mortars. To remove dust from the unhulled grain after threshing and to separate kernels from chaff after hulling, farmers used devices that winnowed grain in the wind, and sieves that sifted grain according to size. Also, a winnowing fan, which created a breeze for winnowing, and the "ten thousand *koku* screener," which used a sifter placed at an angle, came to be used. Needless to say, all of these harvesting instruments were worked manually by the peasants.

In watering and draining rice fields, peasants had to manage the water with great precision. In accordance with the practices established by their village's association on water usage, growers worked carefully to assure their fields the right amount of water. They took steps to guarantee that paddy received sufficient water in hot, dry weather, and in the event of floods during typhoon season or prolonged rainfall, they acted quickly to drain the fields of excess water. During the weeks when the rice plants were growing, not only watchmen appointed by the association but also all the rice growers went around day and night checking water outlets, irrigation ditches, and fields.

In mountain villages where farmers had to obtain water from hot or cold springs, and in villages in colder regions where they had to use melting snow, they converted paddy fields into farm ponds or drew the water along long, serpentine ditches to raise its temperature to optimal levels. In regions where it was not possible to irrigate by means of ditches, they used lifting devices such as water wheels, mounted buckets, and radial treadles. In some villages located on the deltas of large rivers, growers used tread wheels, and in villages with small rivers or canals running through them, they employed water-powered mills.

Vegetation was the chief source of fertilizer for preserving soil fertility, and *karishiki* was the most important method of keeping paddy land fertile. In *karishiki*, rice growers spaded into their fields grass and bushy growth that they had cut and removed from wood and wasteland and the paths and ridges of paddies during the spring. It was necessary, therefore, to have sufficient space for this growth near the fields. The communal use of this wood and wasteland was handled through the village's *iriai* system. When the conversion of wood and wasteland to rice cultivation leveled off from the latter half of the seventeenth century, a major reason was the need to preserve areas where fertilizer material grew.

The cultivation of crops for industrial use, which is discussed below, as well as the expansion of double cropping, with rice as the main crop and wheat or barley following it, and intensified land usage based on advances in farming technique led to improvements in the art of fertilizing, and various fertilizers besides grass came to be spread in the fields. There was compost consisting of barnyard droppings mixed with rice straw, fallen leaves, garbage, and so on. Farmers also used weeds gathered from lakes and ponds, night soil, and any biodegradable rubbish left over from daily use. Besides these homemade fertilizers, there were others that had to be purchased: vegetation, ashes, and such industrial by-products as the residue from cotton and rapeseed oil production, the bran generated by polishing rice, and the cakes of meal that remained after oil had been extracted from sardines and herring.

Farmers in lowland villages lacking brushland and in more commercially advanced areas were the first to apply fast-acting commercial fertilizers to their fields, thereby enhancing their income from farming. The most widely used commercial fertilizer was dried sardines, and as a consequence advances in coastal fishing were closely linked to advances in agricultural productivity. Improvements in the art of soil enrichment involved not only the varieties and quantities of fertilizer to be applied but also the timing of their application, with meticulous care being given to apply the optimal amount of preplanting and postplanting fertilizers.

Weeds and insects were serious threats to crops. Weeds proliferated during the summer because of the heat and humidity, and in the annual round of farm work, peasants had to expend a great deal of labor in weeding. Especially onerous was the weeding of rice paddies, which had to be undertaken several times in the summer heat. A didactic proverb of the time said that the diligent peasant removes weeds before they appear, the middling peasant weeds them after they appear, while the lazy peasant lets them grow rank. The only method for controlling leaf hoppers, which damaged rice, was the application of oil. At first fish oil and rapeseed oil were used, but as the whaling industry grew, whale meat came to be used for food and the oil for protection against leaf hoppers. It is said that one could estimate the extent of insect infestation and the price of rice by checking fluctuations in the market price of whale oil.

The advances in agronomy are represented most tellingly in the breeding of plant varieties made by peasants themselves. In particular, the development of early-, middle-, and late-growing rice increased output, with the different dates of maturation helping peasants to prevent an entire crop from being damaged by typhoons, heavy rain, insects, sharp fluctuations in temperature, and so on. Moreover, the use of early maturing rice permitted more extensive double cropping and enabled peasants to spread out the periods of heaviest labor demand, specifically planting and harvesting. Thus, the development of rice varieties contributed to wide-ranging improvements in farming. From the mid-Tokugawa period, there appeared numerous varieties of rice named after persons, localities, and temples. Efforts at varietal improvement involved crops grown on uplands as well as wet rice. Peasants actively selected superior crops from their own fields and those of fellow villagers, and they exchanged improved varieties across domainal and provincial boundaries, choosing the varieties most suited to the climate and soil of their villages.

Development of Commercial Production

The Tokugawa division of labor, which separated peasants and samurai and distinguished among those engaged in commerce, industry, and agriculture, determined the character of urban centers and farm villages. Castle towns, temple and port towns, and towns along highways tended to be centers of consumption, whereas most of their food and raw materials were supplied by the villages. When military men ceased living in the communities where their land was located, villages became purely communities of working peasants, who, in principle, were economically self-sufficient. In practice, however, villagers were not totally self-sufficient in either their work or their daily lives. For example, they had to purchase iron for farm tools, salt for their food, clothing, and other daily necessities. To do so, they sold whatever farm products were left after taxes and family consumption, using the income to purchase these necessities.

From the latter half of the seventeenth century it became possible for peasants to retain a certain amount of surplus after they had paid their taxes. Instead of simply producing enough to pay the rulers their annual rice tax and ensure their own family's survival, they gradually shifted to the production of cash crops for the commercial market. They began growing specific crops as a way to earn money. As background factors to this development one may cite a rising standard of living among the common people, an increase in spending on consumer goods by the rulers, and the growth of consumption, with the three major cities of Kyoto, Osaka, and Edo leading the way.

The economy of the rulers could not fully function unless lords changed the rice they had extracted from the peasants into money in the central market place. In this sense, rice was the most important commodity in Tokugawa society. The price structure can be indicated by charting the price of rice separately from the prices of other material necessities, which will show the price differential. However, even though rice occupied a core position in the farm commodity market, it cannot be denied that its role was restricted by the rice tax system. For this reason peasants produced commercial crops in uplands that were not subject to rice-tax levies, and specialized dry-field cropping developed throughout the country on the general principle of suitable crops in suitable places. The specialized crops are represented by the so-called four trees and three plants. The four trees were tea, mulberry, lacquer, and paper mulberry; the three plants were hemp, safflower, and indigo. In general, these plants were grown for industrial uses, and other important industrial plants were cotton, rapeseed, and tobacco.

In the first half of the Tokugawa period, a clothing revolution occurred that replaced hemp with cotton as the raw material for clothing. Centered in western Japan, the production of cotton increased rapidly. In villages in commercially more advanced regions, as much as 70 percent of farm acreage came to be devoted to cotton production, with many paddy fields where water could be drawn in or drained efficiently growing cotton and rice alternately in one- or two-year rotations. As for the production of the more refined fabric, silk, after the import of raw silk from China was banned in the mid-seventeenth century, domestic sericulture expanded greatly. Sericulture consists essentially of cultivating mulberry bushes, feeding silkworms, and producing cocoons. However, creating the final product of silk fabric involves the industrial processes of extracting silkworm eggs, nurturing the worms, producing thread, and finally weaving. These requirements gave the sericulture industry the most extensive division of labor of the Tokugawa period.

The growth in cotton production and sericulture increased sharply the demand for dyes to color thread and fabric. As a result, areas specializing in the production of indigo and safflower dyestuffs came into existence. Safflower, which was also used in women's cosmetics, was one of the most highly priced industrial crops.

Peasants produced diverse other commercial materials. Sap from the lacquer tree was processed to make varnish for wooden utensils, while its fruit was used as wax for candles. Paper mulberry provided raw material for Japanese paper, which was used in the voluminous documents composed during the Tokugawa period. Rapeseed had a wide range of usages, being used for illumination, food, oil, animal fodder, green fertilizer, and so on. Even the dregs that remained after the oil had been extracted were deposited in the fields as fertilizer. Specialized production not only provided daily necessities for warriors and common people, but also such luxury goods as tea and tobacco.

These industrial products required both the agricultural processes from planting to harvesting and the manufacturing processes that yielded finished goods. The agricultural processes were handled by peasants as regional specialties throughout the country, but the manufacturing was primarily entrusted to artisans in cities like Kyoto and Osaka, with rural and urban merchants handling distribution of the raw materials and finished products. Thus, there developed a geographical division of labor. Unlike grains such as rice, wheat, and barley, these finished products commanded high prices that included relatively high added values, which made them strong earners even for the peasants. However, it must be admitted that the production of industrial crops required the use of expensive commercial fertilizer and costly horticultural techniques. Moreover, sharp fluctuations in the price of fertilizer and farm products caused farming to become an unstable vocation, so that in villages concentrating on specialized crops some peasants suffered economic ruin.

Another important development was the increase in vegetable production in villages near major urban centers. In the villages surrounding large cities, farming devoted largely to vegetables emerged to meet the needs of the growing population of urban consumers. River boats transported fresh vegetables to the cities and hauled urban waste products, such as rubbish and night soil, back to the villages for use as fertilizer. This arrangement, which is an excellent example of material goods circulation between urban and rural areas, solved the city problem of disposing of rubbish and waste products, while it enabled the surrounding villages to preserve the fertility of their soil.

Producing for the commercial market was not limited to farm villages but penetrated mountain and fishing communities as well. In mountain villages, people went deep into forests to cut timber for use in housing construction. They also cultivated paper mulberry trees and manufactured paper. They provided cities and farm villages with wooden tools and tableware, firewood, and charcoal. In mountain villages located along rivers, where it was possible to float timber downstream, villagers planted cedar and cypress trees, and beautiful forests began to emerge in different parts of the land. In fishing villages, the development of coastal fishing yielded varieties of shellfish and fish that provided protein for the dinner tables of Tokugawa society and whale-oil and fish-meal fertilizer that were essential to farming. In coastal regions where the sea was calm, salt fields were created for the production of salt. These developments were all part of the commercialization of forest and sea products.

The increase in specialized industrial production entangled peasants, merchants, and artisans, and even the rulers in the burgeoning commercial economy because of their interest in the profits. Merchants sought to purchase raw materials from peasants at low prices and to monopolize control of the distribution of manufactured products. *Han* officials encouraged the cultivation and processing of special products in their domains and established monopolies so that the fruits of commercial production would ease their financial difficulties. In its entirety, the nationwide configuration of production was also intimately linked to the development of a distribution network of sea routes, river routes, and highways and to the establishment of central markets in Osaka, Kyoto, and Edo and regional markets in castle towns. Without question the special products that peasants produced invigorated the economy, but at the same time these developments contained in them the economic forces that hastened the dissolution of Tokugawa society.

Writings on Agriculture

Many treatises on agriculture (*nōsho*) were written during the Tokugawa period. Although rice culture was introduced to Japan from the Asian continent almost two thousand years earlier, such works were written for the first time during this period.

These agricultural writings dealt mainly with the technical side of farming, but they also touched broadly such subjects as farm management, peasant thought, and daily life. Also, many other types of works appeared that were similar in content to these treatises. For instance there were works on botany that discussed the collection and efficacy of medicinal herbs and had a scholarly influence on authors of *nōsho*. There were famine-relief manuals that explained how to survive in times of crop failure and starvation by using and storing food substitutes found in woods and meadows, and product catalogues that listed the fauna and flora, minerals, and local specialties found in the different provinces. There were farm almanacs used as textbooks in the temple schools that educated children of commoners. There were civil engineering and riparian construction manuals that discussed the proper management of land essential to farm production. There were compendia of family precepts that instructed descendants on the credo of a proper peasant life, and diaries that carefully recorded how farm work and life were influenced by changes in the four seasons. Finally, there were forestry works that dealt with the organization of production in mountain villages, treatises by agrarian scholars on farm governance, and regional data books that were used by the authorities as comprehensive manuals to govern the peasants.

There also were many derivative farm books that consisted entirely of citations from originals. These plagiarized woodblock editions were sold by urban publishers for commercial purposes and circulated widely among the people. Their scholarly value as books on agronomy was insignificant, but their contribution in broadly diffusing agricultural information and in contributing to the improvement of agricultural technology cannot be denied.

Some farm books did not rely solely on the written word to explain agricultural techniques or peasant life. These devised other means of conveying their contents to illiterate peasants and warriors and townspeople who were not directly engaged in farm production. Some relied on audio-visual techniques, such as picture books that illustrated the chronology of farm work and life in terms of the four seasons. Some of these picture books were merely illustrations inserted in the farm books themselves, while others were independent picture books. Of the latter type, the book that is richest in content is *Nōgyō zue* (Illustrated book on agriculture), which illustrates in full color the farm work and folk culture of villages near the city of Kanazawa in snowy Kaga province on the Japan Sea coast.

As for works utilizing audio-educational methods, there were books that consisted of short poems (*waka*) about farming technique and peasant life, which a reader recited to an audience. For example, *Aizu uta nōsho* (Aizu *nōsho* of poems) summarized in 1,668 *waka* the contents of *Aizu nōsho* (Aizu farm book), which originated in a frigid snow basin in the northeast. The picture books and books of poems on farming deal with agricultural technology of the Tokugawa era, but they are also documents that give us glimpses of peasant literature.

Farm books can be divided into two categories in terms of the authors' objectives as instructional farm books or local farm books. Instructional books were written for the specific purposes of improving farming techniques and disseminating knowledge about agriculture and were published either by the authors at their own expense or by urban publishers who printed woodblock editions for sale. They circulated widely, captured a large readership, and had a significant impact on later developments in farm management and agricultural technology. In contrast, the local farm books, though they were influenced to some extent by the scholarship of the instructional farm books, mainly recorded the indigenous, practical farming technique of the author's home region. They were private accounts that authors wrote for family use to ensure the prosperity of their descendants, and they were only of local utility. Some were copied and circulated among the peasantry, but the existence of others was unknown during the Tokugawa period, many being discovered after World War II when regional history became popular.

The differences between the authors of instructional farm books and local farm books are seen not just in their motives and purpose but also in their social status. The authors of instructional farm books were primarily agricultural scholars or lower-level regional officials. The writings of the three greatest Tokugawa agricultural scholars, Miyazaki Yasusada, Ōkura Nagatsune, and Satō Nobuhiro, belong to the category of instructional farm books. On the other hand, local farm books were written by such people as village officials or wealthy peasants. That is, they were written by the peasants themselves.

Instructional farm books can be divided into general and specialized works, depending on their content and organization. General
farm books contained comprehensive discussions of agriculture as
well as methods of raising specific crops. Their contents usually
were according to consistent systems of agricultural science, as
typified by Miyazaki Yasusada's *Nōgyō zensho* (A comprehensive
book on agriculture) of 1697. This book, which is representative of
general *nōsho*, went through five printings in the Tokugawa period.

Specialized farm books dealt with selected topics such as a single
crop or a particular method of farming. Among these are a series of
works written by Ōkura Nagatsune, who might be called an agrarian journalist. For example, there are his *Nōgu benri ron* (Discourse
on the usefulness of farm tools), which discusses the importance of
selecting tools that are suited to the soil and the crop; *Jokō roku* (On
the extermination of locusts), which deals with the use of whale oil
to prevent infestations of leaf hoppers; *Menpō yōmu* (Essential facts
about cotton fields), which discusses in detail methods of growing
cotton; and *Nōka hibairon* (On farm family use of fertilizers), which
deals with the types and uses of fertilizers in sustaining soil vitality.
In 1859, Ōkura published his *Kōeki kokusankō* (Reflections on highly
beneficial national production), which can be regarded as the culmi-
nation of his lifework. It deals with ordinary crops, special crops,
forest products, and sea products, as well as the products of industrial arts. Ōkura comments on the advantages for farmers of producing these products and discusses the ways in which peasants can
be enriched and the national wealth increased.

Geographically, Japan consists of a long, slender archipelago
that extends north to south, so there is great regional variation in
the natural environment of its agriculture. Differences in such cli-
matic conditions as temperature and snowfall are especially to be
noted. In overall terms, moreover, there were differences in productivity between the area centered on Osaka and Kyoto, which had a
higher level of agricultural productivity, and the Kantō plain with
Edo at its center, which had a lower level. Taking these different factors into consideration, we can divide the local farm books into
works of warm and cold regions. Representative of the former is the
Kagyō den (Commentary on family business), and of the latter, *Aizu
nōsho* cited earlier. The former instructs the author's descendants on
the particulars of the annual work cycle and on the cultivation of

cotton, rice, wheat, edible roots, beans, potatoes, and so on in villages near Osaka. *Aizu nōsho* avoids discussing general aspects of farming technique and focuses on the method of farming relevant to the Aizu region only.

Some local farm books contain accounts of inspection tours and information on farming methods advocated by rural leaders in technically advanced agricultural regions. "Accounts of inquiries made concerning insect control in coastal Kyushu" (*Kyūshū omote mushi fusegikata nado kikiawaseki*) reports the findings of four peasants who toured advanced farm communities in Kyushu and noted their methods of rice cultivation and ways of controlling harmful insects. "Agricultural methods of farmers in the Kyoto region" (*Kamigata nōnin dembata shihōdameshi*) is an account from a farm village that invited peasants from agriculturally advanced communities to come and explain their farming techniques. These accounts are valuable documents for studying interaction among Tokugawa peasants and the diffusion of farming technology.

With the growth of domestic sericulture from the latter half of the seventeenth century, books on the subject were written throughout the country. Of particular note is *Yōsan hiroku* (Secrets of sericulture), which is the prototypical Japanese work on sericulture. It discusses in detail the origin of the art, methods of growing mulberry trees, instruments and facilities needed for silkworm raising, methods of raising silkworms, silk reeling, and so on. It contributed significantly to improvements in the art of sericulture and eventually was translated into French and circulated in Western Europe. Techniques in silk production are the only product of Tokugawa technology that was exported.

These farm-book authors dealt with all the specific issues that concern modern agricultural science. For example, they wrote treatises on farm labor, village farm plots, weather and farming, crops, plant varieties, farm soil, fertilizer, farm tools, and insect control. Still, it is undeniable that these treatises do not completely agree with the principles of modern experimental science.

Most notably, farm books dealing with plant varieties contained distinctive discourses on plant gender. The theory of plant gender, which was influenced by the Chinese concepts of yin-yang and the five elements, held that, just as with animals, so there are male and female plants. So it was believed that in cultivating plants, if seeds were selected by distinguishing between male and female seeds, and female seedlings were planted, the yield would be greater. This theory of gender differences gained such wide popular acceptance that a one-sheet publication called "On the selection of plants" ("*Sōboku senshu roku*"), which consisted of a diagram illustrating the gender differences in thirty-three trees and other plants, became a bestseller.

For controlling insects and plant diseases, whale oil was used, but praying at temples and shrines and performing rituals to drive off insects were also widespread practices. The rituals were performed by groups of villagers from May through August. They made straw dolls and paraded them through the fields while carrying pine torches and beating bells and drums. They ended the ritual by throwing the straw dolls, together with the insects, into the river or sea at the outskirts of the village.

From the perspective of modern scientific agronomy, these Tokugawa farm books have their limitations. Nevertheless, they are documents based on the agricultural methods of the peasants' own experience and are, therefore, records that explain the most effective ways of utilizing natural resources. Since the framework of the modern Japanese economy was erected on the two major pillars of rice and sericulture, and the technical knowledge that came out of these two agricultural enterprises was formulated by Tokugawa peasants themselves by means of these farm books; in the final analysis, those works played a key role in the development of modern Japan.

(Translation by Mikiso Hane)

Chapter Three

The Development of Rural Industry

SATORU NAKAMURA

The modernization of the Japanese economy began with the Meiji Restoration of 1868. A fundamental condition underlying that process, however, was the economic development that had already been achieved prior to Japan's opening to foreign trade and intercourse in 1859. This chapter will attempt to illuminate that economic development, with special attention to the cotton industry. Most industry that has occurred anywhere prior to an industrial revolution has been closely connected with agriculture and commerce. That was especially true of the cotton industry during the Tokugawa period, which developed initially as a rural industry. Therefore, this chapter will also necessarily touch on the connections among industry, agriculture, and commerce.

Cotton is a useful focal point for several reasons: (1) Cotton was a major industry of the Tokugawa period; it was the largest industrial sector in the post-Meiji Restoration period; and since its products were used to clothe the masses, it commanded the largest available market. (2) The cotton industry began to produce commercially in the mid-eighteenth century, and by the Restoration era it was an advanced industrial sector in which capitalism had made considerable strides. (3) After the opening of the ports, American and European—particularly British—industrial products flowed in, creating difficult conditions for domestic industry. Those imports consisted largely of cotton goods, both cloth and thread. (4) Cotton spinning and silk filature were the leading sectors in Japan's industrial revolution, which began around 1880.

1. Cotton Goods and Urbanization

Medieval society in the Kamakura and Muromachi periods and Tokugawa's early-modern society shared the decentralized structure that has traditionally been called feudal. However, in other ways, the two societies were very different. The most important economic difference between them relates to the development of commerce, which was quite far advanced by the early-modern period. Of course, the early-modern commercial economy was still quite distinct from that of the modern period, not only because it was at an earlier stage of development but also in the qualitative sense of having a different character and basic mechanism. That is, early-modern commerce was intended primarily to preserve an economy that was based fundamentally on fief-holding (*ryōshu keizai*).

Nevertheless, the commercial economy that developed in the early-modern era certainly exerted a powerful influence on the development of a modern capitalist economy. For example, the important trading goods of the post-1859 era—silk thread and tea as exports, cotton cloth and sugar as imports—were not really native to Japan. All four had been imported in medieval times, and they only began to be produced in Japan during the transition from the medieval to early-modern era. A technologically backward form of silk-thread production had existed since antiquity, but the silk thread that provided raw material for the advanced production characteristic of the fifteenth century and after—the Nishijin brocade—was all originally imported. Indeed, by the sixteenth and seventeenth centuries, silk thread had become Japan's largest import item.

Nor had cotton cloth always been used in Japan. Records indicate that a certain amount of cotton had been cultivated in ancient and medieval times, but only for limited periods and in specific locales. Cotton became economically significant only in the medieval era when it began to be imported from Korea and China. This import trade began in the late twelfth century and expanded in volume only in the fifteenth. Demand for cotton cloth increased precipitately only during the sixteenth-century period of general warfare, when soldiers used cotton for clothing, matchlock fuses, and sails for ships. In fact, imports increased so rapidly as a result that Korea had to impose export controls to avoid an adverse impact on domestic supplies. Japan was forced to turn to China, and by the late sixteenth century China had become Japan's major source of cotton goods.

Cotton cloth production had begun in India and was rather slow in spreading to East Asia. Cotton goods entered China under the Southern Sung and Yuan dynasties (twelfth–thirteenth centuries), and in the fourteenth century, under the Ming, China began to produce its own. Korea began production in the fifteenth, followed by Japan late in the century. However, the practice did not spread across the country until the sixteenth century.

Cotton cloth is believed to have been very expensive in the beginning, but it became more accessible to the masses as it diffused through the countryside. Hemp had been the most important material for clothing in the medieval period, but in the early-modern era it was replaced by cotton. Indeed, Japan began in late-medieval times to produce a variety of goods that earlier had been imported—not only cotton but also sugar, tobacco, tea, silk cloth, silk thread, and porcelain—and the lives of the people changed markedly as a result. It is also noteworthy that domestic production was commercial from the beginning. Even peasants were forced to engage in commercial relationships in order to make a living.

Cotton spread rapidly across Japan in the sixteenth century, particularly its latter half, and by the beginning of the seventeenth century it seems to have been in common use for clothing. By this time the cultivation and processing of raw cotton, as forms of commodity production, were tending to concentrate in the Kinai, which by that time was economically the most advanced region, and it was also there that agriculture and industry began to diverge. Conditions were unfavorable for cotton cultivation in regions such as Hoku-riku, Tōhoku, and Kyushu, and as a consequence, producers in those areas began to purchase large quantities of raw cotton from the Kinai and to transform them into cotton thread and, finally, cloth. Through this method, even backward agricultural regions such as Tōhoku and Kyushu were able to participate in a national commercial network.

During the seventeenth century, capital accumulation by merchants in Osaka and Edo had not yet progressed very far. Therefore, in the distribution of cotton commodities the *ninushi* (a type of merchant who used his own capital to purchase, store, and sell goods) was often a native of the producing or the consuming region, while the Osaka or Edo wholesale merchants (*ton'ya*) merely lived off commissions and shipping fees as middlemen. Wholesale merchants of this type were often called *niuke-don'ya* or *tsumi-don'ya*. However, beginning in the late seventeenth century, a new breed of large merchant, exemplified by the Mitsui house, appeared in the three largest cities of Edo, Osaka, and Kyoto. In contrast to the practice of the *niuke-don'ya*, these new urban merchants used their own capital to purchase goods from the production area, transport them to the consumers, and sell them. Called *shiire-don'ya*, they did not receive commissions but reaped large profits in return for the considerable risk they incurred in actually purchasing goods prior to putting them on the market. The economy developed considerably from the late seventeenth to the early eighteenth century, and as merchants of this new type rode the crest of that development, their rate of capital accumulation increased. By the eighteenth century they controlled a nationwide system of commodity distribution.

Another economic characteristic of the early-modern era was urbanization. In the Tokugawa period, a variety of large and small cities (up to several hundred in number) emerged all over the country and became an important economic and cultural legacy to modern Japan. The formation of these cities required the accumulation of large quantities of goods essential to the livelihood of city dwellers, especially agricultural products. Agriculturalists had to produce the necessary surplus, and that surplus had to be transported to the cities. Accordingly, the period saw the development of transportation networks and nationwide systems of commodity distribution. It appears that Edo's population reached a million in the early eighteenth century. This made it not only the largest city in the world at that time but also probably the world's first city to reach a million people. Neither ancient Rome nor the medieval Chinese capitals of Ch'ang-An and Loyang ever reached a million, although it appears that Peking in the eighteenth century was in the neighborhood of 800,000 to 900,000. In Europe, it was the early nineteenth century before London reached 860,000 and Paris, 540,000.

Despite the scale of this urban growth, the character, structure, and function of the early-modern city were very different from those of modern cities. Most urban centers were castle towns constructed as the seats of local administration by daimyo. Members of the ruling warrior class (*bushi*) comprised about half the population of such centers, and most of the other residents, including merchants and artisans, existed only in order to contribute in one way or another to the livelihood of the *bushi* or the finances of the domain. Edo became a city of one million because it was itself the castle town of the shogun, and because the *sankin kōtai* system obliged each daimyo to spend every other year in service to the shogun in Edo.

Osaka, which had a population of 400,000 and was about equal to Kyoto as Japan's second-ranking urban area, was a city of townsmen (*chōnin*) where very few members of the warrior class were allowed to reside. It was the center of the country's commercial economy, but it was also the nucleus of the bakufu's distribution control system and had the important function of collecting and transporting—from the center of commerce in western Japan and from elsewhere around the country—many of the goods necessary for Edo's maintenance. For example, cargoes shipped to Osaka in 1714 were valued at the enormous sum of 440,000 *kan* of silver, of which 35.8 percent was accounted for by tax rice (*kuramai* or *nengu-mai*). The bakufu and daimyo took the tax rice they extracted from the peasants in their domains and sold it in Osaka. The proceeds were then either used in Osaka to purchase the goods necessary for the warriors' livelihood, or sent to Edo or the castle town to pay administrative and other costs. The function of Osaka as a commercial city in the early eighteenth century was thus to support and maintain the feudal rule of the shogun and daimyo.

2.   The Development of a Commercial Economy in the Late Eighteenth Century

The early-modern economic structure, in which tax goods were processed through the cities to generate income for the rulers, began to collapse in the mid-eighteenth century. If we look at cargo arriving at Osaka during the first quarter of the nineteenth century, it is evident that a major change transpired in the century or so after

1714. We find that bookings of tax rice stood at about 1,500,000 *koku*, which marks a decided increase in volume over the 1,120,000 *koku* of 1714. However, in terms of price, the rice still amounted to only 13.7 percent of all commodities if we assume that bookings for those commodities for which we lack figures increased during the century at more or less the same rate as those major commodities for which figures are available. This is primarily because of the proliferation of these other commodities, but it also resulted from a decrease in the relative price of rice. If rice is compared to such cotton goods as cloth, thread, and raw cotton (taking rice as 100), cotton goods were 18 in 1714, 31 in 1736, and 105 between 1804 and 1829. In other words, the total value of cotton-related goods eventually exceeded that of rice.

Not only are rice and cotton goods different in substance, but they are different in their essential economic character as well. Whereas rice was used as payment for land tax before it became a commodity, most goods related to cotton were originally produced as commodities by farmers or handicraft workers. Therefore, one could argue that during the century or so from 1714, the Osaka market was transformed from an institution serving the lords into one that served the common people. The case of cotton helps us to see how this transformation took place.

Some important changes became evident in the latter half of the eighteenth century. First was the development of rural industry. In the seventeenth century, the technological level of urban handicrafts in the Kinai was unsurpassed. Technological development stagnated in the eighteenth century, however, as a result of close regulation of the system of guild-like associations (*kabunakama*) for artisans and stricter control of the wholesale merchants. At the same time, industry in the form of commodity production began to take shape in rural areas where guild regulations were absent, wholesale merchants were weak, and wages were low. Such production occurred all across the country as areas where cotton was cultivated also developed their own cotton industries. Even in areas not suited to raising cotton, entrepreneurs brought in raw cotton or cotton thread from elsewhere and established cloth industries.

Between the late eighteenth and early nineteenth centuries, weaving specialists (*oriya*) appeared in the most advanced of the rural cotton industry areas. Many of these specialists did not engage in agriculture at all, but some farmed as a sideline while concentrating primarily on weaving by loom . Most engaged in a petty-capitalistic form of management in that they employed wage labor to work alongside the manager and his family. As the scale of production increased and division of labor was introduced, factory-system handicraft production developed in some places.

Also widespread were a form of wholesaler-controlled cottage industry, which provided virtually no autonomy to the producer, and another system of capitalistic cottage industry under which the producer worked at home but was supplied with raw thread (and often a loom as well) by the capitalist and paid by him on a piece-work basis (this was called *dashibata*).

For example, in Uda-ōtsu village in Izumi in 1842, there were eighteen weaving specialists, fifty family workers, five indentured servants (*hōkōnin*—workers who lived in, and worked on one-year contracts), and eighty-two piecework day-laborers (workers who lived elsewhere and were paid by the day). The manager of the largest enterprise in Uda-ōtsu employed 6 family members and 15 piecework day-laborers for a total of 21 workers. Ten households, including this one, did absolutely no farming. Moreover, in the Bisai

Table 1. Weaving Specialists in the Jurisdiction of the Udasu Deputy in 1844

	Number of Looms	Households		In shop (*uchibata*)		Looms Loaned out (*dashibata*)		Total	
		No.	%	No.	%	No.	%	No.	%
Four main villages	1~5	85	59.0	201	40.8	44	13.9	245	30.3
(Konobu-nakajima,	6~14	51	35.4	232	47.2	171	54.2	403	49.9
Okoshi, Shimo-sofue,	15~29	8	5.6	59	12.0	101	31.9	160	19.8
Yamazaki									
	Total	144	100.0	492	100.0	316	100.0	808	100.0
Other villages	1~5	145	81.4	314	66.5	58	37.4	372	59.3
(38)	6~14	33	18.6	158	33.5	97	62.6	255	40.7
	Total	178	100.0	472	100.0	155	100.0	627	100.0
Total villages	1~5	230	71.4	515	53.3	102	21.6	617	42.8
(42)	6~14	84	26.1	390	40.6	268	57.0	658	46.1
	15~29	8	2.5	59	6.1	101	21.4	160	11.1
	Total	322	100.0	964	100.0	471	100.0	1,435	100.0

Source: Satoru Nakamura and Yasutsugu Kawaura, "Bakumatsu keizai dankai ni kansuru shomondai," *Rekishigaku Kenkyū* 225, p. 75.

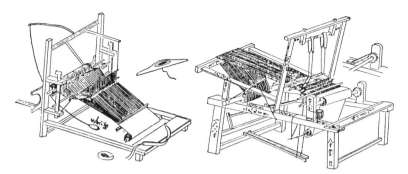

Figure 1. (Left) Traditional loom (*izaribata*) and (right) the tall loom (*takabata*). From Endō Motoo, *Orimono no Nihonshi*, (Japan Broadcast Publishing, 1971)

district of Owari in 1844, there were 322 weaving specialists in some 42 villages and they used 1,435 hand looms (Table 1). Eight of the large-scale weaving specialists used between 15 and 29 looms per household, with about one-third working in-shop (*uchibata*) and two-thirds accepting piecework on a *dashibata* basis. This district produced striped Shima cloth, and inasmuch as each loom was operated by two workers, the stage of factory-system handicraft production was quite advanced.

With regard to development in the social division of labor, not only did cotton cultivation come to be separated from the cotton industry, but within the industry itself the various component processes were split apart and managed separately. Of particular importance was the separation of thread production from cloth production. The varieties of cotton cloth also proliferated, and differences became evident according to region of origin.

Most important technologically was the transition in looms from the traditional looms (*izaribata*) to the "tall loom" (*takabata*), which brought a doubling or even trebling of efficiency (Figure 1). Use of the *takabata* spread directly or indirectly from Kyoto's Nishijin district, and by the nineteenth century it was in common use in the advanced cloth-producing regions.

As this kind of rural industry developed, certain core areas were formed within the regions of rural industry, and these cores gradually developed into industrial towns. Most towns that had emerged in the early-modern period were either consumer centers, such as the castle towns, whose function was primarily political, or a few others like Osaka, which were oriented primarily to commercial functions. These new, small towns, however, differed in that their major purpose was production. Of course, they emerged prior to the industrial revolution, so they were not entirely free of a certain rural character. They were, indeed, rural industrial towns whose central functions were industry and commercial activities related to industry. In the modern period that followed the industrial revolution, a large number of them developed into full-fledged industrial cities.

For example, located close to Osaka was Izumi district, a major center of cotton weaving, and Uda-ōtsu was one of its central villages. By 1843, only 14 percent (40 of Uda-ōtsu's 277) households were engaged in agriculture, while 46 percent were engaged in occupations related to the cotton industry. It was fast becoming what might be called a cotton-industry town. Similarly, the western part of Owari (Bisai district) was one of the foremost producers of Shima cotton. If we look at a village called Okoshi from that area, we find that in 1845, 20 percent of its 262 households were engaged in agriculture, and 31 percent in occupations related to the cotton industry. Since Okoshi was a port on the Kiso River and a post town on the Mino Highway, 22 percent of its households were engaged in occupations related to transportation. Okoshi, also, had ceased to be an agricultural town and had acquired the composition of an urban center devoted to the cotton industry.

Next to Okoshi village was Konobu-nakajima, whose agricultural production by value amounted to only 18 percent of the total, while its industrial production, almost all of which had to do with cotton, was 81.5 percent.

It is also noteworthy that, as shown in Table 1, rural industrial towns such as Okoshi and Konobu-nakajima were the nuclei of the cotton industry in their district and contained concentrations of large-scale weaving specialists. Of the ninety-two specialists who had six or more looms, fifty-nine were in four villages: Okoshi, Konobu-nakajima, Shimo-sofue, and Yamazaki. Moreover, all eight who had fifteen or more looms were located in these four villages. We assume that those listed in Table 1 as *dashibata* employed producers who lived within the village, but this type of rural town also often extended its control of production throughout the surrounding countryside. For example, according to other source materials, in Okoshi village in 1844 there were 464 producers, most of whom were from other villages and were employed on a *dashibata* basis. Industrial towns also became the distribution centers for their districts, and among their hometown merchants were some who accumulated capital and dealt directly with each other over long distances without the good offices of large wholesale merchants such as those in Osaka and Edo.

3. The Developmental Stage of the Economy in the Late Tokugawa Period

Given this proliferation of rural entrepreneurial ventures, it was inevitable that competition among cotton cloth production centers would spread across the nation. As this occurred, those areas that were superior in terms of production—those, for example, in which the social division of labor had progressed, capitalist cottage industry and factory-system handicraft production had developed as forms of industrial organization, and the use of the tall loom had spread—came out ahead in the national competition. In the early nineteenth century, these advanced textile-producing centers included Izumi, Yamato, Owari, Mikawa, and Shimotsuke (especially Ashikaga). Musashi finally joined them after 1840.

If we compare cargo arriving at the Osaka cotton goods market with those of the late nineteenth century, it is apparent that late-eighteenth century production areas changed greatly. The main production centers in the late eighteenth century had been coastal districts on the Seto Inland Sea, such as Harima, Awaji, Bizen, and Suō, while in the late nineteenth century the undisputed leaders were Yamato and Izumi. Textiles from the coast of the Inland Sea did not fade out, but rather were directed toward other markets. For example, in 1847 Fukuoka domain in Kyushu imported a large quantity of cotton cloth (one million *tan*) from the Inland Sea coast. Akita domain in the Tōhoku region also took in great quantities of cotton-related goods in the early nineteenth century, including not only finished goods (cloth), but semi-processed goods (cotton thread) and raw materials (raw cotton) as well. Moreover, by the nineteenth century, Edo, which along with Osaka was the largest market for cotton textiles in the country, was buying primarily from Owari, Mikawa, and Musashi.

Another factor in this change was the collapse of control over distribution once exercised by the *ton'ya* of Osaka and Edo. Why had these merchants been able to establish and then maintain nationwide control of commodity distribution in the late seventeenth and eighteenth centuries? One reason was political: the wholesale merchants were given special prerogatives by the bakufu. Another more important reason was economic. It included the following aspects: (1) The key to the economic control exercised by large wholesale merchants was their ability to offer advances to merchants and producers in the cotton producing areas; (2) the urban handicraft industry was technologically superior and the wholesale merchants controlled advance payments to the handicraft industrialists; and (3) wholesale merchants controlled the means of transport and monopolized advances to the providers of water transportation, which was quite highly developed.

After the close of the eighteenth century, these conditions no longer existed for the following reasons: (1) Capital accumulation progressed in the producing areas, so control by advance payment gradually lost its effectiveness. At the same time, capital accumulation by the large wholesalers tended to stagnate. They had either earned capital by themselves or borrowed it from large-scale money-changers and financiers who made the bulk of their profits by loaning money to daimyo. By the end of the Tokugawa period, however, these financiers had little wealth to deploy because their loans to daimyo had become very risky as the feudal system dissolved and large fief-holders increasingly defaulted. (2) The urban handicraft industries lost their technological superiority as technology flowed into rural areas. Prior to the eighteenth century, urban industries had dominated most final processing, which meant that even the products of rural industry tended to be sent to the cities for final processing before sale. Since the quality of a product is generally determined by this last stage of work, considerable value was added by the urban handicraft industry. From the end of the eighteenth century, the final processing was increasingly done in rural areas, and therefore in this realm, as well, control by wholesale merchants declined. (3) The wholesalers' monopoly over transportation also collapsed. This resulted from the decline of their financial power, which led, in turn, to the dissolution of the control they had exercised through advances, and also from the establishment of new transportation routes and facilities.

These tendencies emerged with final clarity during the Tempo Reforms of 1841–43, when the bakufu instituted a policy designed to dissolve the merchant associations. Rising commodity prices were threatening the livelihood of urban dwellers, and bakufu officials thought that the wholesale merchants' monopoly over distribution was causing inflation. Accordingly, they sought to bring prices down by forcibly dissolving the associations. However, the policy failed to accomplish this objective because the wholesalers' control over distribution had already dissipated, and they had no power to determine prices.

How, then, are we to evaluate the stage of industrial development that Japan had reached by the late Tokugawa period? I am of the view that from the late eighteenth century to the early nineteenth— at the latest, by the Tempo Reforms—Japan entered the stage of early capitalism or proto-industrialization. Early capitalism occurs prior to the industrial revolution and depends upon handicraft technology, but it is also the stage at which capitalistic forms of management, such as factory-system handicraft production, capitalistic cottage industry, and petty-capitalistic management, come to dominate industry. A modern domestic market forms in parallel with this stage. In no country has a full-fledged domestic market formed prior to the industrial revolution, but in Japan such a market was in its formative stage. Moreover, this development constituted a favorable historical condition for the actual development of capitalism once the ports had been opened.

4. The Opening of Ports and the Response of the Cotton Industry

Japan remained closed to the outside world for more than two hundred years from the 1630s, but under pressure from the Western nations, the country finally opened its doors in a process that began in 1854 with the Japan-U.S. treaty of friendship and culminated in 1858 in commercial treaties with the United States, Holland, Russia, England, and France. Trade began the following year. These agreements were typically unequal, being modeled on the Treaty of Tientsin that England and France had just concluded with China.

Japan's trade during the 1860s and 1870s consisted of the import of cotton goods and other industrial products and the export of silk thread, tea, and a smattering of other raw materials, foodstuffs, and semi-processed goods. The other party was almost always a Western nation, usually England. That is, Japan's trade was typical of what we now associate with developing countries.

Cotton textiles were the major item imported by all Asian countries at that time. Cotton cloth was the staple material for plebeian clothing in Asia, and its production was also the major indigenous industry. But as inexpensive goods produced in the modern factories of England and other Western countries flowed into Asia in large quantities, they severely damaged the Asian cotton industries. Japan's was no exception. Nevertheless, the import of cotton goods by Japan was exceptional in some respects:

1. There were rapid increases in the volume of imports. For instance, if we look at import volume per capita (with thread imports converted into cloth equivalents) in 1861, just two years after the ports were opened, we find that imports had already exceeded 0.5 square yards per person, a volume equal to China's imports in 1861 (more than twenty years after the Chinese ports were opened) and India's imports in 1830. By 1865, imports exceeded one yard per person, thereby surpassing China, and in 1879 went on to six yards, reaching the level of contemporary India.

2. In India and China, the impact of cotton imports on domestic industry was very severe in certain regions, but the expansion of their influence to nationwide proportions occurred more rapidly in Japan.

3. The emphasis in cotton imports shifted quickly from cotton cloth to cotton thread. Cotton cloth imports predominated immediately after the harbors opened, but thread imports soon increased, and by 1869 they surpassed cloth. By way of contrast, cloth imports remained consistently high in the Indian case, and in China thread imports did not increase rapidly until after the 1880s.

What accounts for these unusual characteristics of Japanese cotton imports? In India and China, commodity production had developed in the form of a primarily urban, handicraft industry that was oriented to urban consumption and export (there were sizable exports to Europe prior to the early nineteenth century). In the marketplace, this type of commodity production competed directly, in terms of price and quality, with imported goods. Therefore, it did not take long for the imported goods, which represented incomparably greater productivity, to overwhelm the domestic handicraft industry. Of course, the self-sufficient production of textiles through by-employment was widespread in rural areas of China and India, where some 80 percent of the population was located, but goods produced in this manner did not compete directly with imported products at all, so imported cloth scarcely penetrated rural society. Moreover, in quality the imported cloth did not really meet the main rural criteria in terms of weight and strength.

In Japan, by contrast, the commercial production of textiles had progressed during the course of the Tokugawa period, and even in rural areas the production of cotton cloth had already become commercialized. Therefore, imported cloth was able with relative ease to penetrate not only the cities but rural areas as well. Since a national market in cotton cloth had already formed, imported goods could easily spread throughout the country.

Another factor should be taken into account. The weaving specialists who had emerged in the advanced cotton cloth producing areas were already in the habit of purchasing cotton thread for weaving. But as a result of the prodigious development of the domestic cotton cloth industry since the end of the eighteenth century, the supply of cotton thread, which is the raw material for that industry, had been unable to keep pace, and its price had risen. Therefore, when foreign, machine-produced thread became available, weaving specialists quickly substituted it for the domestic variety. Foreign factories began providing an abundant supply of cheap, high-quality thread to the advanced cloth-producing areas, making it possible for those areas to hold their own against the onslaught of imported cloth.

Of course, Japan also had areas where cotton production was backward, and self-sufficient cottage industry was widespread. In these areas, people purchased raw cotton, spun thread, wove cloth, and in some cases even cultivated the raw cotton locally. These textile-producing areas and farm household industries found it very difficult to adjust to the large-scale import of thread, and they eventually fell by the wayside.

Another serious problem confronting the cotton industry following the opening of the ports was excess labor power. Once the cotton cloth industry had converted to imported thread, the production of cotton thread declined steeply, and workers in the thread sector found themselves deprived of jobs. Productivity was lower in thread than in cloth, with eight workers in thread typically needed to supply a single weaver. Therefore, the number of workers affected is believed to have been from 2 to 3 million. Most worked cotton as a form of by-employment; many were farmers' daughters. If we add workers who performed the cotton ginning and willowing, farmers who planted cotton, and cloth producers who lost employment because of competition from imports and from the advanced textile-producing areas, the figures increase to between 2.5 and 4 million. The total population was 35 million, of which 19 million were workers, so the problem was indeed grave. Rural areas were beset by large numbers of semi-employed and had to deal with surplus population. For these reasons, the wage level of workers fell precipitously in the years between the opening of the ports and the early Meiji period. Wages in weaving also declined.

It is now recognized as a characteristic of developing countries that when they engage in trade with advanced nations they soon are plagued with domestic industrial decline, excess population, and expanding numbers of low-income semi-employed. But in the nineteenth century the world economy had not yet reached its present level of development, and neither had the productivity of the advanced nations. Therefore, the surplus population that emerged in developing countries grew more slowly.

At the same time, we should not forget that even in the nineteenth century commercial production and market development were more advanced in Japan than in other Asian countries, so it was with relative rapidity that the problem of surplus population assumed national proportions. Of course, the concomitant decline in wages also strengthened the ability of the cotton-weaving industry to compete with imported goods.

In 1873, Japan imported from France and Austria the "flying shuttle," a loom invented in 1733 in Lancashire, England and applied to cotton weaving in the 1760s. By 1877 it was copied, and its use spread throughout the cotton-weaving areas of Japan where it was called the *battan*. It raised productivity by 1.5 to 2 times over the level of the tall loom.

Under these conditions, from about 1870 onward, the Japanese cotton cloth industry quickly vanquished imports and developed at a rapid pace. Cotton textile production increased 15 percent annually between 1874 and 1880, thus more than doubling the output. Whereas imported cloth had commanded 40 percent of the domestic market in 1874, by 1880 it had fallen to 23 percent, and by 1888 was only 15 percent. Even under the constraints of the unequal treaties, and without any government protection, the industry had succeeded on its own in recovering the domestic market. Moreover, it accomplished this solely by developing the existing weaving industry, without establishing modern factories filled with imported machinery.

It is also interesting to note that the development of the existing weaving industry actually created the market conditions for a modern spinning industry. The rapid development of the cotton cloth industry through the use of foreign thread naturally brought a steep increase in thread imports, but the same increase in domestic demand for thread also made possible the construction and successful operation of a large-scale modern spinning industry. A mechanized cotton-spinning industry developed rapidly from the 1880s, and the defeat of imported thread made virtual self-sufficiency possible by 1890, although high-grade threads did continue to be imported. Moreover, around 1900, Japan exported one-third of its production (to China and Korea), and cotton thread became an export item second only to silk thread. Spinning was the most important sector in Japan's industrial revolution, but its success was made possible by the further development of a cloth industry that predated the industrial revolution. In fact, a number of wholesale merchants who had traditionally dealt in cotton goods were among the major founders and investors behind the development of the spinning industry in Osaka, its modern center. In this respect, too, the modern industry owed much to its early-modern antecedents.

(Translation by J. Victor Koschmann)

Chapter Four

Urban Networks and Information Networks

KATSUHISA MORIYA

Two striking characteristics of the Tokugawa period were the growth in economic integration and social cosmopolitanism. Ever more people became literate, and they developed a keen interest in learning more about the world around them. To satisfy that demand, early modern Japan developed an extensive publication industry and an elaborate communication system that produced and disseminated new information—political, economic, and cultural—throughout society. The three great cities of Kyoto, Osaka, and Edo played, each in its own way, key roles in this activity, but the multitude of lesser towns and the highways and byways that linked them together also were essential to the creation and maintenance of this nationwide information network.

1. The "Three Metropolises" and the Provincial Towns

The urban centers are commonly grouped into two categories: the three major cities and the provincial towns. Even during the Tokugawa period, the great cities of Kyoto, Osaka, and Edo were known collectively as the "Three Metropolises" (*santo*) or "three ports" (*sangatsu*). The remaining urban centers, or provincial towns, which numbered in the hundreds and ranged in population from a few thousand to over a hundred thousand, included castle towns, lesser ports, religious centers, market towns, and highway post towns.

The Development of the Three Metropolises
The three great metropolitan centers of Kyoto, Osaka, and Edo had

large, highly developed communication systems, and the three played roles of inestimable importance. Kyoto and Osaka were located in the Seto-Kinai region of western Japan, which historically was a highly productive and economically powerful area. By contrast, eastern Japan, where Edo was situated, was economically weaker and might be called an economic backwater. Advanced culture developed earlier in western Japan, where it was easier for population to concentrate, and we might say that the early modern period of history commenced in a context of the primacy of western Japan.

Kyoto had been the seat of imperial government since the late eighth century and was the only metropolis in Japan before the seventeenth century. A city on the order of some 200,000 souls, Kyoto monopolized political, economic, and cultural authority, and as a consequence already possessed an extremely powerful information apparatus by late medieval times. Even in the early modern period, the importance of Kyoto did not diminish. Instead, its population grew to between 350,000 and 400,000.

Kyoto was also the greatest industrial city in the early modern period, mainly because of its textile production—spinning, dyeing, and weaving—which constituted the largest-scale handicraft industry in Japan. The city's Nishijin weaving industry was Japan's most powerful textile center and produced its highest quality textiles. Indeed, Nishijin controlled such a large share of the textile market that it might fairly be said to have monopolized the high-quality segment. Nishijin had some seven thousand of the finest looms, the *takabata*, or high looms, which required at least two operators apiece. Adding in the *hirahata*, or flat looms, worked by lone operators, the Nishijin silk industry employed several tens of thousands of weavers. Further, a social division of labor was already well advanced, and when dyers and spinners are figured in, something approaching 100,000 people were working in the Nishijin textile industry alone. This artisan force thus constituted a major portion of Kyoto's total population.

Kyoto was also advanced in the field of design, in which the accumulation of knowledge had been continuous from ancient times. In this area, the city enjoyed overwhelming superiority, and from it information about textiles and design spread nationwide during the eighteenth century, raising the quality of both.

Kyoto was also a cultural center, the hub of Japan's scholarship, letters, and religious thought. Here too it benefited from an accumulated legacy that boasted a great concentration of scholars, writers, and artists. They in turn attracted numerous people who came from all around the land to study with them. The prestige of the city is suggested by the term *jōraku*, "going up to the capital," which people used when going to Kyoto.

The Tokugawa shogun permitted daimyo from all over the country to maintain residences in the three cities, and some 105 or more, about half of them, maintained Kyoto mansions. In each of these, a *rusuiyaku*, or manager while the lord is absent, looked after the mansion. His job was to assure that students sent to Kyoto by their lord were introduced to the right teachers, and to send up-to-the-minute cultural information back to the home domain.

Kyoto was home to the headquarters of many sects of Buddhism and Shintō. Even today, there are over two thousand Buddhist temples and Shintō shrines in the city, and during the seventeenth and eighteenth centuries, they numbered some seven to eight thousand. The monks, nuns, and Shintō priests staffing these institutions ran into the tens of thousands, making Kyoto the greatest religious city in Japan. In each sectarian headquarters, there was a school, and students aspiring to become Buddhist or Shintō clerics came from every region and district of the country to study there. In addition, the city was alive with vast numbers of lay believers, who came on pilgrimages to the headquarters of their sect. On great ceremonial occasions, such as an anniversary of the death of a sect's founder, tens of thousands of people would swarm into Kyoto. The shrines and temples provided lodging, as did the large network of inns in the city.

Kyoto was thus a great information center in terms of industrial production, culture, and religion. The city of Osaka, by contrast, emerged as the key center for economic information. It, too, was an ancient city, where the imperial capital had been situated briefly during the mid-seventh century, but it had fallen to abandonment and ruin. Only in the sixteenth century, after a hiatus of nearly a millennium, did it again enjoy the bustle of urban activity.

Osaka initially revived as a place of religion, the home of a great Buddhist temple complex, but the real urban development of Osaka came under Toyotomi Hideyoshi. In the last years of the sixteenth century, Hideyoshi built his great Osaka Castle, and the city's civilian wards took shape beneath its massive walls. Osaka occupied an exceptionally well-favored geographic situation: located at the head of Osaka Bay, it was positioned to control shipping on the Inland Sea, and it straddled the mouth of the Yodo River, which connected it to Kyoto.

In the early seventeenth century, Osaka passed from the control of the Toyotomi house into the hands of the Tokugawa bakufu. Growing rapidly from the first half of the century, the city underwent a major transformation. Because bakufu leaders considered Osaka Castle far larger than necessary, they tore it down, and when they rebuilt it, a large part of its former precinct was converted into residential area for urban commoners.

The bakufu also undertook major riparian construction projects at Osaka, dredging and filling shallows and islands to construct urban wards and waterfront districts. The projects extended over many years, reshaping the city until it boasted the facilities of a great metropolis. Urban commoners—principally merchants—were encouraged to relocate to the newly reborn city, and many in fact moved in from Kyoto and from such other nearby towns as Fushimi, upriver on the Yodo, and Sakai, south along the shores of Osaka Bay. The influx of people was accompanied, not surprisingly, by the transfer of merchant capital into the city.

Osaka's transformation from a military bastion into a great financial and commercial metropolis was greatly facilitated by the development of the Nishimawari, or "Western Circuit," shipping route, completed in the mid-seventeenth century, which made a long sweep down the Japan Sea coast, through the Shimonoseki Straits, and along the Inland Sea to Osaka. The development of this great sea route, which linked Ezo (Hokkaido, then a remote outpost of Japanese trade), the north and west coasts, and the Inland Sea, immeasurably enhanced Osaka's position as a trading port and commercial terminal. A vast array of goods from along the sea route were brought to Osaka, where traders disposed of them commercially. The bakufu itself promoted these developments as part of its urban policy.

As Osaka developed into the greatest commercial metropolis in Japan from the seventeenth into the eighteenth century, it earned the nickname, "the kitchen of the realm." Functioning as Japan's

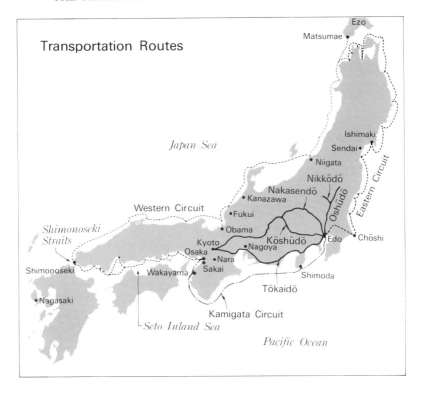

central entrepot, the Osaka market was great enough to affect market movements throughout the country.

In this role, for example, the Osaka market was decisive in establishing the commercial price of rice, which was the most important commodity in the national economy. It also governed the prices of most other commercial goods, as well as the exchange rates among the gold, silver, and copper coinages of the realm. Economic information flowing out of the Osaka market came to control the commerce of the entire country. The eighteenth-century shogun Yoshimune, who went to the extent of receiving in his castle at Edo reports on the daily fluctuations of Osaka rice prices, studied rice prices and policy so closely that he earned the sobriquet "the rice shogun" (*kome shōgun*). By the eighteenth century, the power of the bakufu and, indeed, the realm itself would have been jeopardized had Osaka not existed. With its population of some 400,000 urban commoners, Osaka had earned a secure place in the national economy.

The greatest city in eastern Japan, eventually the greatest metropolis in all Japan, and one of the very greatest cities in the world at the time was Edo, the shogunal capital. Begun as a small medieval town, Edo grew gradually after Ieyasu made it his head-quarters in 1590. A decade later, Ieyasu's rise to national hegemony transformed this small-town Edo into the country's political capital. The functions of a capital had theretofore been fulfilled by Kyoto, but after Ieyasu became shogun in 1603, they moved inexorably to Edo.

After the *sankin kōtai* system of alternate attendance was made compulsory during the 1630s, Edo rapidly expanded to metropoli-tan dimensions. The regular, long-term residence of daimyo in Edo forced them to establish great urban mansions, which caused land development in the city to move forward at a fierce pace. Great land-reclamation projects were carried out, one after another, creat-ing residential wards for the warrior class to occupy. Although the alternate attendance system had been enacted as a scheme to con-trol the daimyo class, it also transformed the Edo landscape. The city's samurai population, including direct retainers of the shogun as well as the resident daimyo and their followers, exceeded 100,000. In addition, the urban commoner population expanded to meet the consumption demands of the samurai populace.

In 1657, much of Edo was destroyed in the great Meireki Fire, but the disaster only occasioned a rebuilding of the metropolis as the boom in urban development continued. By the early eighteenth century, Edo was home to more than a million people and had become far and away the greatest metropolis in all Japan. It is esti-mated that the samurai and commoner populations numbered about a half-million each, so the emergence of this huge metropolis constituted the establishment of a substantial market, to say the least. Goods were shipped in an unending stream to the great con-sumption center that was Edo, a development that had extremely important economic implications.

For all its economic importance as a consumption center, how-ever, Edo was fundamentally a political city. It was a great castle town centered on Edo Castle, in which was located the bakufu, the political apparatus with the shogun at its peak. The political policies of the shogun affected not only the bakufu's own domains but also the daimyo and their domains. Political and administrative information emanated from the bakufu, and the staff in every daimyo's Edo mansion collected the information and transmitted it to their own domain.

Kyoto and Osaka were, of course, under direct shogunal administration. Thus, of the Three Metropolises, Edo actually maintained political control over the other two. It did so through the Kyoto Deputy (*shoshidai*), who was assigned to the old imperial city, and the Keeper of Osaka Castle (*jōdai*) in the great entrepot. As a result of its hegemonic role, Edo's consciousness of itself—and national consciousness of Edo—as the capital of Japan became stronger. Eventually the city, which earlier had been known by the inelegant appellation of Kōfu, or "government by the bay," came to be known by the vernacular title, Tōto, or "Eastern Capital."

The Three Metropolises thus differed in their urban character depending on the historical circumstances of each, and they differed greatly in their social roles and informational functions as well. One might say that they had the strong coloration of a set of branch metropoles, with each perfecting its own individual informational functions and facilities. Each of the three performed vital functions in the development of early modern Japan.

The Growth of Provincial Towns

Of course, early modern Japan did not thrive simply on the strength of the Three Metropolises alone. Nor were the core regions surrounding the Three Metropolises the totality of the Japanese archipelago. From medieval times, castle towns, ports, religious centers, local market towns, and highway post towns had grown up all around the country, eventually comprising a large number of urban areas of varying sizes.

To take the example of major port towns, there were easily twenty such towns along the Japan Sea coast alone during the early modern period, and another twenty along the Pacific coast. When we add to this the many river ports in the interior, we come to a substantial number of port towns throughout the country. In addition, a great many towns grew up at the gates of major Buddhist and Shintō religious and pilgrimage centers. Known generically as *monzen-machi* (gate-front towns), they had their own distinctive developmental characteristics.

But however we approach the subject, there can be no doubt that the castle town was the most important type of provincial town in early modern Japan. Each daimyo, early in the development of his domain, began constructing a castle and its surrounding castle town. In the seventeenth century alone, these newly constructed castle towns numbered over two hundred.

This burst of construction activity lasted less than a century, but during that time it proceeded at a furious pace in all parts of the country. Vast sums of money were invested in building castles and castle towns, and while we cannot begin to calculate their cost, it is no exaggeration to say that they produced a boom in provincial urban construction.

A great number of post towns were also built as the government-designated official post stations along the highways. On the Five Highways (go-kaidō) alone, the trunk highways directly governed by the bakufu (the Tōkaidō, Nakasendō, Kōshūdō, Nikkōdō, and Ōshūdō), well over a hundred new post towns were constructed. When we add to these the post towns built along the major branch highways, the number readily comes to several hundred. In the Osaka-Kyoto region alone, for example, there were over 120 post towns, as well as about forty castle towns. In addition, the region boasted numerous monzen-machi, ports, and local market towns, creating a dense network of provincial towns.

Provincial towns arose during the golden age of the seventeenth-century boom, but their role, especially the role of castle towns, changed during the eighteenth century. In the latter 1600s, economic activity accelerated throughout the archipelago, with the entire economy, including agricultural productivity, developing at a rapid pace. Against this background, provincial towns began to change in character. Most notably, where the castle town initially had a strongly military coloration, it metamorphosed into a provincial economic center, its economic role taking precedence over its soldierly one. This change in castle towns, which was similar to that experienced by Osaka, as noted earlier, bespeaks both the appearance of the provincial town as the center of a regional economic sphere and the formation of that regional economic sphere itself.

The castle town could respond to the changing economy by shedding its military character and showing more strongly the characteristics of an economic town due to changes at the political level. During the early seventeenth century, the bakufu had used the confiscation of domains and transfer of daimyo as principal forms of punishment for major transgressions of shogunal law or for incompetent administration. In consequence, daimyo had frequently had their domains confiscated or transferred from one domain to another. These frequent moves by the rulers imposed severe burdens on the peasants and townspeople whom they governed, in the process serving to destabilize political and economic conditions. From the eighteenth century on, however, the bakufu ceased applying these powerful constraints to daimyo, except in the most extreme cases. This change in policy brought stability to the territory under daimyo governance and new vitality to the provincial towns, particularly the castle towns.

Furthermore, daimyo economic policy changed as well. Instead of concentrating mainly on the production of rice, daimyo fostered a wide variety of regionally specialized products. This policy, which can be called a policy of "industrial production" (*shokusan kōgyō*), had the effect of fleshing out the information network that linked provincial towns because it required the assemblage and dissemination of information on the production, transport, and disposal of diverse local goods. Indeed, had it not been for the strengthening of the provincial information network, this local industrial production would have been impossible.

In discussing industrial production of the early eighteenth century, it is necessary also to consider the connections between the production of regional specialty products and the great central cities and marketplaces. The information network that linked provincial towns closely to the Three Metropolises was formed in this context, with the vital linking role being performed by the mansions and warehouses that the various daimyo had established in the Three Metropolises. Osaka was the arena in which economic information moved most actively, and hence was the place where powerful daimyo built offices and competed with one another. The information that flowed from the daimyo's Osaka office back to the towns in the domain was of such importance that it could change the course of the domainal economy.

Of course, it was not only the domains that sought information in Osaka. Merchants were also active on a major scale, with leading provincial merchants establishing wholesale offices in the three Metropolises. Called *kuni don'ya* (province wholesalers), these merchants dealt in the specialty products of their province, bringing them to the Three Metropolises. What's in demand in the Metropolises right now? What's in demand in the provinces right now? The merchants' judgments on these questions provided the crucial link between provincial town and Metropolis. Catching the right information as it flowed through the metropolis and transmitting it to the provincial town, they brought new goods flowing into the city.

Thus, through their access to information, provincial cities were linked to the center and brought economic development to the provinces. From the eighteenth century, and into the nineteenth, this development moved toward the formation of a broader national market.

2.   The Three Metropolises and the Communication System

The growth in cities and towns, and in the activity that tied them together, both fostered and was facilitated by the development of an extensive communication system. That system eventually came to encompass towns all over the country, but its central segments linked Kyoto, Osaka, and Edo. The three cities dominated the economy and were politically and culturally supreme because of their size and because they constituted parts of the bakufu domain.

The Formation of the Communication System

The infrastructure of overland and maritime transport that promoted communication and trade developed from the very outset of the early modern period. The construction of trunk and branch highways under shogunal control moved at a remarkable pace, while the marine transport system also developed rapidly. In particular, coastal shipping routes—the Western Circuit, mentioned earlier, the Eastern Circuit, and the Kamigata Circuit—were pushed forward from the mid-seventeenth century, stimulating the economy of the entire archipelago while simultaneously multiplying the need for adequate economic information. The Western Circuit, linking Osaka and the Japan Sea coast via the Inland Sea, was the longest route and was the greatest transport artery in Japan. The Eastern Circuit linked ports along the Pacific coast, while the Kami-

Figure 1. Express messengers (*hikyaku*) plying their trade, por-
trayed at Akasaka on the Tōkaidō. *Tōkaidō gojū-san tsugi* (Fifty-
three Stations of the Tōkaidō). By Utagawa Hiroshige. Early
nineteenth century.

gata Circuit connected Osaka and Edo. River transport also flourished, reaching into the interior of the archipelago, and as a result
the center and the provinces, as well as the various provinces, were
linked to each other in a network that developed at a remarkably
rapid rate.

Even as this transport network enmeshed the entire archipelago,
a communications network developed at a comparable pace. Communication arrangements had existed since ancient times, and they
were maintained from the medieval period by a network of express
messengers, known as *hikyaku* (Figure 1). These messengers accumulated a long and rich legacy. Having handled freight and letters,
bills of exchange, and cash during the medieval period, the *hikyaku*
system naturally attracted great official attention at the dawn of the
early modern period.

To establish information links among the three central metropolises, the bakufu moved from the very beginning of the seventeenth
century to employ a government-operated communication system
along the Tōkaidō, the principal overland route linking Edo, Kyoto,
and Osaka. This was the *sando hikyaku* (thrice-monthly express mes-

senger) system. The *sando hikyaku* system was used by bakufu offices in the Kinai cities to send official messages to Edo. Each post town on the Tōkaidō kept three horses in readiness to assure that these messages were transmitted promptly from one station to the next.

In the *tsugi hikyaku* (stage express messenger) system the bakufu employed the post horses and post towns of the Five Highways, which it operated directly, to carry official documents, letters, and freight to both shogunal and daimyo domains. Intermediate stations known as *tsugitate* were established at intervals of approximately eight kilometers, and horses were kept in readiness there to relay messages along the route.

Besides the bakufu, some of the greatest daimyo, most notably the Tokugawa collateral houses at Nagoya and Wakayama and a few other collateral and vassal daimyo, maintained their own separate systems of messengers, often called *shichiri hikyaku* (seven-*ri* express). The seven-*ri* express, also called the daimyo express (*daimyo hikyaku*), took its name from the seven-*ri* interval between the stations where riders changed mounts. The seven-*ri* express messengers serving Wakayama left the daimyo's mansion in Edo at ten-day intervals on the 5th, 15th, and 25th of each month and departed Wakayama for the return trip on the 10th, 20th, and 30th. The other collateral domains employed similar systems, and in their totality they linked domains to one another in an efficient manner.

Despite their efficiency, however, these official post systems were expensive and were plagued with other difficulties, and they collapsed within a few decades of their inception. Another system was born in their place, however, a system of *sando hikyaku* entrepreneurs operated by the private sector. Although known by the same name as their predecessor, they were managed differently. These privately operated *sando hikyaku* postal enterprises, said to have begun in 1664, were known in Edo as *jō bikyaku* (scheduled express messengers), in Kyoto as *junban hikyaku* (sequential express messengers), and in Osaka as *sando hikyaku*.

Kyoto boasted a multitude of *junban hikyaku* houses, some eighty-six separate establishments in the late seventeenth century, while nine *sando hikyaku* shops operated in Osaka. Most of the messenger shops in Edo were branches of the great express companies of Kyoto and Osaka, but there were independent operations as well, which functioned on a relatively small scale. The latter were known as *jōge hikyaku* or *rokkumi hikyaku* ("Edo-to-Kinai" or six-group expresses). These Edo-based express shops generally specialized in serving daimyo of a particular region. The express companies of Kyoto and Osaka likewise specialized, and they quickly began providing service beyond the Tōkaidō, spreading the communications network into the hinterland, to cities like Nagasaki, Kanazawa, Sendai, Fukui, and Nara, and to such provinces as Tamba and Harima.

The *sando hikyaku* of the Three Metropolises generally sent and received messages three times every ten days, or nine times a month. Each company had its set, specialized schedule, with some Osaka companies, for example, dispatching their messengers on days of the month with 2, 5, and 8 in their dates, while others used days with 1, 4, and 7. Osaka thus had eighteen postings for Edo every month. Each express house spent three to four days prior to its next scheduled departure collecting letters, freight, and cash from bakufu offices and from the commercial establishments of the town.

At departure time, a foreman called a *sairyo* supervised the deployment of messengers and horses. He had a great deal of authority, being responsible for the safe delivery of the freight, letters, and cash under his command. Way stations were established along the Tōkaidō where additional personnel and horses were kept ready, and though their locations changed from time to time, there were generally about twenty such stations along the 500-kilometer route.

Thus, from the mid-seventeenth century on, a private-sector communication network took shape centered on the Tōkaidō. Its operating area gradually expanded, and over the years it became an increasingly reliable system for transmitting information.

The Flow of Information: Farther and Faster

The communication network that had taken shape by the end of the seventeenth century changed greatly during the eighteenth. This resulted from economic expansion and the development of market activity, which fostered a growing demand for ever more timely and accurate information. As the demand grew, it accelerated the pace of communication.

In general, communication between the Kinai and Edo, as symbolized in the term *jōroku* (fixed at six), came to require only six days. The distance from Edo to Osaka is approximately five hundred kilometers, so couriers averaged some eighty-five kilometers per day. That was the normal speed in the express-messenger trade, but faster delivery could be arranged by special order.

Travel schedules were regulated because, as the economy expanded during the eighteenth century, so too did the volume of market goods, resulting in traffic jams all along the transportation network. There being insufficient messengers and horses to handle the proliferating freight and correspondence, the goods simply piled up in the post towns.

Reports from Kumagawa station, a small post town on the Wakasa Highway in Ōmi province, contain a humorous tale of freight piling up because of a wounded boar roaming the area. And it appears that the situation at Kumagawa was really quite severe, with some two hundred pack loads of freight piling up for ten days or more.

Conditions like this appeared all around the country. At riverside towns, for example, when flooding forced officials to bar river crossing, freight piled up to phenomenal levels, so that the towns were virtually buried under the accumulated freight, couriers, and other travelers. And once goods had piled up, it took days to move them out again because of the limited supply of horses and manpower. As a consequence, it was no longer possible to make the Edo-Osaka trip in six days. Even high-priority express companies like the *sando hikyaku* and *junban hikyaku* found it difficult to compensate for these delays. So the express companies were unable in practice to stick to their "fixed at six days" schedule, and delivery times of ten or even twelve days became common.

Nevertheless, pressure grew steadily for the express services to stick to their six-day schedules, or even to make their deliveries faster than that. And in fact the services did gradually devise ways to overcome bottlenecks in the system. Some merchants exploited specially privileged transport arrangements to increase their delivery speeds. From earlier times the baggage and correspondence of the old Kyoto civil nobility and priests of imperial descent had borne special labels (called *efu* or picture-stickers) that assured them priority treatment in transit. Some express merchants managed to acquire and employ these labels to gain any advantage possible in speed of dispatch and receipt. This particular maneuver was quickly banned, but demands for speedier deliveries continued to mount.

The bakufu attempted to satisfy these demands for greater communications efficiency. As early as the seventeenth century, it had manned and paid for the highway system by providing subsidies to post stations and levying on nearby villages a corvée of men and horses (*sukegō*) that villagers could convert into cash payments. To cope with the increasing demand for highway service, it later imposed supplemental levies (*zō sukegō*) on the villages and increased the operating subsidies. But these measures did little to ease the pressure.

Despite the obstacles, however, express operators in the private sector, who were under constant pressure from their customers, managed gradually to cut their delivery times to five, four, and even three and a half days. By the time messengers were making the run between Edo and Osaka in three and a half days, they had virtually doubled the speed of the Tōkaidō courier system. They achieved the increase in speed primarily by running at night as well as in the daytime. In addition, they began to skip layovers at intermediate post stations where they formerly had to stop. These *haya hikyaku* (fast-express messengers), as they were called, constituted a new, superexpress, or special delivery system.

Night operations also marked a major change in the system for the messengers themselves. As noted above, transport had formerly operated under the direction of foremen, but round-the-clock operations went on without their supervision. Furthermore, round-the-clock operations reflected the attainment of social conditions that permitted nighttime travel, even with valuable cargo. In the seventeenth century, public safety was not yet sufficiently established to permit travel except during daylight hours. But by the beginning of the eighteenth century, public order had improved visibly. These improved conditions are reflected in many of the writings and documents of the time, including, for example, Tanaka Kyūgū's *Minkan seiyo* (Essential reflections on conditions among the people, 1721). In fact, the improved public order also permitted a great increase in general travel by ordinary people, whether for business, pleasure, or pilgrimage.

The increasing rapidity of communication naturally led to rising costs. The *haya hikyaku* superexpress system was especially expensive. On the Edo-Osaka run, the price listed for three-and-a-half day delivery was 4 *ryō*, roughly equivalent to a year's wage for a domestic servant. Four-day delivery cost 3 1/4 *ryō*, and five-day delivery, 2 3/4 *ryō*. Of course, prices varied from one express company to the next, as well as according to the weight of the cargo or letter. At the high end of the scale is an example of an express company charging from 8 1/2 to 9 *ryō* for three-and-a-half-day delivery. Prices do not appear to have been clearly set, but at the least, these services were expensive. Using rice as a medium of calculation, one *ryō* bought roughly one *koku* at wholesale in the mid-eighteenth century, which was enough to feed one person for one year. Thus, the money spent to mail a single letter with a guaranteed delivery of three-and-a-half-days was enough to feed a family of four for a whole year! Looked at differently, we can see how people were willing to pay staggering sums for the rapid receipt of information.

The acceleration in delivery speeds continued, and by the early nineteenth century, express service between Edo and Kyoto broke the two-day barrier. Averaging close to 250 kilometers per day, the messengers had nearly managed to triple the speed of their "fixed-at-six" seventeenth-century predecessors. The velocity of information seemed capable of acceleration however much social demand required.

Another important change that accompanied the increasing speed of communication was expansion of the communication network. With the development of provinces and provincial towns, the network began to link region with region, and provincial town with provincial town. Starting in the eighteenth century, this network of *jikata hikyaku* (provincial express messengers) grew as metropolitan express companies set up branch offices in the provinces. The Kyoto *junban hikyaku* entrepreneurs led in this development, but later on the express companies of Edo began to advance northward into the provinces of Kōzuke and beyond.

Furthermore, communication arrangements began to develop within the provinces themselves. The *chūma* pack-horse operators who traveled from coast to coast in the Tōkai region between the Nagoya and Sumpu areas are one such example, and they even expanded their network westward into Ōmi province. Itinerant merchants from the Ōmi region, known colloquially as Ōmi *shōnin*, were a particularly famous group. Besides traveling throughout the home provinces around Osaka and Kyoto, they extended their activities into eastern Japan, and even to Ezo, linking them all in their trading network. The informational power of that network, including its capacity for market research, became well-established and served as a model for others. The Ōmi merchants developed a system of bases in the northern and northeastern provinces, to and from which they dispatched express messengers, and the timely transmission of their information became the very lifeblood of the trading network.

Despite their vigor these provincial entrepreneurs did not wrest all the hinterland express business from the hands of city merchants. Rather, the *sando hikyaku* express services continued their active expansion into the provinces. Kyoto companies began specializing in routes to towns in a particular province or region: "Tajima Express," "Etchū Toyama Express," "Inaba Tottori Express," "Tanba Express," and "Tango Express" are but a few examples. Some of these express companies continue to function today, in fact, boasting long histories of operation.

Merchants in the Three Metropolises also developed communication systems within their own cities. These *machi hikyaku* (town express) or *machi kozukai* (town messengers) emerged in conjunction with urban economic development, as local entrepreneurs collected and distributed freight and letters within the towns. At first, entrepreneurs whose specialty was recruiting long-term employees for service in samurai households and commercial establishments began filling their idle time by delivering messages. Gradually, the demand for their services grew until message-delivery became their principal occupation. At first, each delivery was handled separately, and the operators maintained no fixed fee schedules. But over time, they began to collect and deliver letters on set schedules and established fixed rates as well.

The economic growth of the eighteenth century, and the expanding volume of goods and information that accompanied it, required the communication system to improve in quality and expand in scale. And that, in fact, did occur. The system did not always function properly, but its tensions and problems notwithstanding, it is remarkable how profoundly it evolved over the long term. The overall social development that took place in early modern Japan would have been impossible without the transformation of the communication system. Once opened, the gateway to information would not be closed again.

3. Publishing and the Literate Classes

The rise of an urbanized, commercial society bound together by a dense communication system required and encouraged the production of written materials, the spread of literacy, and the accumulation of records relating to all aspects of life. These developments were evident throughout early modern Japan, but they were most visible in the great cities.

The Publishing World in the Three Metropolises

As cities came into existence all over early modern Japan, an interurban communication network became firmly established. Much of the information in the system was political, but the main body of data was economic. Once a town reached a certain level of maturity, however, cultural information also proliferated.

Kyoto had been overwhelmingly the most important cultural center from medieval times—indeed, even from ancient times when it virtually monopolized the production of scholarship, arts and letters, and religious materials. The resulting accumulation of cultural information was found predominantly among the court nobles (*kuge*) and those, like clerics of the great Buddhist monasteries, who were socially or institutionally related to the court. Despite the aristocratic character of its culture, however, because Kyoto was the political capital and the only great urban center in ancient Japan, it had potent means of transmitting its culture to the rest of the country. Lured by the city's grandeur, moreover, many in the provinces went to the capital to acquire the courtly learning.

By late medieval times, the *kuge* had long been isolated from actual political power, but they continued to transmit the culture of the old imperial court from generation to generation, perpetuating it in the form of family specializations or professions. Buddhist clerics operated their own universities and served as an intellectual elite even beyond the religious sphere, maintaining a broad expertise in scholarly and cultural matters. It was only natural, therefore, that large numbers of people continued turning to the cultural riches of Kyoto.

Nor did Kyoto's role in the production and dissemination of culture decline with the coming of the early modern period. Rather, as the times became more settled, more and more people headed for Kyoto, and one might even say that the city's early modern cultural vitality was born of the people who visited it.

The great efflorescence of the publishing industry reflected the general proliferation of cultural activity in early modern Japan, and in that field, as in others, Kyoto initially took the lead. The city had been the center of the publishing industry from medieval times, when it contained publishing enterprises known as "book groves" and "bookshops" (*shorin, shoshi*). The industry grew apace with the increasing social stability of the seventeenth century, and by mid-century, it had spread to Osaka and Edo.

Inoue Takaaki, a specialist in the history of early modern publishing, has studied fluctuations in the number of bookshops in the Three Metropolises. His findings, organized by century, show that during the seventeenth century there were 701 publishers in Kyoto, 185 in Osaka, and 242 in Edo. This figure includes enterprises that came into existence and shortly failed, but even in the single year, 1702, Inoue found seventy-two publishers operating in Kyoto. Clearly, Kyoto dominated Japanese publishing in the seventeenth century.

In the eighteenth century, however, the situation changed, with 536 publishers operating in Kyoto, 564 in Osaka, and 493 in Edo. Kyoto had lost its paramount position, and a rough balance obtained among the Three Metropolises. In the nineteenth century, the situation changed even more, with 494 publishing establishments active in Kyoto, 504 in Osaka, and 917 in Edo. There had been a slight decline in the publishing industries of Kyoto and Osaka, but a doubling in the scale of the industry in Edo. Indeed, Edo had come to wield overwhelming power in publishing, surpassing Kyoto and Osaka in both the quality and quantity of its output. This trend is captured in the early modern epigram, "culture's march eastward."

Provincial publishing also expanded during these centuries. Inoue found forty-three publishers in seven provinces for the seventeenth century and 135 during the eighteenth. For the nineteenth century, he found 407 publishers operating in ten provinces, a nearly tenfold increase in two hundred years.

Early modern publishing was a booming business, but how many titles did publishers issue, and how many copies did they print? Taking the *Kōeki shoseki mokuroku* (Catalog of books that spread benefits) of 1692 as a guide, we find that some 7,300 titles had been published by that date. The catalog lists Kyoto publications principally, but since the fledgling publishers of Osaka and Edo frequently issued titles jointly with Kyoto houses, this figure may be a fair estimate of the total published. An earlier listing of 1685 contained some 6,100 titles, so about 1,200 new titles, or an average of 189 per year, were published during the seven-year span to 1692. Over the full three centuries, the output of publications grew at a formidable pace.

The novel *Genroku taiheiki* (Tales of the great peace of the Genroku era, 1702) describes the boom in publishing in these words: "Fictional tales are published in numbers beyond counting, with fads changing every year, every half-year. Readers scarcely give a second glance to what was fashionable yesterday, for it's old hat today." The lusty appetite of Genroku readers for new information ranged from scholarship to literature and the arts.

Along with the growing number of new titles each year, the size of print runs grew as well. Print runs remained relatively limited, because Japanese publishing had found the carved woodblock preferable to movable type, and this was the medium for most printing. First printings were generally in the neighborhood of three hundred copies, with later runs having a maximum of about five hundred.

During the Genroku era, the production of about two thousand copies of a title over a two-year period was probably the limit. That quantity constituted a great bestseller, although there are accounts, probably exaggerated, of a title selling eight or nine thousand copies. At any rate, mass publishing was a fact of the age, for if an average Genroku year saw 180 new titles, with first printings of some three hundred copies, this alone accounts for some 54,000 volumes a year. Adding in reprintings and revised editions, we can readily surmise a figure of 100,000 to 200,000 volumes a year. In the later Edo period, as many as four thousand copies of some bestsellers were printed in a single year. That number would have entailed recarving the entire set of printing blocks eight times, so a single bestseller like that was enough to keep a publisher busy.

Bookstores, too, proliferated. An 1814 survey of Kyoto found 183 bookstores, more than double the Genroku number, and there were another seventeen rental libraries as well. The two hundred bookstores served a city of between 350,000 and 400,000. Edo and Osaka had many bookstores, too, with rental libraries enjoying extraordinary popularity. According to an Edo record of 1808, there were 656 rental libraries in the metropolis, and around 1830 there were said to be about 800. And Osaka, with its population of 400,000, had some 300 rental libraries in the 1830s.

Book rentals were popular because volumes were extremely expensive to buy. An ordinary romantic tale of the demimonde cost the equivalent of food expenses for one month, and a cheap pornographic story was about two-week's worth of meals. Books on Buddhism or Confucianism cost several times the price of a novel, as did a multivolume serial novel like one of Takizawa Bakin's. Books like these were beyond the purchase of any but the upper strata of the samurai or the wealthy merchant classes, and it was this fact that gave birth to the rental library.

Rental libraries lent for five days at a time, for a price said to be less than one-tenth the purchase price, so that even the urban lower classes could afford to read. In Edo, the rental libraries were organized into twelve groups, and they flourished in the vicinity of both samurai and merchant wards. Most rental libraries were operated by lone peddlers who carried pack loads of books through the neighborhoods of their customers. But there were others with collections of over ten thousand volumes, large shops employing as many as ten clerks.

The great expansion in publishing and book selling was assisted by improvements in printing technology and establishment of the principle of publishers' copyrights. As importantly, expanded production capacity in the paper industry assured publishers the paper they required. The principal raw material for paper was the paper mulberry (kōzō), and it was brought under cultivation, giving birth to a nationwide papermaking industry. Individual papermaking enterprises were extremely small in scale, but as production spread nationwide, total capacity leapt upward.

These several developments permitted the emergence of a huge publishing industry. In the end, however, the industry's vitality required growth in the reading public, which depended on the spread of literacy through the population. This development affected the overall capacity of the society to both generate and receive information, and it is to this development that we now turn.

The Spread of Literacy

In any examination of culture in early modern Japan, one is struck by the large numbers of samurai, urban commoners, and peasants who were literate and thereby equipped to "receive culture." Taking the last category first, there were some 63,000 villages in Tokugawa Japan, each with a core group of about ten men who controlled village affairs. These village officials were required to allocate the village tax obligation among landholders, conduct the annual village census, and perform their other administrative tasks, but they could not do so without the ability to read, write, and do computations on the abacus. The level of skill attained by these officials was high enough so that it may be fair to say there was no great difference, in terms of literacy, between peasant officialdom and samurai.

It is entirely likely, moreover, that there was a considerable pool of literacy among the middle peasantry, even outside the circle of village officeholders, but its extent is difficult to determine from the available sources. Certainly from the turn of the nineteenth century, nearly every village could boast a *terakoya*, an elementary school that often was established in a Buddhist temple or Shintō shrine, and that development greatly increased levels of popular literacy.

Within towns and cities the *chōnin*, or urban commoners, mostly engaged in commerce or pursued occupations as artisans or manual laborers. Especially for the commercial classes, reading, writing, and abacus skills were critical for the handling and analysis of essential business information. Bookkeeping and cost calculations, preparation of orders, invoices, and the like, all required fairly advanced literacy and computational skills. A look at innumerable commercial records left by merchants of the Three Metropolises and provincial towns gives a hint of their high levels of literacy and numeracy. By the eighteenth century, these merchants had independently developed and put into use bookkeeping practices comparable to those used in the commerce of Europe and the Middle East.

During the seventeenth century, at least, commoner literacy

levels were highest in Kyoto. Of course, that city had a cultural tradition tracing back to ancient and medieval times, when it spawned its own large population of merchants and artisans, who received the basic education in reading, writing, and arithmetic that enabled them to pursue their trades. That, however, was not the end of their learning. The basic knowledge they gained through literacy gradually advanced to where townsfolk were seeking higher knowledge in scholarship, literature, and the arts.

Haiku poetry is an example. From the early seventeenth century on, townsfolk joined in the composition of these seventeen-syllable verses, and in response to their demands, publishers began to bring out *haiku* handbooks, explaining the rules of composition and offering sample poems for emulation. By late in the century the population of *haiku* poets had grown substantially. According to the late seventeenth-century chronicle, *Haikai Kyō habutae*, there were as many as 739 *haiku* teachers in Kyoto. Of these, sixty-seven were full-fledged professional *haiku* poets who supported themselves entirely from their poetry or from teaching the art to others. If we assume only ten students for each of these 739 teachers, then the old capital would have had nearly 7,400 *haiku* poets; if twenty, then nearly 15,000. As mentioned above, Kyoto had a population of between 350,000 and 400,000; if 250,000 of them were adults, then better than one Kyoto adult in twenty may have been able to make at least a modest attempt at writing a *haiku* poem.

Indeed, during the second half of the seventeenth century books on *haiku* were second in popularity only to Buddhist texts among the publishers of Kyoto. They published 658 titles of *haiku* poetry, compared with 2,796 Buddhist titles. If we include the many other forms of verse that were popular, more than 1,500 poetry titles were published in Kyoto. Assuming each work came out in ordinary print runs, then the first editions alone comprised the publication of well over 300,000 volumes of poetry during the seventeenth century alone. A publishing industry of this magnitude could only be sustained by a broadly literate populace equipped with a high level of learning.

This expansion in urban literacy came to Edo as well. As we saw above, the publishing industry there grew rapidly during the eighteenth century, reaching and later surpassing the level of Kyoto and Osaka. That growth reflected the spread of literacy in the city, which derived in significant part from the rapid proliferation of *tera-koya* throughout Edo. Although the education policies of Tokugawa Yoshimune, the eighth shogun, contributed to this development, the driving force was the inherent demand of the burgeoning city itself. *Terakoya* education continued to expand as the century advanced, a development revealed in the writings of the day. According to the mid-eighteenth century collection, *Kanpo-Enkyo Kofu fūzoku shi* (A guide to the customs of Edo during the 1740s), "By 1750, just about anyone could become an elementary writing teacher. Tuition has become extremely inexpensive, and school-registration procedures were simplified. It amounts to a bargain sale on education, and as a result, even people of low status have enrolled in *terakoya*, to the point that nowadays 'brushless people' [*muhitsu*—those who can't write] are a rarity. This is a very good thing."

A miscellany published somewhat later, *Asukagawa* (1810), also noted, "In the old days, writing teachers were scarce, but nowadays, there are two or three in every block." Even if this was an exaggeration, it suggests that by the late eighteenth century almost everyone in Edo could read and write. Clearly, educational levels were rising, and the literacy skills needed to obtain the most basic knowledge and information had extended to even the lower levels of Edo society. Without these developments society would have had no way to transmit the great volume of information it now generated.

It goes without saying that the samurai caste required literacy. Those who would govern must accumulate training in the techniques of public administration, and that demands a high level of literacy and knowledge. By the second half of the seventeenth century, governance of the realm could no longer rely solely on the martial arts, even those of the most talented warrior. Rather, it demanded the best of administrative and bureaucratic skills, and from about that time the bakufu and daimyo began competing to persuade the best scholars of Kyoto, as well as the other two metropolises, to establish domain-sponsored schools. The opening of new domain schools continued through the eighteenth century, and into the nineteenth, at an ever-accelerating pace, until virtually no domain was without its official academy.

These developments brought higher levels of intellectual accomplishment to the samurai, who in a sense became one wing of the intelligentsia. Their knowledge advanced the capacity of society to receive and transmit information. And, in its entirety, the rising intellectual level of the samurai, townsfolk, and peasantry played a crucial role in the creation of a national culture.

Records upon Records

As we have already seen, from the eighteenth century on, the efflorescence of publishing, and the expansion of literacy that undergirded it, changed Japanese culture greatly as people came to recognize the importance of information. Moreover, that information generally was of interest not only to the ruling class but to the common people as well.

The information that circulated through early modern Japan was recorded with great energy. The social elite, such as the court nobility, had from ancient times been meticulous in its record-keeping habits. Indeed, leaving records for later generations seems to have amounted to a life's work for some. This tradition was continued in the Edo period, as samurai generated vast quantities of records which they left to posterity. In addition, especially as the eighteenth century progressed, we find a great volume of records being left by urban and rural commoners. They began generating prodigious quantities of political, economic, and cultural information that convey vivid accounts of life as seen through their eyes.

The itinerant merchants of Ōmi, for example, gathered information that consisted of detailed surveys together with their own analysis. The surveys took the form of travel diaries, which were little short of research reports. They discussed the towns and villages along the highways, recording in detail local customs and traits, economic conditions, and plans and projects, as well as noting the prices of various goods and commodities and the consumption habits of the locality. The surveys constituted a sort of market research and sometimes they suggested a marketing plan, reporting that a certain product seemed likely to sell well in a particular locality. Most merchants probably regarded this kind of research and record keeping as a natural activity, and almost certainly they reported their findings back to their home shops. But it is also true that the Ōmi merchants followed a clear set of guidelines in this practice and were quite punctilious in conducting and recording their surveys. It may be fair to say that this single-minded pursuit of information was the source of their strength in commercial competition.

Ōmi merchants were not the only ones to keep travel diaries. Indeed, long-term travelers prepared an immense number of these accounts of the customs, great sights, and important products of the provinces. People of all classes and stations left such diaries, literary figures like the *haiku* poet Bashō, as well as ordinary peasants or officials. Examination of the things they recorded shows the ferment of a developing national consciousness, as they compared their home provinces with other provinces, their hometowns with other towns, becoming aware of differences and similarities among them. This trend is particularly evident in the diaries of the eighteenth and nineteenth centuries.

The demand for more information accelerated even further during the nineteenth century. But rather than being driven by consciousness of a particular purpose, it appears to have been an aimless pursuit of all sorts of information about daily life. Typical examples are the voluminous Osaka chronicle, *Ukiyo no arisama* (How things are in this fleeting world) and the *Fujiokaya nikki* (Fujiokaya diary), which provides a vivid portrait of Edo in the 1800s. Both were collected with no visible purpose, but they contain a wellspring of political, economic, cultural, and ethnographic information. Thus the writer of the *Fujiokaya nikki*, for reasons of his own, no doubt, paid his informants for whatever information they brought him, whether it was news of personnel changes in the bakufu or of a problematic divorce in one of the commoner wards. Even the most outlandish of rumors was recorded vividly in his diary. Rather than saying he gathered information without any purpose, it may be better to say he collected it for its own sake.

At any rate, it would be little exaggeration to say that by the nineteenth century, Japan was flooded with information. Especially in the last years of the Tokugawa period, the country entered an era when fresh international news reached not only the highest councils of the bakufu, but the farthest fringes of commoner society as well. The quality of the information may have been flawed, but great volumes of "tidings," "strange tales," and "records of disturbances (at such-and-such place)" were being published, creating premonitions of a new age. Viewed in this context, the availability of diverse information, the capacity to transmit it, and the recognition of its value, which had taken shape since the seventeenth century, may well be seen as providing the initial motive power that stimulated formation of the modern Japanese nation-state.

(Translation by Ronald P. Toby)

Chapter Five

The
Spatial Structure of Edo

HIDENOBU JINNAI

1. Characteristics of Edo City

Tokyo's precursor was Edo, an enormous, early modern castle town. It centered on Edo Castle which was located on a headland of the Musashino plateau, but the town itself spread broadly enough to encompass both the surrounding bluffs and the low ground of the seashore. Like the other castle towns of early modern Japan, its structure was to some extent determined by the logic of residential segregation according to the status system enforced under the bakuhan system. At the same time, it developed a spatial structure of a sort that could never have resulted from the rational, geometrical urban planning that produced European cities after the Renaissance. The peculiarities of this pattern result largely from the city's relationship to the natural environment. That is, urban structure in Japan is above all characterized by its intimate relationship with nature and topography. Contrary to the modern city, which everywhere tends to create homogeneous space, the early modern Japanese city preserved the particularity of each location and achieved a certain ecological balance.

Edo was built among a particular set of natural conditions that included frontage on the sea and a plethora of hills and rivers—a topography replete with variety. The Shitamachi, Downtown, area that developed along the shores of Edo Bay and the Sumida River was a "city of water" laced with a network of canals. On the other hand, Yamanote, the Upland, which emerged among the plateaus and valleys of the Musashino hills, could be called a "city of fields

Figure 1. *Edo ezu* (Picto-map of Edo). Mid-nineteenth century. Tokyo Central Metropolitan Library.

and gardens" wrapped in green. This dual structure, which developed in close collaboration with nature, is the major characteristic of Edo's urban space, and what makes this Japanese pattern distinctive.

In Edo, the various functions that must be performed in an urban area were skillfully distributed, with close attention to the particular environmental features characteristic of Shitamachi and Yamanote, respectively. Indeed, it is possible to identify precisely the kind of ideal for urban development that is now called a "master plan" even at a relatively early historical stage in the formation of the castle city. Not only was the city appropriately arranged functionally, but urban space, rich in imagery, was differentiated symbolically, using as props the various natural elements, like forests and water. Thus, the city's layout is fascinating even when viewed from the perspective of cosmology.

A number of panoramic representations of Edo were created late in the Tokugawa period. They invariably project toward the west from a vantage high above the Sumida River, thus paying homage to the lifespace of the townsmen (*chōnin*) by faithfully depicting the

watery world of Shitamachi (Figure 1). Casting our eyes from right
to left across this illustration, we follow the lazy flow of the Sumida
as it passes through Shitamachi and finally empties into Edo Bay.
The scene reminds us that Edo's literary space, which was pervaded
by the culture of the townsmen, also developed around the banks of
the Sumida. Indeed, the illustration suggests with nearly palpable
realism the commercial vitality of the canal-crossed townsman area
by depicting the merchant storehouses packed tightly at water's
edge.

Near the center of the picture, halfway back, is placed a symbolic
representation of Edo Castle, and behind it are spread the verdant
hills and valleys of Yamanote, peopled primarily by the samurai
(*bushi*). But high above the political space that contains this ruling
class looms an image of Mount Fuji, highly accentuated so as to
demonstrate its status as the city's most potent symbol and belie its
actual distance from the urban area.

Edo lacked the walls that typically surrounded European cities,
and within its precincts, water, hills, and forests blended with city
streets to create a special urban environment. This essay will
emphasize Edo's bond with nature as a way of understanding its
special urban form and social identity. In doing so, it will pay particular attention to the characteristics of Shitamachi and Yamanote, as
the two major dimensions of Edo's spatial structure.

2.   Shitamachi

We can begin by considering how the urban space of Shitamachi
developed in intimate connection with water. The city streets of
Shitamachi have been fundamentally reconstructed in the aftermath of modern earthquakes, and so retain very little of Edo's original form. On the other hand, the network of rivers and canals that
make up the "city of water" has been relatively well preserved. It is
possible to imagine the original form of these waterways even
where they have been filled in, and it is even possible to travel part
of the network by boat. Therefore, if one considers the city from the
perspective of water, and not only extrapolates imaginatively from
actual experience in urban waterways but also makes good use of

old maps and other pictorial materials, it is quite possible to recon-
struct and analyze the spatial structure of old Edo.

Of course, not even Edo's "city of water" could be a direct reflection or extension of nature. As engineering technology was rapidly
improved in the early Tokugawa period, Shitamachi developed as a
remolding of nature in response to human will. For example, not
even the major artery in Edo's waterworks, the Nihonbashi River,
was allowed to take its natural course. It is thought that the Muro-
machi-period warrior and castle builder Ōta Dōkan rerouted the
original Hirakawa River, which emptied into Hibiya inlet, in the
direction of Nihonbashi. In addition, to prevent water damage to
the streets of the Nihonbashi area (which were themselves the
result of landfill) the Kanda River was dug to redirect the north-
south waterways of the Hirakawa, Koishikawa, and other rivers
eastward into the Sumida. By means of such large engineering
projects, it was possible to eliminate flooding in the lower reaches of
the Hirakawa and thus prevent the silting up of Edo harbor. At the
same time, builders used the earth excavated from the Kanda River
to fill Hibiya inlet and lay the foundation for more city streets.

By replacing and rerouting large natural rivers in the lowlands of
Shitamachi, Edo's engineers were able to arrange an organic network of canals that conformed to the original topography. No doubt
one secret of Edo's urban beauty, whose diversity was always kept
in such good order, lies in the convergence of the uniquely planned
quality of the early modern castle town, on the one hand, with
archaic techniques of skillfully assessing and adapting to natural
conditions, on the other. Of course, the network of waterways had
various functions in addition to transportation. It allowed excess
water from heavy rains or a swelling of the Sumida to accumulate
harmlessly; it also provided a source of water for the miscellaneous
needs of cottage and light industries, and an outlet for their waste
water.

The importance of water in the formation of Shitamachi is clearly
apparent in the central role of the canals in the distribution of goods
(Figure 2). Shitamachi's canals were the veins and arteries of an
enormous consumer economy that nourished the city of the shogun.
In the early modern period, most goods were transported and distributed by water. Cargo vessels from all over Japan converged on

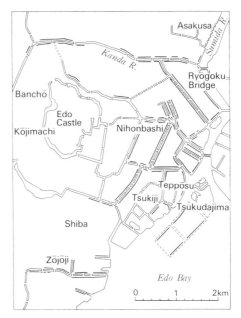

Figure 2. Edo's canals, waterways, and wharves in the late
Tokugawa period. From Suzuki Masafumi, *Edo no kawa, Tokyo no
kawa* (Japan Broadcast Puublishing, 1978).

Edo harbor and lay at anchor off Shinagawa or Teppōsu, while
workmen transshipped their goods to lighters, which were unloaded
at wharves along the city's canal system.

What was the scenery like along these waterways? Early in the
Edo period, the riversides were still rough and simple, with docks
and loading ramps but no stone embankments. However, as Edo's
commercial activity expanded and a distribution system was consolidated, shorelines were improved, giving rise to a uniquely con-
figured waterfront. Canal banks were reinforced with stone facing,
and adjacent storehouses were equipped with boat moorings and
small, planked jetties to facilitate offloading directly into the storage areas. Eventually, in the major centers of urban life, both sides
of the waterways were chock-a-block with such storehouses, presenting the spectacle of gabled roofs in rhythmic patterns over
whitewashed walls, bisected by the busy coming and going of a
variety of boats.

The shoreline was fundamentally public land under the authority
of the bakufu, but the holders of land proximate to the waterways

were allowed to extend their frontage to the water. Such land, with direct access to water transport, was taxed at a premium rate, so naturally the rich wholesalers who were involved in distribution gradually tended to acquire it, and their warehouses soon lined the waterfront. As a result, in the central environs of Shitamachi, facilities relating to transportation and distribution tended to monopolize space near the water. Shops and residences came to be separated from the warehouses, and in the center of the city there emerged the peculiar spatial arrangement by which the potentially very scenic water's edge was thoroughly dominated by storehouses. In Edo, there was no room for the sort of scenery one encounters in Western "cities of water," such as Amsterdam or Venice, where large, public halls are beautifully arranged along the waterfront. Rather, from the early years of the Tokugawa period, Shitamachi was built as a commercial city, and commercial priorities were manifested clearly in its structure and vista.

Among the many functions of the shoreline, the market deserves special emphasis. The several markets that supplied the kitchens of the great capital city were dependent upon water transport. The main vegetable market that operated with special permission of the bakufu was located in Kanda's Tamachi, where it utilized the water transport offered by the Kanda River. Similarly, the fish market was from very early in the Tokugawa period located near the convenient transportation offered by the Nihonbashi waterfront. Tokugawa Ieyasu brought fishermen with him from Settsu, near Kyoto-Osaka, and they settled in Tsukudajima, which served to establish the fish market in that location.

To understand the activities that developed in the vicinity of the markets which emerged near the water, it will suffice to take a look at the area around Edo Bridge, right next to Nihonbashi. In the aftermath of the Meireki Fire, the great Edo fire of 1657, a broad street was cleared here as a fire break. At the water's edge wharves were built, and along the fire break there sprang up large commercial facilities and 108 small shops and stalls that were closely associated with the marketplace. It is only to be expected that barbershops should have appeared where so many people gathered. And tea houses, which provided the masses with a place to rest, were also much in evidence. In a secluded alley off the main thoroughfare were hidden five separate bow-and-arrow shooting galleries and a hall for storytelling. All were small establishments

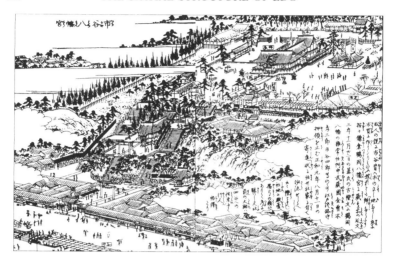

Figure 3. Ichigaya Hachiman Shrine. From *Edo meisho zue* (Illustrated guide to Edo landmarks).

hidden behind reed screens. The alley offered an inconspicuous haven of enjoyment for the crowds visiting the market; at its far end was a shrine dedicated to the harvest deity Inari. All this contributed to making the main thoroughfare at Edo Bridge a busy and prosperous area.

It is noteworthy that what the bakufu had set aside merely as a fire protection area was used by the people for their own purposes, and that it assumed a variety of meanings and functions in relation to its new identity as an entertainment area. Also significant is its location: the open area, bustling with activity, was formed at the base of a bridge, the intersection of water and land. In European cities, it was common for the city square to be symbolically central and permanent, set off by an imposing cathedral or government office building. It is suggestive, therefore, that in the Japanese city such a public area formed rather at the nexus of mobility among people and things, in a neighborhood filled with spirited activity.

The distribution of famous landmarks provides a somewhat different way of looking at Edo's spatial configuration. According to Higuchi Tadahiko, a landscape engineer, the spots that were made famous by continuous displays of popular affection were strongly influenced by topography, mostly being located in the vicinity of either hills or water. In the case of Yamanote, they were located at sites on the Musashino plateau that jutted out in the most obvious way, or in places that were most interior and secluded. On the other hand, in Shitamachi, famous landmarks appeared at the edge of Edo Bay and Sumida River. Moreover, these famous landmarks always formed in close proximity to a temple or shrine that conveyed a sense of permanence.

Thus, if we look at the distribution of temples and shrines in Edo, we find that in the Yamanote area they were at the edge of the hills, surrounded by quiet forests (Figure 3), and in the Shitamachi area they were built at the edge of the land so that behind them stretched a broad expanse of water. In both cases, they were far from the secular space of city streets, and the arrangement of their paths of approach no doubt represented the process by which one is drawn from the profane world into a quiet, religious realm. This pattern illustrates the motif of the interior (*oku*) that the architect Maki Fumihiko has identified as characteristic of Japanese urban and architectural spaces. Indeed, sometimes the grounds of a temple or shrine, wrapped in forest, became the site of performances staged in a makeshift theater while the block outside the temple gate was turned into an entertainment area to attract the masses.

This manner of situating religious facilities in Edo was the exact opposite of the European pattern. In Europe a cathedral, as the religious center of a city, was located at the most prominent place on the square. Moreover, the various parish churches not only held religious services but also administered household registration, collected taxes, and functioned like a combination of our present-day city offices and tax bureaus. Therefore, they tended to be located on neighborhood squares in the center of people's daily lives, where only thick walls or a single door separated the secular world from the sacred space within. European guilds and other artisan leagues often had patron saints and thus were bound by religious fetters. Accordingly, religion played a central role in the constitution of urban daily life.

In Edo, on the other hand, there was no local institution like the European parish church, with its crucial role, nor were there city squares of the sort that, in Europe, were so essential to those institutions. Of course, in Japan every household had a Buddhist ancestral cabinet (*butsudan*) or Shintō family altar (*kamidana*), and on the whole religion was probably more securely integrated into daily life than was the case in Europe, even though Japanese religion was not social in the European manner. Individuals or households worshiped their own ancestors, and the elements of religion played a conspicuous role in daily life. However, religion was not related closely to commerce or production in the city and region, nor was it directly involved in community formation on a daily basis. It is true that as society became disordered in the final years of the Tokugawa period, harvest deities and other objects of worship were placed right in the city streets where they became the focal points of frenetic activity, but there was never any counterpart to the central role in the forming of urban society that religion played in Europe.

In Edo, most religious spaces were located quite apart from the locale of daily life. They were selected for their sacred aura of connection with the world beyond and were often nestled in the greenery of the hills or set next to water, withdrawn from the bustle of the city streets. Accordingly, Japanese religious sites retained an aura of the nonquotidian, or extraordinary (*hare*). It would seem that the shift from quotidian to nonquotidian space is expressed not only at the level of consciousness but also in the distribution of urban geography. If so, this would help explain why some temples and shrines became the nuclei of landmarks that eventually developed into entertainment areas.

The historian Amino Yoshihiko has pointed out that in medieval Japan the places where itinerant artisans, drifters, and entertainers gathered, such as temple and shrine gates, markets, river banks, and bridges, were considered to be exempt from both conventional social norms and clearcut property relationships. They were a kind of "sacred" place where freedom and protection were assured. That is, they constituted sanctuaries (Fr. *asile*). In medieval times, even mountains, forests, rivers, or the sea might be granted a certain sacredness and take on the character of a refuge. Although the special freedom claimed for such places was largely suppressed by the expanding power of the early-modern daimyo and shogun, its distorted remnants survived in such marginal urban precincts as the brothel quarter and theaters.

In fact, if we consider the formation of Edo from this perspective, we find that it illuminates not only the entertainment quarters and

Figure 4. Ryōgoku, in *Shimpan ukiyoe Ryōgokubashi yūsuzumi hanabi kembutsu no zu* (Viewing fireworks in the cool of the evening at Ryōgoku Bridge, new edition). Print by Katsukawa Shunrō/Hokusai).

theaters but the structure of the city as a whole. The insight that medieval mountains, forests, and waters often had a sacred aura that gave them the quality of a sanctuary helps explain the observation that in Edo, religious spaces were located either in the foothills of Yamanote or next to the water in Shitamachi. Moreover, the Edo masses also had access to a kind of *asile*: they could flee the city streets, which were ruled by secular obligations and relationships, and liberate themselves in the grounds of a temple or shrine at the urban edge, or in the entertainment area outside the temple gate. Religious sites were under the jurisdiction of the Edo commissioner for temples and shrines (*jisha bugyō*), and the rules observed there concerning a number of activities were more lenient than those in ordinary urban areas ruled by the Edo city magistrate. The areas in which shows and plays were performed were concentrated on the grounds and outside the gates of the temples and shrines that were often visited by the masses.

Plays and shows were also put on at the water's edge, perhaps on

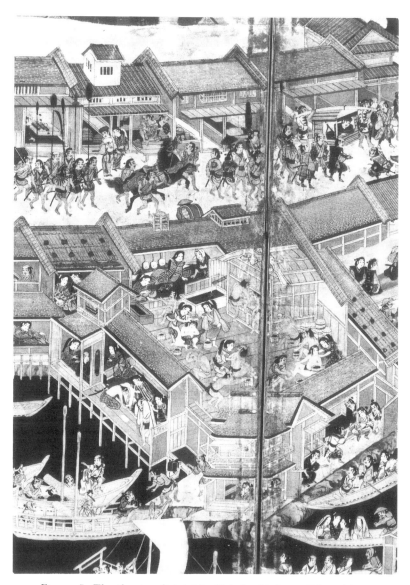

Figure 5. The theater district in Nakabashi, from *Edo meishozu byōbu* (Screen painting of Edo landmarks). Idemitsu Museum of Arts.

an avenue near the foot of a bridge. It appears that the freedom
from social norms and relationships that had since ancient times
been enjoyed in places connected with water, such as river banks
and bridges, was inherited intact by the approaches to bridges in
Edo. This is confirmed by scenes from Ryōgoku Avenue (Figure 4),
a fire break that was established after the great fires in the early
eighteenth century. The foot of Ryōgoku Bridge, where water and
land transportation meet, and Ryōgoku Avenue, which profited
from the expansive scenic beauty of the Sumida River, were transformed into a flourishing entertainment area where an atmosphere
of freedom prevailed and small structures housing sideshows, dramatic recitations, plays, and oral storytelling tightly lined the street.
The area eventually drew sufficient mass attention to become Edo's
largest amusement center.

　　This sort of free space, which liberated the energies of the masses,
also existed elsewhere in Edo, near Edo Bridge and, indeed, near all
of the city's major bridges. In Europe, energy was generated contin-
uously in the public space at the city center. In Edo, however, the
rules and constraints that were found in the usual townsman areas
could be evaded and free activities engaged in by the masses only in
special places that were under direct bakufu control, such as river
banks and the approaches to bridges. One could see this as a peculiarly Japanese logic of spatial formation.

　　In order to explore more fully the meaning of Edo's urban structure, we need to look more closely at the spaces to which drama was
relegated. These changed over time as the city streets developed
and expanded. Particularly as fire breaks were relocated in accord
with the adjustment of ward boundaries, the sites of dramatic productions and entertainment also moved. Overall, however, there
was no change in the practice of staging most dramatic activities in
the vicinity of water and near bridges.

　　The formation of entertainment areas in Edo can be traced well
into the past. The *Edo meishozu byōbu* [Screen painting of Edo land-
marks] (Figure 5) is useful as an aid in ascertaining how the Edo
streets looked before the Meireki Fire. The illustrations demonstrate that the Nakabashi theater district, in a new area facing the
ocean just outside the city center, was very busy at the time. It contained rows of theaters, baths, teahouses (of the sort found in
brothel quarters), and bow-and-arrow galleries. On the water, boats

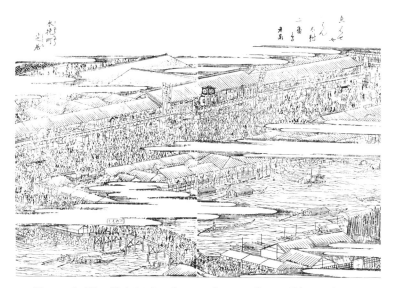

Figure 6. The Kobikichō theater district. From *Edo meisho zue.*

loaded with women of the night or theatergoers jostled each other
as they plied toward the scene. This sort of open, tolerant amusement quarter was eventually the victim of bakufu intervention, but
the practice of arranging a space such as this near the water was
inherited by the later theater districts.

The areas that developed as theater districts with bakufu permission—including the very active Sakaichō and also Fukiyachō—were
located, predictably, in an area just above Nihonbashi that was easily accessible to water transportation. And if we look at the *Edo
meisho zue* (Figure 6), which portrays another theater area called
Kobikichō, we find that it, too, was located near water. It is shown to
be lined with teahouses of open construction that face the canal and
to attract a variety of pleasure barges and the sort of narrow, roof-
less boats (*chokibune*) that carried passengers on the Sumida. The
Edo masses are also shown, crossing the bridge. No doubt this spatial arrangement, in close proximity to water, aroused festive feelings in the hearts of those who came to attend the performances.

This layout, with the theater district constructed in a special corner of the city that was accessible by bridge or boat, would have
been inconceivable in a European city. Restricting the activity in

this manner and employing various spatial contrivances to establish an insular theater ward served to stimulate yet further the libertarian urges of the people and gave rise to a peculiarly Japanese sort of entertainment district.

As we have seen, Edo's shoreline provided the focal point for a number of activities; it served not only commercial and economic but also cultural and entertainment functions and was a great source of urban energy. This tendency of Edo to develop entertainment areas and theaters along shorelines and near bridge abutments was also characteristic of many other early modern cities, such as Osaka, Hakata, Kanazawa, and Niigata. Edo's pattern must be considered typical of an early-modern form of urban development in which a commercial city is constructed around a network of canals situated on a river delta.

As the city expanded, the cultural and amusement areas were uprooted, not only from the political and economic center but also from the daily life spaces of the city dwellers, and moved to the outskirts, where nature was plentiful and an atmosphere of freedom flourished. In contrast to the centripetal structure of European cities, which were integrated around a walled, symbolic center, Edo developed centrifugally so that the concentrations of energy, where residents gathered, drifted toward the fringes. To some extent, of course, bakufu policy was responsible for this, but it might be regarded as a tendency, intrinsic to Japanese urban culture, to differentiate spatially between the everyday and the extraordinary.

In any case, it cannot be denied that the history of the kabuki theater's efflorescence is also the history of its expulsion from the urban center. The theater district was originally in Nakabashi, but it was driven out to Sakaichō, Fukiyachō, and Kobikichō. And finally, in 1842, the district was forced to move to Saruwakachō in Asakusa, a marginal area surrounded by temples and water. The same treatment was administered to the brothel quarter, which even before the theater district—in the immediate aftermath of the Meireki Fire—was expelled to Shin-Yoshiwara.

All this movement notwithstanding, the brothel and theater districts, which played such important roles in Edo culture, remained in close proximity to transportation and water on the city's margin near the Sumida River. The revelers who set out in *chokibune* from the boat livery near Yanagi Bridge and headed up the Sumida River could enjoy the changing scenery on the shoreline while traveling upstream to Asakusa. Water was thus extremely important in enabling Edo residents to escape the routine of daily life and institutions and enjoy themselves in a world of make-believe.

By the latter half of the Tokugawa period the *sakariba*, which were the city's areas for unfettered entertainment, had all become concentrated in the vicinity of Asakusa, Honjō, and Fukagawa. In the course of Edo's development, the Sumida, which originally had been completely outside the city, was gradually drawn into it. For the residents of what had become the world's largest city, the shade trees of the shoreline and the broad panorama of water offered a fine stage on which to liberate themselves from the humdrum of crowded streets.

It seems that the watery world of Shitamachi was possessed of a natural beauty that we can no longer imagine. Aimé Humbert, the head of a Swiss diplomatic delegation that visited Japan in the late Tokugawa period, compared the coastal areas of Edo centering on the Sumida River with the canal banks of Venice, the Queen of the Adriatic.

Nevertheless, the history of Tokyo since the Meiji era is a history of the conversion of a "city of water" to a "city of land." This conversion occurred in conjunction with the development of railways, but that does not necessarily mean that the structure of the city changed radically. The sites of major rail stations in Tokyo, like Shinbashi and Ryōgoku, had emerged originally as centers of water transportation. Furthermore, Tokyo's first real rail-station square (*ekimae hiroba*) appeared at Manseibashi, which was originally an important waterfront on the Kanda River.

The Great Kantō Earthquake of 1923 completely erased the old Edo ambiance from the water-world of Tokyo. However, water transportation remained vital, and post-earthquake restoration projects emphasized shoreline spaces. Bridges, parks, and buildings of excellent design soon gave birth to a modern form of waterfront scenery. More decisive in the long run than the earthquake was the extensive damage done to the "city of water" by the urban renewal that accompanied the rapid economic growth of the post-World War II period. Waterways were left unused, canals were glutted with polluted sludge, and elevated highways were constructed heedlessly across shoreline scenery.

Only in very recent years has the water quality finally been restored. As people have again begun to appreciate the role of water in their lives, they also have gradually reevaluated the shores of the Sumida River, the canals, and Tokyo Harbor.

3. Yamanote

One might think that the urban structure of Tokyo would have changed completely as a result of the dizzying process of modernization, but topographically the various sectors of Yamanote have maintained a surprising degree of historical continuity. By overlaying a current map with information from charts of the Tokugawa period, and considering actual topographical relationships, it is possible to visualize just how the urban space of Edo was organized.

It is especially useful to superimpose a late-Tokugawa period sectional map over a present-day map. If we pay particular attention to the Tokugawa-period network of roads and patterns of land use (i.e., the estates of daimyo and lesser Tokugawa vassals [*hatamoto*], lower-*bushi* residential areas, temple and shrine grounds, commoners' districts, fields, and so on), it becomes clear that in Yamanote the roads and outlines of building sites have remained fundamentally unchanged right down to the present. Indeed, the urban structure of Edo emerges quite clearly from behind the apparent confusion of Tokyo's urban sprawl.

Edo was skillfully laid out so as to follow the contours of hills and valleys. The Yamanote or "upland" region was not merely a flat plateau, its name notwithstanding, because valleys carved by numerous rivers gave the plateau a topography of ridges and indentations. Like Rome, Edo contained seven hills that were separated by a maze of valleys: Ueno, Hongō, Koishikawa-Mejiro, Ushigome, Yotsuya-Kōjimachi, Akasaka-Azabu, and Shiba-Shirogane. Thus, Yamanote had a complex topography consisting of alternating ridges and valleys, which fundamentally determined the pattern of the area's urban growth.

In close conformance to this terrain there developed a skeleton of urban roads and highways. Particularly in Yamanote, these arteries are of two types, ridge roads and valley roads, and they are connected by a number of slopes.

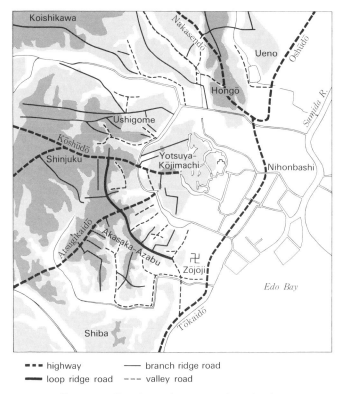

Figure 7. Roads and topography of Edo.

When we superimpose the roads of the Tokugawa period on a map of present-day Tokyo, it is possible to see clearly which roads were of each type (Figure 7). The major highways, such as the Nakasendō and Kōshūdō, which radiated out from the city center like spokes of a wheel and connected the center with broad sectors of the surrounding area, were all of the ridge type. Some important loop roads, also of the ridge type, ran from west of Edo Castle to the south and thus linked these major arteries. Moreover, on the many ridges that projected out from the seven major plateaus, smaller ridge roads were extended from the highways to facilitate the development of residential areas. As a result, a clearly delineated spatial order emerged among the ridge roads that were constructed by opening the forests of adjacent uplands (Figure 8). Along the plateaus organized in this manner there developed a series of samurai

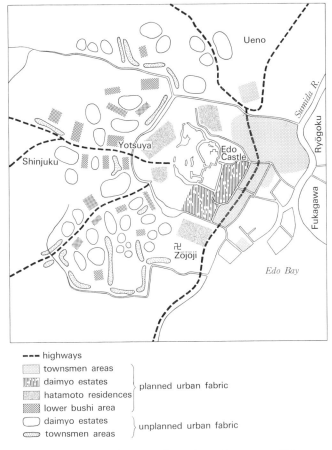

Figure 8. Distribution of residential areas in Edo.

- - - highways
- townsmen areas
- daimyo estates
- hatamoto residences
- lower bushi area
} planned urban fabric
- daimyo estates
- townsmen areas
} unplanned urban fabric

residential areas, with daimyo mansions nearest the center and the homes of low-ranking retainers on the margins.

On the other hand, the narrow valleys that lay between the ridges had been cultivated and dotted with villages since before the Tokugawa period. Roads that wound through the valleys also sometimes crossed the ridges to connect one village with another. As a result of this prior agricultural settlement, therefore, the subsequent formation of Yamanote was guided by a phenomenon peculiar to wet-rice cultivation—the tendency of farmers to settle on the low ground where water was plentiful. That is, as the city blocks of Edo expanded into the Yamanote area, the townsmen took the place of the farmers who already lived in the valleys, eventually giving rise to the bustling settlements that became a kind of Shitamachi within Yamanote.

Yamanote's charm is largely the result of its hilly topography, which, in turn, is responsible for the great diversity among its plethora of tiny towns. Within the same area, the worlds of the samurai on the high ground and commoners in the valleys existed cheek by jowel, connected by Yamanote's innumerable slopes. Whereas the names of streets became the names of wards (*chō*) in the townsman areas, samurai wards remained nameless. Rather, each of the slopes came to be individualized with a popular name.

Thus far, we have looked at the structure of Yamanote as a whole. Next, some examination is due the residential areas, which followed the pattern peculiar to castle towns.

Daimyo were required to live alternate years in Edo in accord with the *sankin kōtai* system, and as it became common for them to maintain not only a principal mansion near the city center but also a second and even a third residence in suburban areas, such residences gradually came to dominate the most desirable areas of Yamanote. Because of their location on the city's outskirts, which were free of the various restrictions governing urban construction, these large estates were not arranged according to any plan or system of allotment. Instead, they were placed very carefully in accord with geographical conditions.

In most cases, daimyo villas were built facing the ridge roads. This meant that the grounds sloped toward the back, making possible the use of topography and water flow to construct ponds and walking gardens. Moreover, it appears that whenever possible the estates were arranged along the south side of the ridge roads, placing the main building on the high ground to the north, and the garden down the incline to the south. This regularity clearly reveals the sense of residential directionality that the Japanese have cultivated since antiquity.

These daimyo estates, so rich in their proximity to natural beauty, were the homes of the privileged *bushi* class, whose members produced nothing and never participated in urban activities. Therefore, in placement and construction these residences were highly individualized and conformed only to the topographical con-

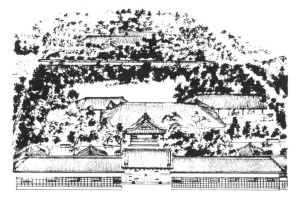

Figure 9. Residence of a 4000–5000 *koku* warrior household
household. From Sasama Yoshihiko, *Edo bakufu yakushoku shūsei*
(Compilation of official positions in the Edo bakufu) (Yūzan-
kaku Shuppan, 1965).

ditions of the terrain. They were, in that sense, very "non-urban." In
a manner directly opposite to the orientation of European aristocratic homes, which were typically urban in their tendency to open
onto a square or street, the daimyo villas adopted a closed, defen-
sive posture, dramatized by their placement of a road lined with a
virtual wall of retainers' rowhouses (*nagaya*) around the outer edge
of the grounds.

Eventually, in the Meiji era, most of these daimyo residences
were confiscated by the government and, without changing the
dimensions of their grounds, transformed into government offices,
embassies, military installations, and various other educational or
cultural facilities. In their new capacity, they played an important
role in the modernization of Tokyo.

The residential patterns of the *hatamoto*, who were typically
middle-ranking samurai, differed markedly from those of the daimyo. Soon after moving to Edo, Tokugawa officials chose Kōjimachi
plateau, to the west of the castle, as an area suitable for *hatamoto*,
because of its favorable topography and ease of development.
Although relatively flat for Yamanote, it still had some undulations.
Particularly the Banchō area, located at the tip of the plateau, was
elaborately incised by two small valleys. Nevertheless, it was
divided in the manner of castle towns into a number of wards (from

Ichibanchō to Rokubanchō) and acquired an extremely systematic layout. Just as in the center of Shitamachi, city blocks were sized on their short side according to the fundamental standard of 60 *ken*, following the precedent of the grid system used in the ancient capital at Kyoto. And, in accord with typical Japanese practice, each block was bisected lengthwise so that house lots measured 30 *ken* in depth.

The typical *hatamoto* residence was inserted compactly into a space comparatively small by daimyo standards but still averaging about 2,000 square meters (Figure 9). And of course the occupant's samurai status was displayed clearly in the arrangement of its gate, approach, and entryway, as well as in the layout of its main building. The *hatamoto* residences were also built with sensitivity to directionality, as a rule with the main house to the north and garden toward the south.

Although the popular image of the large estate that was inherited by post-Meiji Japan is unmistakably that of the daimyo or *hatamoto* residence, most of the free-standing houses with attached gardens that can still be seen in present-day Tokyo are in the tradition of the low-ranking samurai home. A large part of the 70 percent or so of Edo that was set aside for *bushi* residences was covered with the dwellings of these low-ranking samurai. Although these residences conformed to the layout of the blocks and the fundamental requirements of space apportionment, their essential features are still imitated in the heart of the city and comprise an important heritage for middle-class housing.

The lower samurai lived in groups that were constituted according to their official duties, in a manner similar to the way present-day employees often live in company or government dormitories. Land leased from the bakufu was bisected by a road, and then each side of the road was divided into orderly lots with uniform frontage. Lots were generally from 300 to 600 square meters in size, and of course the residences expressed the *bushi* status of their occupants in the quality of gate and entryway. The typical house plan approximated that of a present-day middle-salaried worker's home, but since the lot was large in proportion to the house, it was not unusual for even lower-ranking samurai to have a vegetable garden.

Early in the Tokugawa period, these lower-*bushi* residences were built on high ground in desirable locations and arranged in system-

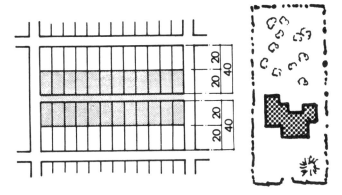

Figure 10. (Left) Layout of a lower *bushi* residential module and (right) artist's conception of a residential plot. In the lefthand figure, the shaded area represents one group's residential area.

atic patterns that obviously reflected an ideal conception with city blocks 40 *ken* in width and house lots half that in depth (Figure 10). However, in Yamanote, ideal plans were not imposed mechanically over large areas as they had been on the flat land of Shitamachi. Rather, the residential unit was treated as a module that could be adjusted as necessary to accord with local topography. The result was a mosaic pattern of organic connectedness. Clearly, the organization of the plots was determined by a balance between the planning that was characteristic of castle towns and a more flexible conformance to topography.

Urban sprawl and crowding advanced considerably in the second half of the Tokugawa period. By this time, all the really desirable locations had been occupied either by daimyo mansions or the middle and lower-*bushi* housing that had been constructed early in the period. Therefore, new housing for lower *bushi* had to be located in the less attractive spots along the north side of slopes, at the base of cliffs, or in lowlands and hollows.

The main actors in the formation of Yamanote were by no means all samurai. If one walked far enough along a plateau occupied by their residences, one would soon come to the edge of a slope or hollow, and the world of the townspeople would be spread out below. In the early eighteenth century, the belt of close suburbs, notably Koishikawa, Ushigome, Ichigaya, Yotsuya, Akasaka, and Azabu, were designated wards and brought formally within the boundaries of the city. It was also in this era that many of the valley settlements of Yamanote were established, as the city population spread outward.

These commoners' settlements followed the twists and bends in valley roads, springing up spontaneously in the narrow areas between road and hillside. Whereas the standard residential pattern for Shitamachi was for a block of 60 *ken* width to be divided into three parts, each 20 *ken* in depth and bisected by a back alley lined with rowhouses between the townsmen's homes, here it was unusual for a block to achieve even 20 *ken* in depth. Nevertheless, where space was available, there was a tendency to place townsmen's residences and rowhouses in a pattern that duplicated the standard commoners' life-space of Edo. Merchants who retailed fruit, sundries, and other goods built their homes along the roads, and in the rowhouses lining the back alleys must have lived the artisans, carpenters and plasterers who serviced the estates on the plateaus.

Thus, in the castle town of Edo, the urban structure of Yamanote was formed in close correspondence to the region's hilly topography, and that heritage is still reflected in the diversity of modern Tokyo's various sections. Whereas the old samurai housing areas along the ridge roads have now been transformed into quiet residences, schools, and other facilities, one can still find, along the valley streets below, the bustling commercial and entertainment centers characteristic of the townsmen's culture of Edo.

(Translation by J. Victor Koschmann)

Chapter Six

The Management Practices of Family Business

YŌTARŌ SAKUDŌ

"Japanese-style management" has recently been a topic of considerable public interest. However, to understand it properly, one must recognize its antecedents in the commercial practices of the Tokugawa period. Those practices took shape as the economy grew and changed, shaped by the interplay of commercial influences from Edo, the castle towns of the daimyo, and, most importantly, Osaka. Privileged merchant families, such as the Yodoya, dominated the commercial life of seventeenth-century Japan, but by century's end new entrepreneurs, such as Mitsui Takatoshi, were displacing them. The organizational structures and procedures and the ideology of management developed by such entrepreneurial families as Mitsui, Sumitomo, and Kōnoike became the antecedents of modern Japanese managerial style.

1. Three Paradigms: Osaka, Edo, and Castle Towns

Tokugawa society was organized around a rice-based economy in which agricultural productivity was the principal measure of wealth. Thus, the domain of Kaga was defined as a one-million-*koku* domain by the estimated productivity of its fields. Both the bakufu, with its seven million *koku* of scattered domain, and the 270-odd daimyo, with their twenty-five million total, needed to exchange their tax rice for cash. This need gave rise to central markets where large quantities of tax rice could be exchanged and capital resources secured for purchasing other commodities. Osaka handled much of this rice trade and as a consequence became the nucleus for protective trade associations (*kabunakama*), which received from the bakufu special privileges for controlling commercial transactions. Known as "the kitchen of Japan," Osaka became a sort of privileged city where wholesalers (*ton'ya*) and brokers (*nakagai*) were concentrated and where facilities for commodity exchanges became established.

The daimyo domains, in addition to shipping their tax rice to Osaka warehouses for sale, exported to Osaka wholesalers special products from their domains, such as cotton cloth, rapeseed oil, paper, sugar, salt, wax, and iron ore. In some instances, domain authorities classified products as monopoly goods (*senbaihin*) that could be purchased only by domain agents. Some domains issued special currencies (*hansatsu*) for purchasing these monopoly items or for other purposes, and they established domain-managed monopsonies that actively encouraged the production of goods for the national market. Through such activities as these, a monetized commodity economy arose from the agricultural foundation of Tokugawa Japan.

Within this overall process of commercial development three patterns or paradigms of family business management practices arose. One was that of Edo, the political center of Japan. Edo's growth into an enormous city followed the implementation of the system of alternate attendance and the forced residence of daimyo and their retainers in the city. As a result, Edo became the locus of bakufu politics and a prosperous consumption center with an eighteenth-century population of over one million people. As the city grew, large-scale family business enterprises like the Mitsui Dry Goods Stores (Echigoya) arose to handle its commerce.

In contrast to the Edo paradigm of huge family businesses were the small family businesses found in the castle towns of the various daimyo domains, towns that in many respects were miniature versions of the shogunal capital. Daimyo required their retainers to reside in their castle towns, and they assembled various kinds of merchants and artisans who provided them with military supplies and articles of daily use. These provisioners tended to be settled in assigned areas of town in accord with their professions, which created neighborhoods of specialized merchants and artisans. Many castle towns had neighborhoods with names like Gofuku-machi, which concentrated clothing stores, Teppō-chō (firearms dealers),

Daiku-machi (carpenters), Kawara-machi (tile makers), Tatamiya-chō (floor mat makers), Kon'ya-chō (indigo dyers), Chaya-machi (tea dealers), Yaoya-machi (greengrocers), or Sakana-machi (fish merchants). In addition to these diverse business neighborhoods, castle towns had areas set aside for samurai residences and for temples and shrines, clearly giving the towns three types of use-specific districts. These towns generally were artificially located, planned communities, although a few were located on the sites of existing temple towns (Kanazawa, Suwa, and Shingū, for example), post towns (Takasaki and Sekiyado), or port towns (Kuwana, Amagasaki, and Hakata).

Most of these castle towns were built during the few years between 1580 and 1610. The development of the domain economies, which centered on these castle towns, was tied closely to the growth of the three great cities of Edo, Kyoto, and Osaka, with the consequence that they constituted indispensable components in the growth of the economy as a whole. Following the Meiji Restoration, many of these castle towns became prefectural capitals and served as regional administrative centers. Former castle towns thus played a major role in modern economic growth, the nature of their role influenced by the historical character of their pre-Meiji economies.

Whereas Edo functioned as a major consumer center, and castle towns as regional economic centers, Osaka, the "kitchen of Japan," emerged as a central market city for the whole country. Besides handling the rice tax business of bakufu and daimyo, Osaka was closely linked to Kyoto, where the emperor resided, as well as the ancient city of Nara. It maintained close economic ties with the nearby port of Hyōgo and with the province of Ōmi, which was a central transit point for traffic between eastern and western Japan. With this rich array of connections, it was natural that Osaka should attain the position of a central market city where a national commodity market arose and prospered.

Osaka developed as a commercial city due to its important role since ancient times in both domestic and overseas transportation routes. In A.D. 416, Emperor Nintoku established his capital at the port of Naniwa (ancient Osaka) and there constructed his Takatsunomiya palace. Subsequently, in 645, Emperor Kōtoku situated his capital there, and a century later, in 744, Emperor Shōmu moved his court to Naniwa from Ōmi, making it the locus of imperial authority for the third time. Thereafter, political authority resided elsewhere, but Naniwa remained the port from which Japanese ambassadors embarked for the Sui and T'ang empires of China and to which foreign representatives from T'ang and the Korean kingdom of Paekche came to Japan.

As the national port city of ancient Japan, Naniwa continued to prosper. Immigrants to Japan were settled in the Uemachi plateau vicinity. There they taught engineering, shipbuilding, seamanship, weaving, and other technical skills, in the process helping to keep the Osaka area an economically progressive region.

During the Tokugawa period, the historical traditions that dated from ancient times continued to influence the Osaka economy. They fostered the city's frank character and pioneering spirit. And they underlay the energetic entrepreneurial spirit that seized upon foreign technologies and introduced them to Japan.

2. The Role of Privileged Merchant Families During the Early Tokugawa Period

During the early Tokugawa period, the leaders of the urban economy were privileged merchants who were closely linked to and dependent on the patronage of the bakufu and daimyo. Subsequently, in the second half of the seventeenth century, a new class of merchants emerged, men who rose to positions of economic power and influence by seizing the opportunities associated with the development of a national commodity economy. Their number included successful merchants from such cities as Hakata and Nagasaki in the west, Edo in the east, and the Kyoto-Osaka vicinity in central Japan. Four of the most famous were were Yodoya Jōan and his son Koan in Osaka and Suminokura Ryōi and Chaya Shirōjirō in Kyoto.

Among these merchants, the Yodoya house was important for constructing the foundations of the Osaka economy. Jōan, the first-generation house head, came to Osaka from the nearby province of Yamashiro during the heyday of Toyotomi Hideyoshi. In the city he operated a lumber business and participated as a merchant administrator in building embankments along the Yodo River. Later, at the time of the sieges of Osaka Castle in 1614 and 1615, he built the

Chausuyama headquarters used by Tokugawa Ieyasu and the Okayama headquarters used by Tokugawa Hidetada. The completion of these strongholds made an important contribution to the establishment of stable political authority under the Tokugawa shogunate.

Around 1615 or 1616, Jōan established a market for vegetables and fish on land adjoining the Yodoya residence on the Yodo River, and the market, later relocated, became known as the Temma produce market. The Tokugawa bakufu asked Jōan to develop Nakanoshima, an island on the river that bisects Osaka, and he completed the task in 1619. A large number of daimyo constructed rice warehouses there, and Nakanoshima became a central location for business transactions in Osaka. By the end of the century, there were ninety-five daimyo rice warehouses in the city, and it had emerged as the commercial capital of Japan.

Jōan died in 1622 and was succeeded by his son, Koan, who constructed a rice market at Kitahama that constituted the prototype for the Dōjima Rice Market, which eventually dominated the city's grain trade. Koan also engaged in the shipping business, and he transported 10,000 *koku* of tax rice from Kanazawa domain to Osaka, helping to establish a long-distance trade route between the Hokuriku region of northern Japan and the Osaka market. This resulted in the development of regularized shipping service from the Hokuriku region around the western end of Honshū to the city. Moreover, Koan handled the tax rice shipments of many daimyo and was the first merchant to serve as a government warehouse intendant (*kuramoto*). He was also the first merchant to provide loans to various domains. In 1624, he constructed the Kaifu canal in Osaka and established the Utsubo Marine Products Market, where salted and dried fish and dried sardines were traded. Koan died in 1643, but by then the mercantile foundation of the Yodoya house was secure, and the basis of Osaka's role as the "kitchen of Japan" had been established.

By creating the Osaka marketplace during the early Tokugawa period, the privileged merchants had a major impact on those Kyoto merchant houses that had preserved family business traditions from the ancient and medieval periods. As the third Mitsui house head, Takafusa, noted in his *Chōnin kōkenroku* (Some observations on merchants), during the early Tokugawa period Kyoto

bankers (*ryōgaeya*) provided loans to daimyo and were more important than bankers from Osaka. However, changing economic circumstances and the development of new business methods by the
Osaka bankers, who secured daimyo loans by linking them to future
delivery of domain goods to the Osaka market, resulted in the business operations of the Kyoto bankers gradually fading away as they
were displaced by bankers from Osaka.

As reported in the *Naniwa suzume*, a shopping guide to Osaka
business published in 1679, many merchants from Kyoto and
Fushimi had by then relocated their operations to Osaka to take
advantage of opportunities available there. The Osaka market
activities that privileged merchants developed had shifted the
power center of the Kyoto-Osaka market in the direction of Osaka,
but the merchants' success was leading to their eclipse. By then the
Sumitomo family had relocated its base of operations from Kyoto to
Osaka, and the Kōnoike house, originally from Kōnoike village in
Settsu province, had moved its residence to Osaka. They and other
newly established merchant houses were becoming more active
than the traditional privileged merchants, setting the stage for their
displacement.

3. The Management Practices of "New" Merchant Families

In general, the Kōnoike, Sumitomo, and Mitsui, the three great merchant families of the Tokugawa period, can be considered representative of the newly established merchants. Unlike the Yodoya
family, they were all descended from generals or local castle holders
of the era of the warring states. For example, Yamanaka Shinroku,
founder of the Kōnoike house, was the eldest son of the famous warrior Yamanaka Shikanosuke Yukimori. The founder of the Kōnoike
banking business, Kōnoike Zen'emon, was the eighth son of Shinroku. In the case of the Sumitomo house, the founder, Masatomo,
was the second son of Masatsura, son of the lord of Maruoka castle,
Sumitomo Masatoshi. Masatomo served as a warrior under Shibata
Katsuie, but following Katsuie's death, he moved with his mother to
Kyoto and opened a pharmacy and a printing shop. A remote
ancestor of the Mitsui house was Mitsui Takahisa, a relative of the

Sasaki warrior house of Ōmi and commander of his own castle. Later, during the lifetime of Mitsui Takayasu, the family moved from Ōmi to Ise. By the time of Takayasu's successor, the first Mitsui Takatoshi (father of the business founder, Takatoshi, who used a variant of his father's name), the family had built a residence in the town of Matsusaka in Ise province. By 1673, the younger Takatoshi, fourth son of the first Takatoshi, had established dry goods stores in Kyoto and Edo. In 1683 he set up a money-changing shop in Edo, and in 1686 he established a similar business in Kyoto. By 1691, he was operating dry goods and money-changing businesses in Osaka, and the Mitsui sphere of business activity embraced the three major cities of Tokugawa Japan.

In this manner, the Kōnoike, Sumitomo, and Mitsui all changed their status from warriors to merchants. In the process they brought creative innovations to the newly emerging merchant society. Thus, Shinroku, founder of the Kōnoike house, established a sake brewery in Kōnoike village in 1600, and by around 1604 he was successfully shipping sake to Edo. In 1615, the house branched out to Osaka and in addition to the sake-brewing business engaged in shipping, transporting tax rice from western daimyo domains to Osaka along regular trade routes. They also contributed to the establishment of a commodity shipping system between Osaka and Edo.

Most important among the business activities of the Kōnoike family was the money-changing business that Kōnoike Zen'emon established in Osaka in 1656. When the Kōnoike had first entered the banking business in 1628, they modeled their business practices on those of Tennōjiya Gohei, the founder of the Osaka money-changing business. But by 1670, when a banking group that consisted of the ten most representative Osaka money-changing houses was appointed to oversee the banking community, Kōnoike was one of the ten, placing the family on a par with Tennōjiya Gohei as an official banker (goyō ryōgae) for the bakufu. By around 1696, Kōnoike banks were engaged in business transactions with thirty-two daimyo domains, and their primary business had changed from the merchant loans of the early Tokugawa period to daimyo loans. Subsequently, a total of 110 daimyo domains received loans from the Kōnoike house, making its banks a source of capital for well over 30 percent of the daimyo houses.

By the time of the third house head, Munetoshi, the family business of providing loans to daimyo had made the Kōnoike house extremely prosperous. Using accumulated interest income, in 1705 the Kōnoike purchased a tract of ponds and swampland in Wakae-gun in Kawachi province and reclaimed around 220 hectares for cultivating new paddy fields (*shinden*). Upon the project's completion, 120 households numbering 750 men and women from nearby villages, as well as 360 households from other areas, migrated to the new fields. This Kōnoike *shinden* was typical of land reclaimed under merchant supervision.

That same year, even as the new merchant family Kōnoike reclaimed land, the bakufu confiscated all the wealth and property of Yodoya, the privileged merchant family then led by its fifth-generation house head, Tatsugorō. The confiscation was punishment for the extravagant lifestyle of the Yodoya family, which was accused of exceeding the boundaries of behavior appropriate for members of the merchant class. This incident, together with the development of the Kōnoike *shinden*, can be said to illustrate the downfall of the privileged merchant families of the early Tokugawa period and the coming to power of the newly established merchant families.

The Sumitomo merchant house, which along with Kōnoike ranked among the great commercial families of the Tokugawa period, was founded in Kyoto by Sumitomo Masatomo, as noted above. The individual who founded Sumitomo's basic metallurgical business was Soga Riemon, the husband of Masatomo's elder sister. In 1591, he learned from Western traders at the port of Sakai the so-called *nanban-buki* technique for separating copper and silver, and he used this technique to advance the Sumitomo family business. Because of Riemon's contributions to Sumitomo interests, Masatomo adopted his eldest son Tomomochi as his own son-in-law and designated him heir. In this manner the lineages of the house founder and the business founder were joined together.

Tomomochi, as the second-generation house head, moved the family business from Kyoto to Osaka in either 1623 or 1624. He shared the Western smelting technique with members of the Osaka copper guild, thereby establishing his own position in the city. In addition to smelting, Tomomochi engaged in copper exporting. Together with his father Riemon, he traveled to the ports of Naga-saki, Hakata, and Hirado in Kyushu where he sold copper to foreign merchants. In these activities the Sumitomo were playing a pioneering role as international traders. Later, in 1662, a younger brother of the third-generation house head expanded the family business into banking by opening a money-changing store in Osaka. However, the period of Sumitomo's greatest expansion came after 1691, with the excavation of the Besshi Copper Mine in Iyo province on Shikoku. Previously, the Sumitomo had operated mines in the Tōhoku, Kantō, and Chūgoku regions, but after the Besshi Mine opened, it became the primary source of the family's wealth.

While copper smelting was the core of the Sumitomo family business, it also had many other facets. In 1746 the family established a *fudasashi* business in the Asakusa district of Edo where it made loans to shogunal vassals (*hatamoto* and *gokenin*) and even engaged in financial transactions with the *bushi* secured by their rice stipends. In this manner, the Sumitomo became active in financing members of the samurai class. They were also active in the money-changing business at their Nakabashi store in Edo, which was established in 1805 in the name of Izumiya Kichijirō, the founder of the business. There is evidence, moreover, that the Sumitomo were actively involved in money-changing in Edo even before that date.

Next, let us examine the case of the Mitsui family. The major turning point for the Mitsui enterprise occurred in 1683 when the house founder, Takatoshi, relocated his dry goods business in Edo from Honchō to Suruga-chō and introduced new methods of doing business. These methods included cash sales at cheap and marked prices and a large volume of goods. That same year the Mitsui established a money-changing store in Edo, and in 1691, they were appointed official merchants in service to the bakufu (*goyōtasshi shōnin*) and were charged with handling the conversion of gold and silver notes issued by the bakufu. They reaped great profits in all their business enterprises.

As their businesses proliferated, Mitsui leaders took steps to strengthen their control over the family's various interests. In 1705, they established the so-called *hondana ichimaki* family council to control their dry goods stores in Kyoto, Edo, and Osaka. In 1710, they created a central business office for all their enterprises, and in 1719, a family banking council to oversee the operations of their money-changing shops in the three cities.

In 1694, the Mitsui founder, Takatoshi, died, leaving his business in the hands of four mature sons aged thirty-six to forty-one. These four engaged in group leadership of the extended family unit (*dōzoku*), maintaining an indivisible joint ownership of Mitsui resources that helped sustain the family enterprises over long periods of time. Their strategy was evident in organizational reforms effected between 1705 and 1719, and it was subsequently stipulated in the codified Mitsui Family Bylaws, the *Sōchikuisho* of 1722. This Mitsui strategy will be discussed further below.

Thus, the three great Tokugawa-period merchant houses of Kōnoike, Sumitomo, and Mitsui differed substantially in the diversity and organization of their family enterprises. The Kōnoike concentrated their activities in Osaka and prospered by making loans to daimyo. The Sumitomo located their main copper-smelting business in Osaka and joined to it the management of their Besshi Copper Mine and Nagasaki copper sales outlet, while simultaneously prospering from their banking businesses in Edo. The Mitsui successfully extended their network of shops to all three of Japan's great cities and concentrated their efforts on the dry goods trade and money-changing. Each of the families followed different business strategies, and all contributed to the development of a monetized economy during the Tokugawa period. And finally, be it noted, they developed the capital resources and family enterprise management systems that enabled them in the years following the Meiji Restoration to found family holding companies, the modern zaibatsu.

4. The Organization of Family Businesses

If we examine the enterprise structure of Tokugawa-period family businesses, we find that many of them constituted extended-family enterprises or family associations. The Kōnoike, Sumitomo, and Mitsui examples were all characterized by the basic *dōzoku* elements of *honke* (main house), *bunke* (related branch houses), and *bekke* (unrelated branch houses).

Looking specifically at the Mitsui family, as evident in Table 1, Organization of the Mitsui Family Business Enterprises, the family business was organized as a *dōzoku* under the leadership of the central business office (*ōmotokata*). The *dōzoku's* leader was the head of

Table 1 Organization of Mitsui Family Business Enterprises in the 1730s

Central Business Office (ōmotokata) in Kyoto		
Main Stores	Banking	Matsusaka Store
Kyoto Main Store* (Echigoya Hachirōemon)	Kyoto Money-Changing Store (Mitsui Saburōsuke)	(Mitsui Sokuemon)
Edo Main Store (Echigoya Hachirōemon)	Osaka Money-Changing Store (Mitsui Motonosuke)	
Osaka Main Store (Echigoya Hachirōemon)	Edo Money-Changing Store (Mitsui Jirōemon)	
Edo Mukōdana Store (Echigoya Hachirōbei)	Kyoto Thread Store (Echigoya Kiemon)	
Edo Shibaguchi Store (Matsusakaya Hachisuke)	Kyoto Ainomachi Store (Hinoya Jirōbei)	
Kyoto Kaminomise Store (Echigoya Kizaemon)		
Kyoto Accounting Office (Echigoya Hachirōemon)		
Kyoto Red Dye Store (Mitsui Sokuemon)		
Edo Thread Store (Echigoya Kizaemon)		

Notes: * Main house of group.
          Family names in parentheses.
Source: Nakai Nobuhiko, "Mitsui-ke no keiei: Shiyōnin seido to sono un'ei," *Shakai Keizai Shigaku*, Vol. 31, No. 9, 1966.

the senior house (*sōryōke*), who took the hereditary house name Echigoya Hachirōemon. He controlled the main dry goods stores in the three cities and was responsible for the central family accounting office in Kyoto. Besides the senior house, Mitsui had five main houses, including most notably the house of Mitsui Saburōsuke, in charge of the Kyoto money-changing business, that of Mitsui Motonosuke, which controlled the Osaka money-changing operation, and Mitsui Jirōemon, who handled the money-changing in Edo. In addition, three affiliated houses (*renke*), most notably the house of Mitsui Sokuemon, handled other enterprises, Sokuemon was descended from an older brother of the Mitsui founder, Takatoshi, and was responsible for both the Kyoto red dye (*beni*) store and the Matsusaka dry goods store. This latter was the initial Mitsui business in Ise from which the family was descended. In each of these instances, the house head was personally responsible for the operation of his own family's enterprise.

During the early eighteenth century, the Mitsui family thus consisted of nine houses (one senior house, five main houses, and three affiliated houses) that were responsible for the various stores under the family's control. Later, during the tenure of the third-generation house head, two additional affiliated houses—Masatoshi (Iehara house) and Takanobu (Nagai house)—were added, expanding the Mitsui *dōzoku* to an eleven-house structure. This eleven-house organization continued in place until the dissolution of the Mitsui zaibatsu after World War II.

The distribution of the Mitsui *dōzoku's* collective assets was codified in the Mitsui Family Bylaws of 1722, as mentioned above, and they were shared among the existing houses in the following manner. The Bylaws assigned Mitsui's business assets a total value of 220 units and allocated them to the several houses in terms of these units. Thus Hachirōemon house was allotted 62 units (28 percent of the total), Motonosuke 30 (13.6 percent), Saburōsuke 27 (12.3 percent), Jirōemon 25 (11.4 percent), Hachirōjirō 22.5 (10.2 percent), Sōhachi 22.5 (10.2 percent), Sokuemon 8 (3.6 percent), Kichirōemon 6 (2.7 percent), Hachisuke 7 (3.2 percent), and a balance of 10 (4.5 percent) unspecified in the distribution of total family assets.

As the pinnacle of the Mitsui family business structure, the central business office, *ōmotokata*, organized an assembly of house heads that decided family financial policies. The *ōmotokata* would advance investment capital and working capital to each enterprise to finance its operations. Semiannually, each enterprise then repaid the *ōmotokata* a fixed percentage of the advance. Each enterprise was financially independent and used its funds at its own discretion. The value of the semiannual repayments to the *ōmotokata* varied from one enterprise to the next, reflecting the earnings of each store. On average, they amounted to around 12 percent of the funds advanced. As a consequence, the relationship between the *ōmotokata* and each Mitsui store can be considered similar to that between a contemporary holding company and its affiliated enterprises. However, because the *ōmotokata* had unlimited liability for the management of each individual enterprise, it seems more appropriate to liken the relationship to that between the main and branch stores of a single enterprise.

The personnel practices of the Mitsui house developed along with this enterprise structure, with the procedures for appointments, salaries, promotions, training, and retirement of employees being consolidated some time after 1703. Initially family leaders considered it important that all employees be raised from infancy within the Mitsui house, but later outsiders were accepted at a young age. The rank system for employees was complex and included many gradations whose particulars changed from one period to another. The dry goods stores, which had at least sixteen different ranks, extending from apprentices and shop boys to foremen, administrators, representatives, and managers, illustrates the complexity of employee gradations.

When young men from other families were brought into Mitsui enterprises, they were completely cut off from their past social attachments and were brought up to adhere to the norms of the business. At the Kyoto dry goods store, it was forbidden to employ individuals from either Kyoto or communities within sixty kilometers of the city. At the Edo store, people from Kyoto or from communities within twelve kilometers of Kyoto were employed. Until the 1720s, seniority was used as the basis for promotions. However, after around 1735, while employees to the rank of group foreman were advanced according to established principles of seniority, those promoted to higher ranks were selected on the basis of their performance.

Most employees were hired between the ages of eleven and thirteen and were promoted to head clerk after serving for ten to fifteen years. It usually took from twelve to eighteen years to advance to the rank of group foreman. Very few employees were promoted from this level to ranks above commuting manager, and around 5 percent of all employees advanced further. In the Kyoto dry goods store, 239 children were hired as apprentices between 1696 and 1730. Twenty-eight of them died while employed, 19 retired due to illness, 7 requested release from employment, 77 were discharged for incompetence, and 13 retired after the satisfactory completion of their service contracts. This totals 174 employees. The employment histories of the remaining 65 employees are unknown. However, as evident from the above, only around 5 percent rose above

Figure 1. Scene of the Echigoya store. The curtains have the
shop logo, the character "Mitsu" in a box within a circle. Print
by Okumura Masanobu. Eighteenth century. Courtesy of the
Mitsukoshi Collection.

the rank of commuting manager and went on to honorable retirement.

In the Mitsui family, the *ōmotokata* permitted those who had been
employed at the lowest managerial rank (*hirayaku*) or above and
who retired after the satisfactory completion of their employment
contracts to use some form of the Echigoya store name and the
Echigoya shop curtain if they went into business as *bekke*. There
were three gradations among those who received these privileges.
Those who retired as *hirayaku* were granted the shop name Echigoya and the right to hang a shop curtain with the character "Echi"
in a circle. Those who retired from the main store with the next
three higher ranks of group foreman (*jōza* to *yaku-gashira*), or up to
the highest group foreman rank (*kumi-gashira*) from branch stores,
received the Echigoya name and the right to hang a shop curtain
with the character for "Mitsu" in a boxed logo, but without the
circle. Those who retired from the main store with the highest rank
of group foreman or above, or from branch stores as manager or
above, received the Echigoya shop name and the right to use the

same shop curtain as the five Mitsui main houses, that is, a circle surrounding a boxed logo containing the character for "Mitsu" (Figure 1). These rights were conferred only to those employees who had attained the appropriate rank prior to retirement, and the status distinctions were adhered to strictly.

Next, let us examine the case of the Kōnoike family. In the early eighteenth century, the Kōnoike established five related branch houses and twenty-two unrelated branches, a system unlike that of Mitsui with its unique arrangement of senior, main, and affiliated houses. In the Mitsui family, as a consequence of the authority of the *ōmotokata* system, each of the enterprises in Kyoto, Edo, and Osaka had an independently determined profit system and each paid independently negotiated rates of return on capital advanced by the *ōmotokata*. In the case of Kōnoike, after the mid-eighteenth century the business affairs of related branches were included within those of the main house, and the operation of their enterprises depended on economic assistance from the main house. In this centralized arrangement, the Kōnoike, with their focus on making loans to daimyo, used a management style which differed from that of the Mitsui. The latter focused their energies on their dry goods stores while engaging simultaneously in the money-changing business as well, in the process serving the needs of large numbers of customers in the three major cities and their hinterlands.

An employee of the Kōnoike family usually required ten years to rise from clerk to a position from which he could obtain permission to establish a separate enterprise or *bekke*. The house laws codified in 1723 stipulated that there were to be twenty-two such unrelated branch houses, but from the 1740s, we see fewer and fewer examples of employees being authorized to establish their own businesses. Moreover, these *bekke*, depending on their individual qualifications, increasingly participated in the loan activities of the main house and became, in effect, extensions of that house.

Kōnoike employee records reveal that it was common to begin an apprenticeship at age twelve. Then one rose to the rank of clerk and after twenty years or so of employment attained the rank of manager-in-training. After two or three more years, it was common to be promoted to the rank of manager and, after an additional two or three years, employees were authorized to form branch houses. These individuals were referred to as branch house managers, while those not authorized to form branch houses were called resident managers. For example, if one were promoted to the rank of clerk at age eighteen, one might be a manager-in-training at thirty-eight, a manager at forty or forty-one, and a branch house manager at forty-two or forty-three. While apprentices were unsalaried, employees at the rank of clerk and above received compensation that commenced at about 50–60 *momme* of silver every two months. For employees at the rank of manager-in-training or above, annual salaries ranged from 300 or 400 *momme* up to 3 *kan* (3,000 *momme*) of silver, depending on the rank.

In addition to these basic salaries, employees were given special payments called *moyaigin* and *nazukegin.* The first was an annual bonus payment of 200 *momme* and the second a payment given every two or three years from the age of twenty-one or twenty-two to those whom Kōnoike had employed since their youth. Even those who had been hired at more advanced ages, called outside (*tozama*) employees, customarily received special allowances beginning in their eighth or ninth year of employment.

The employees, however, did not actually receive the *nazukegin* payments until the time of their retirement or their reception of the right to open a branch shop. They thus constituted forms of compulsory savings that were designed to provide the capital resources needed when employees established their own independent businesses. This practice was somewhat similar to the modern corporate use of compulsory savings plans as a means of preventing employee resignations or early retirements.

No more than 10 percent of all Kōnoike family employees were promoted to the status of *bekke.* According to the family records, from 1719 to 1741, fifty-one employees resigned or retired. Eight of them died, three were adopted as heirs in other houses, eight asked to be released from their employment contracts, and thirty-two, by far the largest category, were dismissed by Kōnoike. Twenty-seven of those dismissed were categorized as unsatisfactory workers, incompetents, scoundrels, or as employees who reached appropriate retirement age. The other five were specifically cited as one who lost money from the business, one who misplaced funds from the kitchen account, one dismissed as a thief, and two dismissed for illness.

The personnel practices of Kōnoike and Mitsui were widely

adopted by the mid-Tokugawa period in both the primary cities of Kyoto, Edo, and Osaka and in provincial castle towns. While the numbers of employees varied from one enterprise to another, these employment patterns were increasingly popular.

5. The Management Ideology of Merchant Families

Kōnoike, Sumitomo, and Mitsui had all codified their house laws by the eighteenth century. The process of developing such laws began well before then, however. In 1614, the Kōnoike founder, Yamanaka Shinroku (also known as Yukimoto), wrote his *Yukimoto shison seishi jōmoku* (Precepts for the descendants of Yukimoto). Similarly, before his death in 1652, Masatomo, founder of the Sumitomo family and posthumously named Monjuin, drew up his *Monjuin shiisho* (Monjuin's admonitions to his descendants) as regulations for the management of the family business activities. In the Mitsui family as well, the house founder Takatoshi codified his *Shohatto shū* (Collected precepts) in 1673, and in 1675 and 1676 he appended bylaws to it. In 1695, the year after Takatoshi's death, his successor Mitsui Takahira compiled the *Kanai shikihō chō* (Mitsui house laws).

Each of these families had thus codified its house laws prior to the eighteenth century, but their systematic implementation in business activities did not occur until somewhat later. In the Sumitomo family, new house regulations for the operation of the Besshi Copper Mine and the Nagasaki export store were stipulated in 1721. In the case of Mitsui, the *Sōchikuisho*, or Family Bylaws, were implemented in 1722, and the Kōnoike house laws, the *Iesadame kiroku oboe*, were compiled the following year. In each case, these regulations were collections of previously established house laws. Through this codifying activity and the content of the rules we have been given a detailed portrait of the merchant houses and the laws that governed them.

The common features of these house laws can be summarized in the following five points. To begin with, they codified a system that established the primacy of the main house. Branch houses (*bunke, bekke,* or *renke*) were expected to cooperate with it, and family authority was carefully placed in the hands of the main house to insure compliance. Second, they forbade involvement in innovative business activities and admonished family members to follow established house practices to insure adherence to sound business principles. Members were to focus on a single type of business, and imprudent diversification was strongly discouraged. Third, they encouraged frugality, resourcefulness, and careful accounting—the three cardinal tenets of Tokugawa business law—and specified the standards of appropriate business behavior. Fourth, many house laws rejected arbitrary rule and stipulated the use of deliberative councils to make business decisions. Actually, Tokugawa merchant families frequently practiced one-man management from the top down, and perhaps in reaction to this, house laws stressed the importance of consultation. Fifth, many contained specific regulations covering the theory and practice of long-term employment, seniority, good treatment of employees, and "familyism," in effect the elements of "family-style management principles" that constitute the historical roots of Japanese-style management as implemented widely from late Meiji onward.

The overall codification of these house laws by the mid-eighteenth century was linked to the broader historical situation of those years when the eighth shogun, Yoshimune, undertook to revitalize the political and economic systems of the bakuhan order. In much the same spirit, merchant house leaders codified their rules as measures to strengthen their enterprises.

6.   The Antecedents of "Japanese-Style Management"

Japanese-style management, with its distinctive lifetime employment and seniority systems, paternalism toward employees, and enterprise unions, is thought to have become generally established from around 1900 to the 1930s. Some scholars, however, see it taking form after World War II. Opinions thus differ about when this managerial style arose, and also about the relationship between it and cultural traditions. While we lack space to examine these topics here, I would like to describe briefly how the roots of Japanese-style management can be found in the structure and ideology of Tokugawa merchant family management.

The Tokugawa period saw the dramatic development of commercial capital, which provided a stable foundation for the creation of industrial capital following the Meiji Restoration. The historical framework for this development included the formation of the *kokudaka* system and the creation of central markets to dispose of the rulers' annual tax rice; the separation of warriors and peasants and the building of castle towns throughout the country; the creation of an urban network focused on the three major cities of Edo, Kyoto, and Osaka and the development of a well-regulated system of commodity circulation; the implementation of a policy of national isolation and the replacement of privileged merchants with a new type of great merchant family represented by the Kōnoike, Sumitomo, and Mitsui; the development of a monetized commodity economy in conjunction with enforcement of the alternate attendance system; and the establishment of unified values and mercantile ethics based on Confucian morality.

These elements were all in place prior to industrialization, which followed the Meiji Restoration. An "urban revolution" had occurred with the building of the three great cities and the castle towns, and a "commercial revolution" had occurred due to the vigorous entrepreneurial activities of the early privileged merchants and the new merchant class that succeeded them. Also we find that a "commercial culture" had developed as an analog to the "industrial culture" of modern society.

Further, as Hayami Akira, an economic historian, has pointed out, an "industrious revolution" occurred during the Tokugawa period prior to Japan's industrial revolution. Economic incentives came to influence both peasant and merchant conduct and ideology, causing the highly touted industriousness of Japanese workers to become a widely shared value. This industriousness was essential for family business management systems which had to survive in a highly competitive environment and develop in the chaos of the urban and commercial revolutions. Frugality, resourcefulness, and careful accounting, the three articles of faith in the house laws of great merchant families, placed frugality at the head of the list. This reinforced the spirit of self-denial that was the basis of the industrious revolution. The Kōnoike, Sumitomo, and Mitsui were able to manage and expand their family businesses in an intensely competitive society by basing their family-like associations on group principles.

Among the three great merchant families, it was the Mitsui house that maintained the strongest management system and most thorough capital control network throughout its holdings. Taking advantage of the new opportunities created by the turmoil of the Meiji Restoration, Mitsui was the first merchant house to build a comprehensive family holding company (zaibatsu). It was able to do so because the prototype for its zaibatsu existed in the family management system that already was firmly established in the preceding period. This seems to verify that the starting point for Japanese-style management of modern enterprises can be found in the development and expansion of family business management systems in the Tokugawa period.

(Translation by William B. Hauser)

Chapter Seven

The Common People
and Painting

TATSURŌ AKAI

In all periods of history, common people have been able to catch occasional glimpses of paintings, but in Japan it was not until the seventeenth century that they could gain a close understanding of pictures, and even own them. Furthermore, it was only after the beginning of the Tokugawa period that common people began to regard pictures as objects of aesthetic appreciation rather than objects of religious veneration.

Before this period, it is true, commoners had contact with painting, but the connection was weak and the content of the art differed from that of the Tokugawa period. There were public explanations of religious paintings (*e-toki*) that showed scenes from the lives of founders of religious sects, notably Hōnen and Shinran. And there also were public displays of pictures of hell (*jigoku-e*) at temple festivals held in spring and autumn. These, however, were limited only to Kyoto, with its many temples and monasteries, and a few other towns. In the second half of the sixteenth century, tradesmen artists (*machi-eshi*) created illustrated handscrolls and picture books from popular medieval tales (*otogi-zōshi*) in which sardine or fried fish sellers and the like were the main characters. These had a distinctly plebeian character, but since they were manuscripts, each one laboriously copied by hand, they were not produced in quantity and were not widely available to the common people.

From the second half of the sixteenth century, female ecclesiastics called Kumano nuns (Kumano *bikuni*) traveled the provinces, employing large pictures of hell and paradise in sermons that they usually delivered to women. In the seventeenth century, Kumano nuns began singing popular songs as a way of explaining their religious pictures, and they even started appearing as the heroines of puppet plays. In a sense, they were becoming public entertainers. Contemporaneously, workshops of the Honganji Temple in Kyoto started producing large numbers of pictorial biographies of Shinran for distribution to branch temples throughout the country. Finally, public exhibitions of shrine and temple treasures (*kaichō*) became increasingly frequent, and outings to such exhibitions proved as popular with common people as trips to kabuki theater and the pleasure quarters.

Popular medieval tales were full of girls who had been bullied by cruel stepmothers and grew up to become beautiful princesses, or lads of humble origins who become splendid courtiers. Theirs were lives of hardship that led to romantically happy endings. The popular novels of the late seventeenth century (*ukiyo-zōshi*), in contrast, were peopled by townsmen who sang the joys of contemporary life. What is more, these *ukiyo-zōshi* were produced as woodblock printed books with illustrations, and consequently they reached the hands of a far larger number of readers than did the medieval tales produced in manuscript.

Remarkable advances in printing technology during this period permitted development of single sheet ukiyo-e prints, which were based on the figures of courtesans and kabuki actors that had previously appeared as illustrations in books. Ukiyo-e were created as cheap commercial products, and the low price more than anything else ensured that they would always respond quickly to the tastes and needs of common people. Indeed, in a sense, ukiyo-e constituted a self-portrait of the common people of each successive generation. In this chapter, I should like to examine the relationship of common people to painting by considering two topics: public explanations of religious paintings and the nature of ukiyo-e.

1.   Popular Faiths and Explanations of Religious Paintings

Kumano nuns played an important role in explaining religious paintings to common people, and itinerant preachers also contributed to the diffusion of religious insight. In addition, temples placed their religious treasures on public exhibit, and those of the True Pure Land (Jōdo Shin) sect encouraged priests to employ pictures when preaching to their congregations.

Figure 1. A festival at the Sumiyoshi Shrine, detail. Courtesy of the Freer Gallery of Art, Smithsoninan Institution, Washington, D.C. (00.25)

Kumano Nuns

People looking at pictures or people showing pictures to others seldom appear in works of art or literature. However, Kumano nuns are described rather frequently in works of literature of the Tokugawa period and are faithfully depicted in genre paintings of the late sixteenth and early seventeenth centuries. The Kumano nuns who appear in Ihara Saikaku's novel *Seken mune san'yō* (Worldly mental calculation) are leading people in worship before paintings of hell and paradise and soliciting donations while singing popular songs for all they are worth. But they are still unable to fill the wooden ladle, which they always wear pushed through their belts, with contributions.

Just such a scene of nuns also appears in one of a pair of folding screens showing "A Festival at the Sumiyoshi Shrine" (*Sumiyoshi*

Figure 2. *Kumano kanshin jikkai* mandala, a mandala depicting hell and paradise. Gotō Family Collection, Kanaimachi, Niigata Prefecture

jinja saireizu byōbu, Figure 1). In this seventeenth-century work, the nuns have hung a large hell and paradise painting called a *Kumano kanshin jikkai* mandala (Figure 2) at the approach to a bridge, and one of them is pointing at the picture with a stick while explaining the transient nature of human existence. In front of the large box used to carry the picture and the amulets that the nuns distribute, a young *bikuni* assistant is carrying her wooden ladle and soliciting donations from the spectators.

It is difficult to determine exactly the words and melody of the sermons sung by Kumano nuns to explain religious paintings, but we can get an idea from Chikamatsu Monzaemon's puppet play, *Shume no hōgan Morihisa*. This play, which might be described as a female version of the famous kabuki drama *Kanjinchō* (The subscription list), involves two women who masquerade as Kumano nuns to pass through a control barrier on the highway. They carry large paintings of paradise and hell folded up inside their small portable shrine. At the control barrier they unfold the paintings and begin to explain their scenes in rhythmic seven- and five-syllable meter, all the while pointing out such features as blood-spattered victims falling into the Hell of Blood Lake and barren women in the hell where they must dig up bamboo shoots using nothing more than oil-lamp wicks.

The *Kumano kanshin jikkai* mandala mentioned above shows a long, arching path that passes through the seasons from spring blossoms to winter snow, and on it a person's life plays out from infancy through youth to old age. Paradise is depicted inside its sweeping curve, and the bottom two-thirds of the composition shows a whole range of different hells crowded together. Moreover, the manner of depiction is such that the image seems to speak to the viewer: the entire background to the paradise and hells is filled in with a plain yellow ocher color so that there is no sense of depth and each individual motif stands out clearly.

The *Kanshin jikkai* mandala, which is associated with the legend that Oda Nobunaga's daughter became a Kumano nun and traveled to the island of Sado, has inscribed here and there on it explanations of scenes such as "Blood Saucer Lake," "heavenly beings," and the "path of beasts." There are also ten slips of paper pasted on, with poems such as this:

> Climbing the Slope of Old Age,
> They stop and look back.
> How far the way already come:
> How short the way to go.

The poems were very useful for explaining the painting, and they undoubtedly were recited to a melody.

Engelbert Kaempfer, a doctor in the service of the Dutch East India Company, who traveled from Nagasaki to Edo in 1691, wrote that the Kumano nuns he met on the Tōkaidō highway were the most beautiful women he saw on his journey and that, "with their short walking sticks they put one in mind of romantic shepherdesses." During the same period the priest and author Asai Ryōi also described how the women wore a most beguiling black headdress and looked like courtesans. The nuns may have been beautiful, but they were also shrewd, he reported. They would hang up their paintings of paradise and hell and draw the attention of a crowd of

women and children. But they would not hurry to explain the hell
for childless women or the hell for men who loved two women at
once. Only when the audience begged them, would they say, "'Give
us 120 *mon* for votive lanterns'." And then, "they explained the pictures in a manner that got the women all worked up, and the nuns
took their money in a trice."

We know from puppet plays such as Chikamatsu's *Shume no hōgan
Morihisa* that in return for donations the nuns distributed leaves of
the *nagi* (*Podocarpus Nagi*) tree, which was a kind of talisman for
women. The *nagi* leaf has strong longitudinal veins that will not tear
across and so was regarded as a charm for peaceful union between
husband and wife. It was believed that if you inserted the leaf
behind a mirror it would bring happiness. A folk song sung during
the play reveals the thoughts of country women as they waited for
the nuns to come and perform: "When you come, bring me a *nagi*
leaf from the mountains of Kumano." The explanation of the
Kanshin jikkai mandala given by Kumano nuns was thus very much
an art performed by women for women.

Itinerant Preachers Who Explained Paintings

There is a group of paintings, the shrine and temple pilgrimage
mandalas (*shaji sankei mandara*), which displays a technique very
similar to that of the *Kanshin jikkai* mandalas. These works are preserved at the thirty-three pilgrimage temples and monasteries associated with the Bodhisattva Kannon and at the Ise Grand Shrine,
the Zenkōji Temple, and elsewhere. Large paintings of about 170
centimeters square, they present a landscape view of the particular
temple concerned. Even though they are called mandalas, however,
their subject is not the Shintō or Buddhist deities normally associated with religious paintings, but rather the throngs of pilgrims who
visit a site—ordinary men and women of the times, itinerant *biwa*
players, and the like. Yet this is not pure genre painting. Generally
the sun and moon, symbolic of Shintō and Buddhist deities, are
placed at the top of the paintings, and the deity worshiped at the
shrine or temple is often depicted, or scenes from the history of its
founding may be included. In short, they are paintings which tell of
the shrine or temple's miraculous manifestations and of the efficacy
and virtue associated with it.

In the temple pilgrimage mandala for Sefukuji Temple, which lies south of Osaka and is the fourth stage on the Kannon pilgrimage route, tiny scenes relating to the history of the temple are included among the comings and goings of worshipers. These scenes include the interview between an Imperial messenger and the monk Gyōman, who founded the temple in the sixth century; the mid-eighth century monk Hōkai worshiping a thousand-armed Kannon who appeared from the sea; and a scene of the monk Kūkai taking the tonsure after he had determined to enter holy orders at the temple. A person explaining the painting could use these scenes to introduce many stories.

The pilgrimage mandala for the Ise Grand Shrine not only shows the hustle and bustle of pilgrims around the two worship halls of the Inner and Outer Shrines, but also here and there pieces of information necessary for worshiping at the shrine: such as the act of purifying oneself in the river before commencing the approach; the etiquette of worship in the deity's presence; and the location of the *kokuya*, office of contributions. In the case of the pilgrimage mandala for the Kiyomizu and Chinnō temples in Kyoto, the artist does not forget to show the pleasures of pilgrimage and worship: he illustrates the tea shops selling tea and sweet dumplings in front of the gateway. In the Nachi pilgrimage mandala for Seiganto Temple, which is situated in the mountains of southeastern Kii province and is the first stage on the Kannon pilgrimage route, a pair of white-robed pilgrims appear several times in the painting. It is thought that this conspicuous pair are in fact a husband and wife on pilgrimage. Surely, people looking at these figures, simply painted in earth pigments, must have imagined themselves as the couple.

Who would have explained these pilgrimage mandalas, and where would they have done so? In this connection we should note that nearly all bear the marks of having been folded up, which suggests that paintings now mounted as hanging scrolls were originally folded. We saw this earlier in the case of the puppet play, *Shume no hangan Morihisa*, where Kumano nuns walked along carrying a box with the *Kanshin jikkai* mandala folded up inside. For the pilgrimage mandalas, it was a Buddhist or Shintō layperson (*oshi*) from a temple or shrine who carried the paintings around. A segment of the pilgrimage circuit became fixed as the *oshi's* territory, and he would travel that segment, stopping at various places to unfold the mandala and tell groups of pilgrims of the miraculous manifesta-

Figure 3. A priest explaining the Tateyama mandala at Daitokuji in Kyoto.

tions of the deities and the pleasures of pilgrimage. His job was to
encourage those pilgrims to visit his shrine or temple, and he
assisted them in their devotions and with their lodgings. It is true
that the relationship between the *oshi* and his pilgrims was only
short-lived—for the duration of their passage through his territory—
but it generally came to be a very special kind of relationship in
which he gave them assistance, distributed talismans, and even provided medicines.

The text that *oshi* used in explaining this group of pilgrimage
mandalas has not yet been discovered. But the text does survive for
the Tateyama mandala (Figure 3), which is associated with the cult
of Mt. Tate and would have been carried about on his route and
explained in the same way by an *oshi* working that pilgrimage route.
Mt. Tate in the depths of Etchū province was known from ancient
times as a mountain where miraculous manifestations frequently
occurred, and it was believed that an actual hell existed there. The
Tateyama mandala depicts the hells on Mt. Tate and recounts
stories about Saeki Ariyori, the legendary figure who supposedly
was the first to climb Mt. Tate and worship the Buddha there.

The Tateyama mandala consists of four hanging scrolls that together form one large composition. The text used by *oshi* when explaining the painting is made up of three parts: a history of the Tateyama cult; information for climbing Mt. Tate; and material on the Tateyama hell. Scattered through the main body of the text are lines to be spoken when pointing one's stick at particular spots on the painting. "This rock cave has that name because you could see bear's paw marks on it," or, "This is called Mt. Karada and is the Pure Land Paradise of the Bodhisattva Jizō." There are even jokes, such as: "Well I've certainly talked for a long time today. If it was interesting you probably would have woken up, but I've droned on like I was scouring the bottom of a kettle, so I'm sure you're getting sleepy instead." This commentary gives us a good idea of the lively atmosphere at one of these explanations of religious paintings.

Explanations of Paintings at Exhibitions of Temple Treasures

To people in farming and fishing villages, the visiting Kumano nun or Tateyama *oshi* was not just a religious figure who distributed talismans but also a performer who showed pictures and told stories. The city, however, had many more entertainments to offer, including theater and street performances. There were ukiyo-e, as we note below, and also regular public exhibitions of art works, both *shogakai*, or calligraphy and painting meetings, and *kaichō*, or exhibitions of temple treasures.

Shogakai generally were exhibitions held in city restaurants. Artists, calligraphers, poets, and playwrights gathered there to display their wares and execute paintings or calligraphic works to order. Painters belonged to all schools, from ink painters to members of the Maruyama/Shijō or ukiyo-e schools. The ukiyo-e artist Utagawa Hiroshige, for instance, held a *shogakai* in an Edo restaurant on the occasion of a change in his art-name. In Kyoto, *shogakai* called the Higashiyama Exhibition of New Painting and Calligraphy (*Higashiyama shin shoga tenkan*) were held every spring and autumn for some seventy years after 1792. The artisans who mounted the paintings appear to have organized the exhibits on a public subscription basis, their venture being financed with exhibition fees. The exhibitors came not solely from Kyoto but also from Osaka and Edo, and they were of all different schools. In the case of calligraphy the exhibitors included men and women of all ages and backgrounds, from ten-year-old girls to 110-year-old centenarians. The fact that a restaurant in the Higashiyama entertainment district was chosen for the show suggests the free and easy atmosphere of the exhibits.

Whereas *shogakai* were exhibitions of contemporary art, *kaichō* were public showings of ancient works of art. Temples displayed their secret images and holy treasures for the purpose of raising funds, generally showing them in the temple itself, but on occasion provincial temples brought their treasures for display in Edo or Kyoto.

Kaichō in Edo rivaled the pleasure quarters and theater in popularity. During the exhibit, tea shops and restaurants set up stalls in front of the temple's gateway, and even within its precincts, small enclosures were erected for acrobats and other street entertainers. There was a terrific furor when the Fudō Temple at Narita exhibited its treasures in Edo; and the popular actor Ichikawa Danjūrō even appeared in the guise of the deity Fudō Myōō in a special performance of kabuki. In Kyoto, with its many temples and shrines, there were annual public exhibitions of Buddhist sculptures and paintings on such occasions as the equinoxes and the anniversary of Buddha's death. Exhibitions of treasures from provincial temples also were a frequent event there. In 1699, for example, when a temple in Mino placed the treasures of its Benzaiten Shrine on exhibition in Kyoto, Chikamatsu Monzaemon's kabuki play *Keisei Edozakura* was specially staged in honor of the deity. In Kyoto, as well as Edo, *kaichō* were thus events of considerable interest for citizens.

Of course, *kaichō* were not limited to Edo and Kyoto but also took place in castle towns. In Nagoya, an Owari samurai, Kōriki Tanenobu Enkōan, left many illustrated records of *kaichō* held there, giving us a clear idea of what they entailed. In the spring of 1829, for instance, Kōriki's illustrated *Kaichō danwa* (Chats about *kaichō*) records that an exhibition of treasures from the Taema Temple in Yamato was held at Nagoya's Seian Temple (Figure 4). An impressive selection of paintings, calligraphies, and other objets d'art were displayed cheek by jowl in seven rooms of Seian Temple, including the main worship hall, the study, and even the corridors. At the center of the display in room six was an enormous painting some 4 meters square of the Pure Land Paradise, which was intended to explain the Sutra of Infinite Light (*Kammuryōju-kyō*). A single priest

Figure 4. An explanation of temple treasures, from *Kaichō danwa*. 1820s. Hōsa Bunko, Nagoya.

using a stick explained the original painting to an audience of about thirty worshipers, but the explanation was not limited to this central painting. Rather, it covered everything from statues of Buddhist deities and portrait sculptures of founders of the sect to the bones and letters of famous monks. The text of this narrative survives. It is a short piece that takes only about five or six minutes to read aloud, and it includes notations on when the reader should strike his small gong. There were also poems to recite, and one can imagine that the text itself was performed to some kind of melody.

During a *kaichō* a temple often put on sale woodblock prints showing the layout of the temple and describing its history and related miraculous manifestations. In the case of this *kaichō* at the Seian Temple, a reduced version of the Pure Land Paradise painting was offered for sale.

Explanations of the Illustrated Biography of Shinran

There survive today almost no explanations of the paintings (*e-toki*) that were presented with melodies or the narrative histories that were read to melodies. It appears, however, that a style of preaching set to melody, *fushidan sekkyō* or "explanations of pictures with melodies," remained popular until about 1880. In September 1875, the headquarters temple of the Higashi Honganji sect in Kyoto sent Regulations Concerning Preaching to all its branch temples in the provinces. Priests were admonished, "When preaching, you are to refrain from vulgar and bawdy joking while you speak, and it is forbidden to add hand or body movements." We may infer that such preaching was not uncommon at the time. In May 1877, Higashi Honganji sent out an additional notice: "Explaining paintings while preaching is not only against the preaching regulations but also gives rise to many mistaken teachings that can corrupt basic religious tenets. Henceforth you shall not engage in such practices." Similarly, in the summer of 1870, the Nishi Honganji sect, which equaled Higashi Honganji a as major nationwide sect, put out the following ordinance forbidding the explanation of paintings: "It seems that there are persons who hang up the *Holy Pictorial Biography* when preaching and give explanations of the paintings. This is most undesirable."

The *Holy Pictorial Biography* was an illustrated handscroll of the life of Shinran, founder of the Honganji sect, that was produced by his great-grandson Kakunyo. To show the handscroll to more people, Kakunyo's son Zonkaku converted it into a set of hanging scrolls. Later it was reproduced in sets of one, two, even six hanging scrolls and was widely used in preaching to spread the doctrine of Shinran's True Pure Land sect. From the time of Rennyo, the sect's eighth-generation head, however, it became customary to display the hanging scrolls in the main worship hall of a temple only at the annual service on the anniversary of Shinran's death. On that occasion, the biography was recited aloud without reference to the paintings. Yet the basic nature of the *Holy Pictorial Biography*—a biography in pictures that was to be narrated—meant that it could not easily be restricted to such a narrow ceremonial role. By the second half of the eighteenth century, farming villages were increasingly prosperous and almost all branch temples of the Honganji sect came to own a set of the *Holy Pictorial Biography*. Under the influence of the vogue for *fushidan sekkyō*, in which Shinran's life was recounted to a melody, explaining the *Holy Pictorial Biography* with a melody seems to have become increasingly common as well. The fact that Higashi Honganji issued a series of edicts banning the explanation of pictures, as noted above, surely suggests the degree of popularity of this custom.

2.   Ukiyo-e and Townspeople

The popular art works surveyed above, such as those associated with Kumano nuns and temple exhibitions, were religious in character and valued roughly in proportion to their venerability. There also developed during the Tokugawa period an important artistic tradition that was essentially secular in character and that was treasured for its up-to-dateness. This was the tradition of ukiyo-e, or pictures of the floating world.

The Floating World and Its Art

One of the earliest uses of the word ukiyo-e seems to be in the following line of Ihara Saikaku's novel *Kōshoku ichidai otoko* (The life of an amorous man), "a folding fan with a picture of the floating world painted by Miyazaki Yuzen." In this reference to a painting by a late-seventeenth-century artist and dyer, the word appears within a list of items fashionable at the time, such as purses in colored leather or socks in woven fabric. So ukiyo-e meant something like "an up-to-date picture." Yet the noun ukiyo, or "floating world," was a word that included many other notions, as Saikaku frequently explained.

The most obvious example is the name of Saikaku's amorous hero, Yonosuke, which is in fact an abbreviation of Ukiyonosuke. Another example is Ukiyobō, who is the hero of *Ukiyo monogatari* (Tales of the floating world), and who might be described as the precursor of Yonosuke. The preface to that novel, which appeared around 1665, includes a famous definition of what the floating world is all about. "In this world everything is a source of interest. And yet just one step ahead lies darkness. So we should cast off all gloomy thoughts about our earthly lot and enjoy the pleasures of snow, moon, flowers, and autumn leaves, singing songs and drinking wine; living our lives like a gourd bobbing buoyantly downstream. This is the floating world."

The word ukiyo appears in literature as early as the fourteenth century and can be found in the songs of commoners in Kyoto and Sakai around the beginning of the seventeenth century. In these instances, however, the characters used to write ukiyo have the meaning, "world of sorrow," the medieval or Buddhist notion of a transient, sorrow-ridden world that stands in implicit contrast to the paradise of the Pure Land. The word ukiyo in *Ukiyo monogatari* is rather different from this medieval usage. Though it includes the meaning of the world of sorrow in the reference to "one step ahead lies darkness," it ultimately embraces the hedonistic sense of seeking to enjoy life without being gloomy.

The hero of *Ukiyo monogatari*, Ukiyobō, epitomizes this kind of floating world. Hyōtarō, the son of a Kyoto townsman who frequents the Shimabara pleasure quarter, has reduced himself to penury and there is nothing for it but to renounce the world. He takes the priestly name Ukiyobō, but he has led such a dissolute life that he is forced to leave Kyoto and seclude himself in the countryside. Hoping to reconnoiter Kyoto once more, he decides to make a pilgrimage to the city's shrines and temples. But instead of visiting shrines and temples, he spends his time at kabuki and *jōruri* performances held on the dry riverbed of the Kamo river at Shijō. Thus the floating world manifests itself most directly in the pleasure quarters and kabuki theater.

As suggested by the traditional accounts of wealthy merchants and nobles vying for the favors of the courtesan Yoshino at Rokujō-misujimachi pleasure quarter, the pleasure quarters initially were not frequented by common people; rather, they were a sort of aristocratic salon. The pleasure quarter at Rokujō-misujimachi came to be regarded as detrimental to public morals, however, and in 1640 it was forced to move to Shimabara on the outskirts of Kyoto. That move led to a change in the class of customers, with wealthy merchants and nobles giving way to self-employed tradesmen.

After about the middle of the seventeenth century, therefore, customers would have been the types of characters Chikamatsu Monzaemon wrote into his puppet plays: the owner of a stationery store; a farmer-turned-proprietor of a messenger service; and even their servants.

When Yonosuke and his friends visited Shimabara, in Saikaku's *Kōshoku ichidai otoko*, they referred to the place as a bad place (*akusho* or *akubasho*). But rather than just meaning the bad of "good and bad," the term included a seductive sense of dissipation, as in the words *akusho-gurui* ("crazy about the bad places"); *akusho kotoba* ("language of the bad places"); *akusho-bon* ("book about the bad places"). The interesting thing is that in each of these cases the term ukiyo was interchangeable with *akusho* (*ukiyo-gurui, ukiyo kotoba, ukiyo-bon*), a place of dissipation being synonymous with the floating world. Just as the pleasure quarters of the various cities—Yoshiwara in Edo, Shimabara in Kyoto, Shimmachi in Osaka—were confined to specified locations, so also was it forbidden to perform kabuki, another source of entertainment, outside a limited area. It was not until the early nineteenth century that kabuki theater came to be referred to as an *akusho* in the same way as the pleasure quarters, but the kabuki performance was a source of dissipation, just like the pleasure quarters, and an important part of the floating world.

I suggested at the beginning that the word ukiyo-e was first written down in about 1680, but examining the issue more closely, we find that ukiyo-e themselves first appeared among the illustrations of woodblock-printed books during the 1650s. At the time two types of illustrated books were being printed from woodblocks: *kana-zōshi*, or simple novels, and *jōruri seihon*, or libretti for the puppet theater. After the great fire in Edo in 1657, two other types of *kana-zōshi* appeared: *meishoki*, or guides to famous places in Edo and Kyoto; and *hyōbanki*, or critiques of courtesans and actors.

The appearance of these new publications coincided with a considerable development in the techniques of woodblock printing, and a distinctively elegant new pictorial world rapidly emerged. The illustrations accompanying the critiques, which show figures of courtesans and actors, certainly can be regarded as ukiyo-e, and the artist Hishikawa Moronobu who appeared in 1672, consolidated the foundations of the ukiyo-e school in two decades of work. Though Moronobu produced illustrated books that included people of all classes and occupations, as well as many outdoor scenes, his works mostly treated the theater and pleasure quarters. After Moronobu, ukiyo-e became specialized in various ways, as with the theatrical works of the Torii school or Suzuki Harunobu's pictures of women, but at no time did it abandon the twin subjects of theater and pleasure quarter. Viewing it in another way, we can say that though feudal morality might regard them as bad places, the theater and

Figure 5. Trademarks and censorship seals on ukiyo-e prints.

pleasure quarters that appeared in ukiyo-e were topics of endless fascination as far as common people were concerned.

Ukiyo-e as Commercial Products

Looking at an ukiyo-e print closely, one notices two seals in addition to the title and signature of the artist. One of these is a circle containing the single character *kiwame* ("examined"), showing that the design passed censorship before publication (Figure 5). The Edo City Magistrate (*machi bugyō*) required the guild of wholesale publishers to select several members who acted as censors, preventing the publication of works that satirized politics or were detrimental to public morals. For decades ukiyo-e showing courtesans and actors had been subject to restriction by the City Magistrate, but the *kiwame* seal came to be impressed on prints only from about 1790.

The other mountain- or flower-shaped seal with a character inside, which often is found impressed under the artist's signature as if it were his seal, is in fact the trademark of the publisher who issued the print. The publisher's shop name may also appear on flags or umbrellas carried by figures in the design itself. It was customary from the earliest printing of ukiyo-e in the late seventeenth century to put some kind of trademark on the image, so ukiyo-e was in the strange position of being an art form that bore both a trademark and a censorship seal. In fact, as far as contemporaries were concerned, ukiyo-e prints were not "works of art" to be put in a frame and admired, but rather more intimate "commercial products," and they paid no particular attention to the trademark.

Ukiyo-e originated in the Kyoto-Osaka vicinity when those cities were the center of urban cultural life, but during the eighteenth century, Edo bypassed them, and by century's end contemporary sources as often as not used the terms *Edo-e* (Edo picture) and *nishiki-e* (brocade picture) rather than ukiyo-e when discussing prints. It is clear that ukiyo-e prints were thought of as a special product of Edo, and they were taken to castle towns and post stations all over the country as souvenirs of that city.

The importance of Edo in the history of ukiyo-e was reflected in the Edo City Magistrate's role in censoring the content of prints. That importance was evident again in the summer of 1842, when the Magistrate issued the following prohibition to the guild of illustrated booksellers: "To make woodblock prints of kabuki actors, courtesans, and geisha is detrimental to public morals. Henceforth the publication of new works [of this kind] as well as the sale of previously procured stocks is strictly forbidden. In the future you are to select designs that are based on loyalty and filial piety and which serve to educate women and children. And you must ensure that they are not luxurious."

As mentioned earlier, ukiyo-e depicted the "bad places" located in the restricted areas of the theater district and pleasure quarters. To outlaw pictures of kabuki actors or courtesans and geisha amounted, therefore, to a complete ban on ukiyo-e. Admittedly, the publication of the two great series, "Thirty-six Views of Mt. Fuji" (*Fūgaku sanjū-rokkei*), begun by Katsushika Hokusai in 1829, and "Fifty-three Stations of the Tōkaidō" (*Tōkaidō gojū-san tsugi*), begun by Utagawa Hiroshige in 1832, had recently established the genre of landscape prints in ukiyo-e, but in terms of the woodblock print's long history this development only constituted a new and untested artistic phase. Furthermore, even though Hokusai and Hiroshige were then at the height of their popularity, pictures of actors and beautiful women continued to be as common as ever. The prohibition of 1842 thus hit at the very heart of the ukiyo-e world.

Late that same year, as if to pursue the attack further, the City Magistrate tightened regulations concerning format and price.

Figure 6. Bookseller Tsutaya Jūsaburō's shop, from *Ehon azuma asobi.* Print by Katsushika Hokusai.

Coloring of ukiyo-e prints was limited to seven or eight color blocks, and prices of more than 16 *mon* per sheet were prohibited.

Very little information survives about the prices of ukiyo-e, but in an illustrated novel of 1805, the author, Santō Kyōden, recorded that the price of the most common type of ukiyo-e, a large brocade print (*ō-nishiki*) was 20 *mon*. And we can ascertain from another source that the price of a three-sheet print in 1848 was 60 to 72 *mon*. The price of single sheets may well have been about 20 *mon*, with little alteration since the end of the seventeenth century. Around 1840 noodle shops in Edo were advertising "two-eight *soba*" (*nihachi soba*), which meant you could get a bowl of buckwheat noodles for

16 *mon*. As revealed in comic stories of the era, such noodles were a common evening meal for the artisans of Edo; so ukiyo-e were being sold for little more than the price of a bowl of *soba*. Particularly luxurious prints, such as Sharaku and Utamaro portraits with mica backgrounds, surely could not have been purchased for 20 *mon*, but one could be the proud owner of an ordinary actor print, the print of a beauty, or a landscape by Hokusai or Hiroshige by going without a noodle dinner.

Looking at the shops of print sellers, the one pictured in 1802 by Hokusai in his *Ehon azuma asobi* (Illustrated pleasures of Edo) is that of Tsutaya Jūsaburō, who published and sold prints by Sharaku, Utamaro, and others (Figure 6). The sign board bears the publisher's mark of an ivy leaf that also appears on Sharaku's prints, and in the store front is a display of single sheet prints and illustrated books. Among the customers is a samurai wearing swords, but there also are travelers who have probably come to buy ukiyo-e as souvenirs of their trip to Edo. Utamaro and Toyokuni III (Utagawa Kunisada) also drew the store fronts of print sellers, showing all kinds of people enjoying ukiyo-e, from fancily dressed young girls to married women with children.

Before he could offer a print for sale, a publisher had to lay out considerable capital, including a fee to the artist who designed the print, the price of enough large planks of cherry wood to make the printing blocks, a fee to the engraver to cut them, the cost of paper of a quality that could withstand the many printings required for a color print, and a fee to the printer to print them. To sell one sheet for about 20 *mon* and still make a profit, the publisher had to print a large enough number to keep down his basic unit costs.

Information on the size of ukiyo-e editions is extremely scarce, and practically nothing is known about such printing before the nineteenth century. According to a diary written in 1848 by a tradesman called Fujiokaya, no sooner had he started selling for 72 *mon* three-sheet prints showing the shogun hunting at the foot of Mt. Fuji than he was able to sell 8,000 sets. He also recorded, however, the case of another triptych, priced at 60 *mon*, that showed a group of turtles with their faces drawn to look like famous actors. Though he printed 1,000 sets, he was only able to sell 50. Another interesting diary entry for that year reported that Fujiokaya was able to sell 8,000 sets of *Seichū gishi den* (Biographies of loyal retain-

Figure 7. Tarui post station, from the series "Sixty-nine Stations along the Kiso Highway." Print by Utagawa Hiroshige.

ers), portraits drawn by Kuniyoshi of the forty-seven samurai and other characters involved in the famous Chūshingura vendetta, with explanatory text by Keisai Eisen. This series had fifty-one designs in it, meaning a grand total of 408,000 sheets if he sold 8,000 complete sets.

Ukiyo-e series that contained large numbers of designs, such as "Fifty-three Stations of the Tōkaidō" (fifty-five designs) or "Thirty-six Views of Mt. Fuji" (forty-six designs), were not published as complete sets to start with. Instead, they were issued a few at a time and sold as a set only when the series had been completed. It is hard to say, therefore, if the figure of 408,000 sheets is really accurate, but the number certainly must have approached that.

According to Fujiokaya's diary, almost all ukiyo-e of this period were published in units of one thousand sheets. Considering also that in the nineteenth century actor prints came to be published in large numbers in Osaka and Kyoto, where previously single-sheet ukiyo-e had not been produced, one must conclude that from the late eighteenth century a colossal amount of good quality paper was used for woodblock prints.

What is more, certain types of novels, such as kibyōshi and gōkan, which were published from the middle of the eighteenth century as reading material for common people, had illustrations by ukiyo-e artists on every page, and these can justifiably be called illustrated

Figure 8. Mariko post station, from the series "Fifty-three Stations of the Tōkaidō." Print by Utagawa Hiroshige.

books. So we can see that common people of the time, particularly those living in the cities, had the opportunity to own a considerable number of pictures, not just single-sheet prints for 16 *mon* each, but also the simple picture books designed by ukiyo-e artists. The fact that ukiyo-e circulated as commercial products in this way meant that the townspeople who enjoyed them were not merely serving as passive consumers. Rather, a relationship evolved in which the producers, publishers, and artists were responding to their consumers' tastes and desires even as they influenced them. And we can suggest that the more prints were mass produced, the stronger this relationship became.

The Kinds of People Who Purchased Ukiyo-e

In the comic novel *Ukiyo-buro* (Floating world bathhouse) by Shikitei Samba, which was published over a period of thirteen years from 1809, there are references to common people enjoying ukiyo-e. The novel is set entirely in a public bathhouse, and characters from all professions and walks of life, from old people to children, mingle there, giving us a vivid portrait of life in the city.

Near the novel's beginning, boys in the men's bath start mimicking kabuki actors, and when the talk turns to actor prints by Utagawa Toyokuni, the children say things like: "Toyokuni's prints are really powerful," or "at our house everybody loves Toyokuni. We

Figure 9. Women admiring books and prints in *Oshiegusa nyōbō katagi*. Print by Toyokuni III. ca. 1846.

always take Toyokuni prints as presents when we go to Kansai or when we visit the master's house." Similarly, in volume two, mothers are in the women's bath complaining about their children. "Children have gotten really extravagant, the lot of them. My girl has a box full of actor prints that she bought, and my third boy buys *gōkan* [multivolume illustrated novels] whenever they come out. He's collected a big box-full too. These days children even remember the names of artists—'I like Toyokuni' or 'I like Kunisada'—pretending they're so grown up!" "You're right. And to think, when we were kids all we got were those simple picture books." Famous ukiyo-e artists thus were stars, just like kabuki actors, with even children knowing their names.

The designs of quite a few ukiyo-e reveal that it was customary for common people to paste prints on the walls of their houses. Good examples are the prints of the post stations at Tarui and Mariko, by Hiroshige (Figures 7 and 8). In them one can make out many prints pasted to the walls of tea shops, including prints of actors and a landscape that looks like one of Hokusai's "Thirty-six

Views of Mt. Fuji." These prints also illustrates, incidentally, how ukiyo-e found their way to the provinces. In other words, ukiyo-e were not works of art to be put in a frame, but rather something one would not think twice about pasting to the wall to cheer up travelers.

After about 1790 a genre of popular romances called *ninjō-bon* (or sometimes *naki-bon*—"tear jerkers"), which were written with women readers particularly in mind, became very popular. Ukiyo-e, too, appealed to women, especially those who were crazy about kabuki or dreamed about the actors' gorgeous costumes. The cover illustration to *Oshiegusa nyōbō katagi* (Precepts for the ideal wife), which Toyokuni III designed, shows married women happily taking illustrated books and single-sheet actor prints out of a large box (Figure 9). People of the day would have recognized all the publishers' seals on the books and prints that appeared in Toyokuni's illustration, and this recognition must have made them feel even closer to the novel that followed.

As to how common people got hold of ukiyo-e, obviously they could buy prints themselves, but another common way was to borrow illustrated books from itinerant book lenders (*kashi hon'ya*). Book lenders made the rounds of their customers, carrying a large stock of books on their backs. They first appeared around 1750, and by about 1800, 656 individuals were recorded as operating in twelve groups in Edo. It is said that each man normally had a round of customers of about 180 households. Rental was inexpensive, being 8 *mon* for five days in the case of illustrated books. The kinds of books carried by lenders ranged from serious Confucian tracts to illustrated novels and even erotica. Santō Kyōden, the most prolific novelist of the late eighteenth and early nineteenth centuries, likened his works to a young bride: "My design is her face; preparing the blocks is her makeup; printing them is her wedding dress; the kind reader is the bridegroom; and the book lender is the go-between." The book lender was indeed the "messenger" of literature and painting.

Ukiyo-e was principally an art for common people, but of course it was enjoyed by other classes as well. Rich townspeople, samurai, and even daimyo admired it. For example, Yanagisawa Nobutoki, daimyo of Yamato Kōriyama fief until 1773, was an intellectual with a deep knowledge of national learning (*kokugaku*), Chinese studies, and history. But he was also one of the central figures in Edo *haikai* poetry in the 1780s and an ardent fan of the theater. Using his servants as actors, Nobutoki held kabuki performances in his mansion, and he even made actor prints of them. He often mentioned ukiyo-e in his diary, *En'yū nikki*. At New Year's, in particular, he received from acquaintances many gift prints, illustrated books, and *surimono* (single-sheet prints designed by ukiyo-e artists and inscribed with haiku poems), and in return he sent such *surimono* to his friends. Nobutoki was also a patron of the leading kabuki actor Nakamura Nakazō, and when prints of Nakazō were put on sale, he went to the bookseller in town to buy them himself. He also received prints of Nakazō directly from the actor, as well as fans decorated with his portrait.

A contemporary of Nobutoki was Sakai Hōitsu, second son of the Lord of Himeji. He composed comic verse (*kyōka*) under the satirical pen name Shiriyake Sarundo ("Burnt Buttocks Monkey Man), included his poems in anthologies of comic verse with illustrations by Utamaro, and was a friend of the Tsutaya Jūsaburō who published the prints of Sharaku and others. Then there is the example of Ōta Nampo (Shokusanjin), a retainer of the bakufu who, as well as being the central figure among Edo *kyōka* versifiers, was also a leading author of popular fiction (*gesaku*). During the 1830s, Ryūtei Tanehiko, another retainer of the bakufu, published the enormously popular *Inaka Genji* (A rustic Genji), a parody of the classical *Tale of Genji*, with illustrations by Toyokuni III. It was a runaway bestseller, issued in a total of seventy-six volumes over a period of ten years.

This state of affairs was already being lamented in 1816 in the *Seji kemmon roku* (A record of things seen and heard). "Manners are normally something learned from above, but these days it is the manners of the common people that are being transferred to the elite." Ukiyo-e was basically an art form of the townspeople, but it appealed nevertheless to daimyo such as Nobutoki and other members of the warrior class. Many other examples also show that ukiyo-e was a "manner of the common people that transferred to their betters." Hosoda Tokitomi, a samurai of high rank who had been in close attendance to the shogun, painted ukiyo-e pictures of beautiful women using the name Chōbunsai Eishi. And a lower-ranking samurai in the fire-fighting unit of Edo Castle, Andō

Jūemon designed the series "Fifty-three Stations of the Tōkaidō Highway" under the nom de plume Utagawa Hiroshige. In conclusion, we can say that during the later Tokugawa period the culture of townspeople underwent tremendous expansion, subsuming even the culture of the warrior classes.

(Translation by Timothy Clark)

Chapter Eight

Kabuki and
Its Social Background

MASAKATSU GUNJI

1. Popular Culture and Kabuki

The kabuki theater and prostitution quarters were the two great fountainheads of urban popular culture in Tokugawa society. Officially, however, these two centers of entertainment were stigmatized as evil places (*aku-basho*) and were subject to an inordinate degree of supervision and suppression. Both enterprises were banished from the central areas of cities and forced to occupy outlying districts both remote and inaccessible.

Kabuki, to limit the discussion, had its origins in pantomimes given in the bed of the Kamo River at Shijō Avenue in Kyoto. Consequently, those who engaged in this form of theater were branded riverbed beggars (*kawara kojiki*) and were the object of official scorn. At the same time, however, for the general public the world of the kabuki theater was an object of yearning and fascination.

The enthusiasm of the masses for kabuki even permeated everyday existence. It added color and panache to life and extended into novels, ukiyo-e woodblock prints, and fashions. Popular opinion maintained that a thousand *ryō* in gold exchanged hands daily in three locations only: the Yoshiwara prostitution quarter, the Uogashi fishmarket, and the theaters. Kabuki was hailed as the crowning glory of Edo.

Theaters and Actors

The theater system operated under official licensing. Initially, the three metropolitan areas of Kyoto, Osaka, and Edo were restricted to four theaters apiece. In 1714 in Edo, however, Ejima, a senior lady-in-waiting in the women's quarters of the shogunal castle, caused a scandal by her illicit liaison with the actor Ikushima Shingorō, and in retribution the authorities demolished one of the theaters. From the time of this episode until the end of the shogunate, the three surviving theaters (the Nakamura-za, Ichimura-za, and Morita-za) constituted the theatrical establishment of Edo. These officially licensed theaters were known as grand playhouses or ō-shibai, yet smaller, unlicensed theaters operated in their shadow. These were the little playhouses (ko-shibai), hundred-day playhouses (hyakunichi-shibai), and shrine precinct playhouses (miyaji-shibai). The first three types fell under the jurisdiction of the city magistrates; the miyaji-shibai were under the jurisdiction of the superintendents of temples and shrines.

In the provinces there existed a virtually unlimited assortment of local playhouses (ji-shibai). Most were found in the castle towns of daimyo or before the gates of major temples or shrines, yet their popularity reached even remote farming and fishing villages. Urban and provincial troupes went on tour and gave performances on the road. The materials these itinerant troupes reworked or produced were based for the most part on the productions of the three major urban centers of Kyoto, Osaka, and Edo. Since peasants were forbidden to perform kabuki as such, these local productions received sanction under the name of gesture dancing (teodori) and were permitted as offerings at shrine and temple festivals.

While normally tolerating, even protecting kabuki, the bakufu exercised a severe degree of repression. Early "women's" or "courtesan" kabuki, as practiced by Okuni from Izumo, was banned in 1629 after stabilization of the official system of licensed prostitution quarters. Kabuki performed by men only, the so-called youth (wakashu) kabuki, immediately replaced it, but this, too, was banned in 1652 on grounds of its deleterious effect on morals. Thereafter, kabuki was performed exclusively by adult males, the so-called fellows' (yarō) kabuki, and this is the form that has been transmitted to the present day. During this formative period, the term kabuki itself was banned, and for a time, performances were permitted only under the title of monomane kyōgen-zukushi—roughly, complete revue of mimicking farces.

The theatrical world, like the world of licensed prostitution, was controlled by a "ghetto" system. All those associated with theaters were officially required to live in the immediate theater district, and they were forbidden to live elsewhere. In point of fact, star actors did own and inhabit villas and estates throughout the city, but these town houses were always registered under the name of an agent, while the actors themselves, for official purposes, continued to be considered residents of the theater district.

The restraints that the bakufu imposed on actors were harsh: whenever they were in public places, for example, they were required to hide their faces with sedge hats; on stage, they were to wear only simple cotton costumes. Officially, the social status of actors was akin to that of the lowliest paupers. They were considered outcasts, outside the hierarchy that informed every aspect of their society. At the time of the Tempō Reforms of 1841–43, actors did not even enjoy full status as human beings: official documents counted them with the suffix -*hiki*, like so many dumb animals. In principle, then, actors were rigorously isolated from all commerce with society at large, and dwelled in the theater district. In reality, however, this was merely an official façade: not only did actors venture out in public, even daimyo enjoyed their company.

Actors who ranked as star performers lived the sumptuous lives of daimyo. Surrounded by hordes of disciples and servants, they maintained villas and squandered money lavishly on sprees and excursions. In its last years the bakufu banished two actors, Nakamura Tomijūrō II and Ichikawa Danjūrō VII from Osaka and Edo respectively, on charges of unseemly ostentation and extravagance.

Examples of richly paid actors abound. Tamagawa Sennojō, renowned throughout the 1660s, drew an annual salary of 200 gold *ryō*. Sakata Tōjūrō, a top star of the Genroku period, reputedly enjoyed a salary of 600 *ryō*. A few years later, Yoshizawa Ayame, the first actor to earn 1,000 *ryō* in a year, was publicly celebrated as a thousand-*ryō* actor (*senryō-yakusha*). During the 1820s, Ichikawa Danjūrō VII and Iwai Hanshirō V each earned 1,000 *ryō* a year, and Bandō Mitsugorō III, 1,300 *ryō*; while Nakamura Utaemon III commanded a stipend of 1,400 *ryō*.

Ordinances and edicts repeatedly prohibited the unwarranted magnificence of kabuki stage costumes. Whenever the bakufu relaxed its vigilance, however, the earlier opulence returned in force. Year after year, theaters vied with one another in the glamour and artistry of their costumes, wigs, and accessories. The patterns and colors of stage costumes formed the basis of numerous fashion crazes, and their influence on society at large was enormous.

The actors' professional hierarchy, reflecting the feudal society around it, became hereditary. As professional cliques and powerful actors became ever more prominent features of the theatrical scene, it became progressively more difficult in the latter Tokugawa period to succeed solely by one's innate talents. Even as acting positions became hereditary, stage roles became fixed, with each role developing along its own specialized line. Kabuki became increasingly distinguished by its stylization.

The main features of the theatrical industry became standardized shortly after the beginning of the Tokugawa period. Financing was supplied anew for every production by several capital investors (*kinshu*). These theatrical investors, like the financiers of land reclamation projects or gold mining operations, were involving themselves in a risky business and might end up "overnight paupers" as readily as "overnight millionaires."

Once enough capital had been amassed, the first essential was to contract a troupe of actors for the year by providing salary advances. Through this contract an employer-employee bond developed between the theater manager and his actors. In the late Tokugawa period, when actors' salaries increased by leaps and bounds, theater management frequently fell into difficult financial straits because of these elevated salaries. As another consequence, the cost of admission to the theater soared, and the masses grew increasingly estranged from performances. Admission charges fluctuated on a daily basis: as a general rule, when the house was well attended, admission prices rose sharply; when attendance figures fell, prices dropped with them.

From about the 1660s onward, an actor's term of employment was generally one year, running from the Eleventh Month of one year through the Tenth Month of the next. Once the actors had been selected and the employment contract drawn up, the principals went to the office of the city magistrate and affixed their seals to the contracts. At the very end of the Tokugawa period, as exchanges of actors between Edo and Kyoto-Osaka theaters became commonplace, this contractual practice fell into disarray. After 1868, contracts were drawn up for single productions, and

Figure 1. Interior of the Nakamura-za in the 1790s. The play *Shibaraku* is being performed by Ichikawa Danjūrō V, with the hero on the raised entryway (*hanamichi*) on the left. Note the seating arrangements, from expensive boxed balcony seats and raised compartments to the cheaper compartments in the general pit. Courtesy of Tsubouchi Memorial Theatre Museum. Waseda University.

eventually the system of year-long contracts lapsed completely.

Once the roster of actors in a troupe had been established by one-year contracts, the first events of the new theatrical year were the performances of the Eleventh Month, known as showing the face (*kaomise*), which were conducted with the utmost pomp and splendor. The booklets of actor critiques (*yakusha hyōbanki*) published in the First Month of each new year were, for the most part, critical records of these *kaomise* performances. The roster of actors was published and sold to the public in the form of a ranked listing of actors. The annual cycle of performances after the *kaomise* production of the Eleventh Month was fixed: the early spring plays of the First Month, the Third Month and Fifth Month plays, and then from the middle of the Sixth Month, the summer season, during which theaters staged plays performed by junior actors at reduced admission fees. During the Ninth Month, guest actors visiting Edo from Kyoto and Osaka joined their Edo colleagues in commemorating the visitors' coming departure by performing farewell plays, which also were known as autumn or Bon festival plays. In this way, the calendar of new productions kept step with the old courtly calendar of ceremonies, so that changes in the playbill coincided with the most important festivals of the year.

The length of a full program, to take one example from 1814, was from 6:00 A.M. until 7:30 P.M.—a good 13.5 hours. The price of admission to the Ichimura-za in the Seventh Month of 1813 ranged from one *bu* for box seats to twelve *mon* for a compartment in a raised portion of the pit, and two *shu* for a compartment, which sat six or more people in the general pit. These summer performances, moreover, were cheaper than those in other months. In an era when the annual salary of a shop clerk or maid in domestic service was in the neighborhood of 3 *ryō*, these prices of admission were prohibitive, and the lower classes mostly converged on the cheaper "little playhouses." We are told, however, that the "grand theaters" were free to all on the opening day of a performance.

The distinction between "great" and "little" theaters was rigidly maintained. A turret (*yagura*) over the entrance to the theater was solely the prerogative of the "great" theaters as a symbol of their official licensing. "Little" theaters were not allowed to erect such turrets, much less to beat a drum from one, as the grand theaters did during their performance runs. What is more, the "little" theaters, by law, could spread only coarse straw matting on their floors and were forbidden to construct raised entryways (*hanamichi*) or revolving stages. Since they were also forbidden the draw curtain of the "great" theaters, they used a simple drop curtain (*donchō*) pulled up and down on a roller—from which stemmed their disparaging designation, drop-curtain playhouses or *donchō shibai*. No matter how skilled the actors of these "little" theaters might be, moreover, they bore the epithet drop-curtain actor (*donchō yakusha*) and were forbidden to perform in the "great" theaters.

The Audience and Critiques

The kabuki audience was a cross section of the general populace, but samurai, too, attended. Officially the bakufu prohibited any participation by samurai in the kabuki theater, but this taboo was merely another empty formalism. In fact, enthusiastic admirers of

Figure 2. A bustling crowd of theatergoers in front of the Naka-mura-za in the early nineteenth century. Print by Utagawa

kabuki were to be found even among the ranks of daimyo, some of whom, like Matsudaira Naonori and Yanagisawa Yoshiyasu, went so far as to keep journals of their theatergoing. Lesser samurai, too, followed their example, though the bakufu frowned on any contact between samurai and the theater. Especially after the Ejima-Ikushima scandal, samurai ceased to enjoy the freedom of their ear-lier, uninhibited theatergoing.

Among spectators in Edo, there were wealthy townsmen from the Uogashi fish market, the rice brokerages of Kuramae, the Yoshi-wara prostitution quarter, and elsewhere who organized themselves into large fan clubs and functioned as patrons of the theater. The same system prevailed in Osaka and in Kyoto. At performances of

Toyokuni. Courtesy of Tsubouchi Memorial Theatre Museum,
Waseda University.

Sukeroku, one of the eighteen famous plays of the kabuki repertoire,
custom demanded first of all a respectful salutation to the Yoshiwara. The Yoshiwara, in return, shouldered a customary obligation
to donate the parasols, headbands, or paper lanterns used during
the performance. The delivery of these favors constituted a sort of
ritual or ceremony in itself. When the members of actors' fan clubs
attended the theater as a group, they followed prescribed cadences
of applause and shouted words of praise (*home-kotoba*)—spontaneous
or premeditated accolades for their favorites on stage. According to
the *Kyakusha hyōbanki* (Critique book of audiences), permanent
booster clubs developed from local associations in every city ward.
The success of performances throughout the year, the same source

continues, especially at the *kaomise* premieres, and above all in Edo, hinged largely on the solicitude of these clubs of backers.

The booklets of actor critiques appeared from the seventeenth century through the nineteenth, constituting an uninterrupted critical literature without parallel outside Japan. Spectators based their own judgments concerning the skill of actors on appraisals found in the critiques, and they assessed their relative merits and debated the validity of their published rankings. Kabuki spectators included both the discerning and well-to-do and the broad masses. The opinions of the two groups were differentiated in the *hyōbanki* by reference to theater seating arrangements: the box-seat spectators as opposed to those in the pit. The typical actor critique employed a dialogue between these two contrasting points of view to present its assessment. The viewers in box seats could afford a fairly elevated price of admission, and ranged from the senior officials of daimyo in Edo to the wealthiest of the merchant families. The spectators in the pit consisted of ordinary *chōnin*, their shop clerks, and the mass of ordinary tradesmen.

Actor critiques were published in sets of three volumes—one volume for each of the three metropolises, where kabuki was most flourishing and where the works themselves were produced. Critical opinion in each of the three cities had its own idiosyncrasies, and standards of appreciation varied, and preferences for and support of specific actors varied accordingly. One *hyōbanki, Yakusha hanasugoroku* (Actors' floral *sugoroku* game), described the process leading up to the composition of an actual *hyōbanki*. The critiques and ratings, it emphasized, were based on a judicious canvassing of some twenty-two or twenty-three contemporary sources, not merely three to five individual opinions. Any personal bias in the compilation of such a work, it asserted, would foredoom the critique to poor sales. And if the work failed to reflect public consensus, it would hardly be worthy of the designation "critique."

Kuraizuke ranking was a system of symbols denoting grades of actors. In earliest times, this only denoted superior, middling, and inferior grades, but by the Genroku period, the *jō-jō* (doubly superior) rank had been added and then surpassed by the addition of the character for auspicious (*kichi*) to form a new supreme level. Later, commentators prefixed ultimate (*goku*) to this, and the superlative designation became *goku-jō-jō-kichi* (ultimate-doubly-superior-auspicious). As if this were not enough, subsequent evaluations tacked on the characters for peerless (*burui*). These symbols or ranking designations, originally intended for actors, became widespread, and their influence extended even to graded rosters of painters or scholars, to mention but a few.

2. The Development of Kabuki

The Early Phases

It is recorded that in 1603, Okuni from Izumo performed her kabuki dance (*kabuki odori*) in Kyoto. The dance associated with Okuni differed from that of medieval *nō* drama, deriving from *fūryū- odori* or processional dancing, rather than the dance styles characteristic of *nō*. Among the points of divergence from the medieval *nō* were the lack of masks, the basic motions of the dance, since the kabuki dance emphasized vigorous, angular dancing rather than the sweeping, rotating *mai* dance of the *nō*, and the gender of the dancer, because the *nō* was performed entirely by men whereas this kabuki was performed by women. As noted earlier, however, after the prohibition of women dancers, kabuki troupes consisted entirely of men, a situation that still prevails today.

During the earliest phases of kabuki, when women and then young men served as actors, the chief function of the performance was as a preliminary to prostitution. After women and young men had been banned from the stage, however, the form evolved into a display of acting techniques. A few decades thereafter followed the Genroku period, the first golden age of kabuki. It coincided with the ruinous decline of the older privileged merchant class and the rise in its place of a new class of merchants based in Kyoto and Osaka. Kabuki was to achieve a dazzling development within this new economic and social setting.

During the Genroku period, when there were three officially licensed theaters in Kyoto and four each in Osaka and Edo, the financial foundations of the theater industry became firmly established in the three metropolitan centers. Among the noteworthy characteristics of kabuki during this period were successful commercial tie-ups with fairs (*kaichō*) on the grounds of temples and shrines, a noticeable advance in the quality of plays, the fostering of independent playwrights, and the rapid emergence of an entire generation of celebrated actors.

During these years, moreover, the theater developed from its initial primitive form, centered on song and dance, to an essentially dramatic form based on dialogue. And, the regularly published actor critiques advanced from works that emphasized an actor's personal appearance to discussions of acting skills, thereby heightening the critical acuity of audiences and confirming kabuki's development in an artistic direction. Dramatists like Chikamatsu Monzaemon made their debut during the Genroku period and provided works of superior content. Celebrated actors emerged and adapted these works to the stage at a high level of effectiveness. Actors like Sakata Tōjūrō, Yoshizawa Ayame, the original Ichikawa Danjūrō, and Nakamura Shichisaburō were active in the Genroku theater and perfected the sentimental (*wagoto*), rough (*aragoto*), and scandal-piece (*sewa-goto*) styles of acting. Plays dealing with such current social issues as crime and double love-suicide gave the stage a fresh air of topicality and breathed vitality into performances. The disorders in daimyo houses (*oie sōdō*) occupied much of Genroku kabuki—a reflection, one might say, of the unrest in the upper strata of warrior society. In any event, the golden age of kabuki had arrived—a worthy reflection of the high level of Genroku culture.

In 1714, the Ejima-Ikushima scandal occurred—a watershed event that precipitated a major transition in the history of kabuki. Ejima, a senior lady-in-waiting in the shogunal women's quarters, had rested with her party in the theater district while returning from a pilgrimage to Zōjōji temple. During the rest stop she concluded a confidential tryst with Ikushima Shingorō, as well as other actors then in the heyday of their popularity. The incident became known and gravely offended bakufu sensibilities, and as a consequence, the Yamamura-za, one of the four officially licensed theaters of Edo, was utterly demolished, reducing to three the theaters in Edo that retained official licenses to perform. In a sense this incident was merely a case of government scapegoating, but as a result the zest and vitality of the Genroku theatrical troupes promptly showed signs of declining.

The plays about disorders in daimyo houses reflected a gathering crisis in feudal society that culminated during the Kyōhō period when the clamor of popular resentment against the bakufu filled the air. The difficulties led to the Kyōhō Reforms, undertaken during the 1720s and 1730s by the eighth shogun, Yoshimune. His policies of moral reform and economic retrenchment extended even to the mores of urban life. The practice· of *shinjū*, double love suicide, exalted in Genroku drama as an earnest demonstration of natural human feeling, found its claim to sincerity denied. New regulations insisted on the label *aitai-jini* (death by accomplice) and prohibited the burial of the corpses of the lovers, ordaining instead exposure and abandonment of the suicides' bodies. If one lover survived the suicide pact, the decrees further enjoined, he or she was to be accounted a criminal. If the suicide attempt was entirely unsuccessful, the survivors were to be exposed to public humiliation and reduced to servitude as subordinates of the *hinin* class of outcasts. Symptomatic of the times, dramatizations of love suicides greatly decreased, while plays portraying fraudulent or feigned love suicides held the stage.

The renewed efforts of the bakufu to distance the upper classes from the theater reenforced the old prejudices that held kabuki actors to be mere "riverbed vagrants" and fostered contempt for their profession. Repressive attitudes took concrete form in regulations designed to isolate the theater from society as a whole, and the force of these regulations stripped actors of dignity in both their personal lives and their art. Regulations prohibited the use of contemporary personal or place names in plays and strictly forbade the dramatization of current events or stories of topical interest, as well as any allusions to politics. As a result, the fantastic elements gained the upper hand in kabuki, and the stylization of form accelerated.

Furthermore, since the right to manage performances was granted as a special hereditary privilege to a select few, relationships between these hereditary theater managers and their actors evolved into feudal relationships between lord and retainer. The actors, in turn, laid increasing emphasis on their own hereditary system, establishing the importance of professional family affiliations and the bequeathing of artistic names to appointed successors. One outstanding characteristic of this period was the increasing improbability of an actor's succeeding, however talented, without the requisite professional lineage.

In the theater troupes of the early eighteenth century, Ichikawa

Danjūrō II cut an outstanding figure in Edo, matching his talent against that of Sawamura Sōjūrō, an actor whose origin lay in the samurai class. Danjūrō's rough style, with its incorporated senti- mental style, as well as Sōjūrō's soft-mature style (*wa-jitsu*) became firmly established.

These independent acting styles, however, were overshadowed by the predominance of the puppet theater (*jōruri*). Things reached the point where, to quote one contemporary, "Kabuki exists, but might as well not." In Osaka, the Takemoto-za and Toyotake-za puppet theaters engaged in a titanic rivalry and produced in rapid succession the three masterpieces *Kanadehon chūshingura* (The treas- ury of loyal retainers), *Yoshitsune senbon-zakura* (Yoshitsune and the thousand cherry trees), and *Sugawara denju tenarai kagami* (Suga- wara's secrets of calligraphy). The system of using three manipu- lators for each puppet reached perfection, and there was an astonishing progress in stage machinery and in the mechanics of performances. These advances in the puppet theater were influ- enced perhaps by developments in society at large, which, as a result of social petrification, stereotyping of social roles, and loss of human freedoms, was itself moving in the direction of doll-like mechanical manipulation.

During this period, kabuki found material for its plays in the mas- terworks of the puppet theater and assimilated much of its theatri- cal rival's stylization and love of the spectacular. In 1758, Namiki Shōzō, an Osaka native who had turned from writing *jōruri* to com- posing kabuki dramas, used his experience to devise a rotating stage. This device, together with the raised entryway that had been perfected earlier in the century, constituted the two great technical innovations of the kabuki stage. There also was progress in other items of stage machinery, notably trapdoors and elevators, scenery flats mounted on wheels, and the *gandō-gaeshi*, a method of hanging sets that allowed rapid rotation and replacement of one entire set with another. All these innovations markedly enhanced the visual quality of kabuki.

The eventual reaction to the austerity of the Kyōhō Reforms was the so-called Tanuma era of the 1780s, an age of extravagance and luxury renowned for its political venality. During this more gener- ous era, the well-nourished buds of Tokugawa culture bloomed, and the initiative among kabuki troupes passed to Edo from the Kyoto-

Osaka region that had spawned the technical innovations and adaptations of puppet theater.

The Heyday of Edo Kabuki

The late eighteenth century, then, was the heyday of Edo kabuki. In the miscellany *Shizu no odamaki* (Bobbin for native stuff), the compiler, himself a retainer to the bakufu, notes that of late, shogunal retainers (*hatamoto*) from the most respectable families gather here and there, mimic kabuki, or even stage their own amateur productions. For orchestral accompaniment, he notes, their second or third sons join in and strum away on musical instruments.

The *chōnin* of Edo, who managed both the city's rice markets and its financial institutions, were well placed to take advantage of this samurai taste for luxuries. The official rice brokers used their great store of capital to overwhelm the samurai and dominate Edo culture. From this affluent merchant class sprang the "eighteen great *tsū*," the profligate connoisseurs of pleasure representative of contemporary culture. The character Sukeroku, namesake of one of the "eighteen famous plays" of the Ichikawa family, personified this wealthy class on stage and became the object of popular adulation with audiences cheering and applauding his defiance of the samurai class.

Buoyed by the support of wealthy *chōnin*, both the Yoshiwara prostitution quarter and the theater district reached their zenith as the two great central fixtures of Edo culture. This, too, was the age when shamisen music was at the height of its popularity. To quote once more from *Shizu no odamaki*, "The popularity of the shamisen today is of formidable proportions: scions of noble families, eldest sons and heirs, second sons, third sons—none fails to strum the three-stringed shamisen. In mountain or in moor, from dawn till dusk, its sound echoes incessantly."

Dazai Shundai, an earlier scholar, asserted in his own miscellany, *Hitorigoto* (Words to myself), that the immediate cause of the current moral chaos was in fact the music of the shamisen. Officials evidently agreed because in 1739, Bungo-*bushi*, a representative school of shamisen music was totally banned. Before long, however, the Tomimoto and Tokiwazu schools, both offshoots of Bungo-*bushi*, reached the heights of their prosperity as theatrical music. Moreover, Katō-*bushi*, a style patronized by the affluent warehouse brokers at Kuramae, Ogie-*bushi*, derived from theatrical music, *meriyasu* or mood music, and other styles emerged in the world of shamisen music. The 1770s and 1780s were the most brilliant decades of shamisen music, and that music in turn exerted a powerful influence on the development of theatrical dance.

It was an unwritten law of the kabuki theater that dance was the exclusive province of the *onnagata*, or specialist in female roles, and that other actors must not usurp this special prerogative. In the era under discussion, however, the convention was broken in Edo by Nakamura Nakazō, a celebrated performer of male lead parts. Classics still extant today, like the dance-pantomime *Seki no to* (Snowbound barrier of love), *Modori-kago* (Palanquin homeward bound), and *Futaomote* (Double possession), were Nakazō's creations, and first performed by him. Even though his was an age of actors' cliques, factionalism, and hereditary positions, Nakazō rose from the ranks of lower actors to become the chief actor of his troupe. And in the course of his career, he introduced a number of new staging concepts or techniques, thus inaugurating a new phase in the theater. Kabuki enjoyed a new breath of freedom, but theater managements repeatedly encountered difficulties during this era, as a result of steep increases in actor salaries and the cost of their training.

A reaction to the liberality of the 1780s was evident in the Kansei Reforms of the next period. As part of a general campaign of frugality, the bakufu ordered a reduction in actors' salaries. However, objections to the order were surprisingly vigorous, and it came to naught. Kabuki continued to thrive.

Namiki Gohei, a playwright who accompanied the actor Sawamura Sōjūrō III from the Kyoto-Osaka region to Edo in 1794, is known for his attempts to transplant the rationalizing principles of the Kyoto-Osaka playwrights to the Edo stage. Thanks to a masterfully detailed psychological style, his works such as *Godairiki koi no fūjime* (Five guardian bodhisattvas cachet of love) laid a firm foundation for the establishment of realistic domestic plays (*sewa-kyōgen*) in Edo. The category of plays known as severed affection pieces (*enkiri mono*), which derived from *Godairiki koi no fūjime*, was characteristic of Edo kabuki in this latter period and directly contrasted with the lovers' suicide plays of the Genroku period. In these pieces, a woman, despite her unabated real affection for her lover, announces that she has fallen out of love with him and gives up her claims to his affection—all to help him launch his career and advance in the world unhampered. In a typical conclusion, the man, enraged at his lover's apparent feckless change of heart, murders her. In place of the Genroku double-suicide scene, these plays introduced a murder scene in which the two lovers confronted one another, their desires at cross purposes, all communication at an impasse. For these lovers there was to be no salvation, in contrast to the Genroku suicides whose hearts continued their sympathetic communion even beyond death. These were murders born of wild desperation—troubled reflections of a decadent age.

New Patterns of Taste

The Bunka and Bunsei periods constitute the era during which kabuki was most popular among the population at large, with regional playhouses spreading throughout the country. Still, the momentum and greatest vitality of the kabuki troupes during this period remained firmly fixed in Edo, and talented actors journeyed from the western metropolitan areas to Edo to make their reputations. A figure like Nakamura Utaemon III, though greatly disliked by the chauvinistic native sons of Edo, penetrated the bastion of the Edo theater on the strength of his talents alone, and his progress could not be stopped—testimony to the national stature the shogunal capital had assumed during this period. The influx of western actors also suggests that with the growth of merchant capital in Kyoto and Osaka, merchants from those cities had moved to Edo in ever increasing numbers, and that in consequence the very essence of Edo urban culture had begun to alter and new patterns of taste to arise.

On the Edo stage, one might almost designate this period as the age of abusive language (*akutai*), so popular was cynical or abusive language and behavior. This trend derived some of its vitality from the boastful native son of Edo who, according to popular wisdom, "kept no money overnight." At the same time, this trend toward abusive language and manners reflected the resentment of Edo merchants at their ebbing prosperity, threatened as they were by the strength of Kyoto and Osaka merchant capital.

During this later phase of kabuki, plays depicting the activities of petty criminals and rogues who made their living by fraud and extortion won increasing favor. In *Sato namari* (Accent of the prostitution quarter) we see an early expression of this trend. A Yoshiwara prostitute goes so far as to criticize samurai for "promising to fight a war when there's no war to be fought, and all the while drawing emoluments or whatever it is you call them." The cynicism of the day was evident in the dialogue of *Kirare Otomi* (Slashed Otomi). We find the hero commenting: "Come on, do you really think you can go on brooding about obligation and duty, like everybody else, and still go tippling from morning till night? I got rid of you because I wanted a little glory. People live a mere fifty years—and half of that they're asleep, so let's say twenty-five years. While there's still life in you, it makes good sense to 'make arrangements.' Or that's the fashion nowadays, at least." As the excerpt demonstrates, society applauded cynical lines whose import was to reject entirely the decadent latter-day versions of social obligation (*giri*) and personal sentiment (*ninjō*).

In this age, too, there appeared masterpieces like *Tōkaidō Yotsuya kaidan* (Yotsuya ghost stories) which described life in the lower ranks of the samurai class. In stage dialogue of a play of the period, *Nenriki yatate sugi* (Divine strength writing kit cedar), we find this passage: "You receive your official stipend, barely enough to cover the palm of your hand, and eke out a living from day to day repapering parasols or making cheap twine. To keep warm you toast your precious person over a lump of dying charcoal, but even in this miserable, stingy existence, you still go on calling yourself a warrior, a samurai?"

Tsuruya Nanboku IV, the author of *Tōkaidō Yotsuya kaidan*, was a genius in stature comparable to Chikamatsu Monzaemon of the Genroku period. Nanboku often painted the seamy side of a society in its decadent phase. By capturing these aspects of life through a vivid, fantastic stylization, he inaugurated the social theater of raw life (*ki-zewa*) and established a new genre that contrasted with the gentler domestic *sewa-mono* plays of the Genroku period.

In the realm of acting technique, too, we note during this late phase of kabuki the increasingly realistic stage manner of Matsumoto Kōshirō V, reputed to be incomparable in the roles of petty urban criminals, playing villain roles very unlike those of earlier kabuki. Iwai Hanshirō V created the evil crone (*akuba*), a type without precedent among existing female roles. Versatile actors skilled at the combining of roles in a single play also made their appearance, among them Onoe Kikugorō III and Nakamura Utaemon IV. The traditional classification of role types was growing disorganized, and the trend toward a "star system" of versatile individual actors was reaching new heights.

The Tempo Reforms of 1841–43, promulgated by Mizuno Tadakuni, leader of the final reactionary government of the Tokugawa period, were unable to rescue society from its state of decay, despite a thoroughgoing administrative program. Indeed, the reforms served only to fuel public resentment.

Nevertheless, the impact of the reforms on kabuki troupes was significant. Most notably, the theaters were completely dismantled and kabuki itself driven to the brink of extinction. Kabuki did escape obliteration, however, thanks to intercession by the respected city magistrate, Tōyama Kagemoto. But the theaters themselves, which since their founding had stood in the very heart of Edo, were ordered to relocate to Saruwakachō, in the remote Asakusa district. From then until the Meiji period, kabuki lived through its Saruwakachō period, so this new location served as Edo's theater district during the terminal years of the bakufu.

Besides forcing theaters to relocate, the Tempo Reforms heightened social discrimination against actors, set limits on their salaries, and added a host of restrictions to actors' lives, all to curb any presumptuous ambitions to rise in the world. Ichikawa Danjūrō VII was even banished from Edo on charges of extravagance.

The works of the playwright Kawatake Mokuami and the acting techniques of the celebrated Ichikawa Kodanji IV epitomize the characteristics of kabuki during the final years of the bakufu. Mokuami's works lack any high ideals or insightful critique of human life; they display no special individuality, nor do they initiate a new phase in the life of the theater. Rather, their great merit lies in precise articulation of the sentiments of contemporary plebeian life, never deficient nor excessive, thanks to the artful exercise of a fertile dramatic genius in a fitting vehicle of poetic sentiment and lyrical dialogue. Mokuami's rival, Segawa Jokō III, has left masterpieces like *Kirare Yosa* (Yosa the carved) and *Sakura Sōgo* (Tale of the righteous champion of Sakura), the latter dealing with the unusual topic of a peasant uprising. In his later years, though, even Jokō was completely eclipsed by Mokuami.

The tendency of plays during this period was to pursue truth and sincerity even in the midst of decadence. The earnest simplicity of country folk is depicted in plays like *Chijimiya Shinsuke* (Shinsuke the crepe dealer), *Sano Jirōzaemon*, and *Sakura Sōgo*. That a play like *Sakura Sōgo*, whose plot described a peasant uprising, did not suffer a ban is perhaps indicative of an increasing laxity on the part of the bakufu.

Among the pieces composed by Mokuami for performance by Ichikawa Kodanji IV, an artistic emigrant from the Kyoto-Osaka region, the robber plays (*shiranami-mono*), including *Nezumi Kozō* (Mouse Boy), *Sannin Kichisa* (The three Kichisa), and *Shiranami gonin otoko* (Five bandits) are particularly noteworthy. These works are still performed and are considered typical examples of Mokuami's art. Throughout these robber plays a wider background of social malaise surrounds the appearance of the individual thieves and bandits, and among the thieves are some virtuous men whose sense of duty and whose inclination toward compassion even exceed those of the world at large. Throughout these brigand plays, moreover, Mokuami emphasized an "aesthetic of evil." In the very midst of a decline in moral fiber during the late Tokugawa period, the theater at least served as a forum for the sad resistance and dreams of the common people.

On still another level, we find a distinctive group of Mokuami plays that includes *Kozaru Shichinosuke*, whose plot deals with the problem of rape; *Murai Chōan*, in which a coldblooded killer eliminates his own kinsmen; and *Ikake Matsu* (Matsugorō the tinker), which preaches a gospel of hedonism—all plays perhaps best termed social drama for a society that has lost its access to the light. The staging and acting techniques of these plays, in conjunction with their distinctive, sensationally erotic, gory, or masochistic scenes of love, murder, and extortion created a theater of mesmerizing power through appealing stylization and musicality.

Ichikawa Kodanji IV, whose performances best typified these staging and acting techniques, was the son of a vendor of *hinawa* (the match cord used for lighting pipe tobacco)—an occupation held in low esteem even in theater society. Once, brutally kicked by a superior, young Kodanji fell headlong from a building's second story and lost consciousness. After a wretched childhood in Edo, Kodanji pursued his artistic apprenticeship during an adolescence in the Kyoto-Osaka region. As a full-fledged actor, during the mid-1800s he took back with him to the Edo troupes the realism and stylization of the western theater style. He was not favored by nature with an attractive physical appearance, but the feverish intensity of his art in the title roles of *Chijimiya Shinsuke, Ikake Matsu,* or *Sakura Sōgo* was exceedingly true to life. In 1866, during his performance in *Ikake Matsu,* a notice from the office of the Edo magistrate decreed: "During recent years, dramas depicting current life have probed too far into human feelings. Since this tendency is detrimental to the manners of society, plays should reflect human feelings as little as possible." At this, Kodanji could only grieve: he had no way to express his resentment, nor any choice but to give up acting. The very next day his health began a rapid decline; death followed shortly at age fifty-five, at the very pinnacle of his career.

In an intensely lineage-conscious society, Kodanji had raised himself from the ranks of lower actors to become the chief actor of his troupe, very like Nakamura Nakazō in the 1780s. It was tragic that he died after being deprived of the foundation of the art on which he had staked his very life. If Kodanji had not been ruined by the bakufu, but instead had lived and developed his artistic mastery still further, perhaps the kabuki we see today would display a more realistic face.

It took time for the social revolution following the Meiji Restoration to influence the kabuki world. The restrictive three-theater system of Edo disappeared, and Tokyo's theaters then embarked on an age of open competition. To capitalize on this situation, in 1872 the Morita-za, long the underdog among the three official theaters of Edo, relocated under the direction of Morita Kan'ya XII from Saruwakachō to the heart of Tokyo, where it flourished. Actors were emancipated from their special discriminatory status in society, and a classification system based on taxation was adopted.

Zangiri-mono or "flowing hair plays" depicting the new manners of the day evolved from the traditional domestic plays following the introduction of foreign customs during Meiji. Stage adaptations of Western novels also appeared, but their content was identical with what had preceded. Until the later innovations of the synthetic Shinpa movement or the truly Western Shingeki theater, modern theater in the truest sense cannot be said to have emerged. The traditional historical pieces (*jidai-mono*) of the kabuki repertoire came

to be considered absurd, and a new, more authentic form of historical drama, the living history play (*katsureki-mono*) was introduced to
replace them. These new creations, though, were lacking in dramatic quality, and were at best insipid productions that never rose
above the academic depiction of historical manners. A new kabuki
was to be born only later, under the guidance of Western dramatic
theory in the Shin-kabuki or "Neo-kabuki" of the 1910s and 1920s.

(Translation by Andrew L. Markus)

Chapter Nine

Tokugawa Society

CHIE NAKANE

The Tokugawa period provided the foundation of present-day Japan in the sense that many elements now considered characteristic of Japanese society originated then. One can attribute the development of those characteristics to policies of the bakufu that penetrated every corner of the country and to widespread increases in productivity that resulted from developments in agricultural technology.

The basic order of Tokugawa society was established with the policy of separating samurai from the peasantry and defining society as a four-status strata of samurai, peasants, artisans, and merchants. Regardless of strata, the primary unit of a community was the *ie*, or household. Clusters of peasant *ie* constituted villages, which were stable, well-organized communities, and merchant communities tended to replicate basic characteristics of these villages. The samurai, who lived in castle towns, were in essence a modestly stipended, hereditary bureaucratic class. They were the elite of the society, forming 6 percent of the total population, but they did not monopolize scholastic and cultural activities, with the result that learning spread widely through urban society, and arts and letters flourished among the common people.

1. The Effect of the Policy of Separating Samurai and Peasants

The official four-status strata of samurai, peasant, artisan, and merchant is distinctive of the Tokugawa period, but most noteworthy is the thorough-going segregation of samurai and peasants. Samurai

213

were forced to settle in castle towns. Peasants, denied weapons and required to till the land, lived in villages. The samurai, who were compelled to depend on stipends and gradually turned into administrators, were effectively prevented from establishing ties to the land, which precluded their development into wealthy landholders. Instead, peasants had to pay annual revenue in kind directly to the lord of their domain. Similarly, merchants and artisans were forbidden to own land and had to live in towns.

There were some two hundred castle towns in Tokugawa Japan. Their sizes varied according to the production of the daimyo's fief, but in other ways they were all very similar. The typical castle town was laid out with samurai houses clustered near the castle and merchant and artisan houses arranged in neighborhoods by occupational type. The width of roads, the layout of streets, and the appearance of samurai and merchant houses were essentially the same everywhere, the countrywide uniformity testifying to the pervasive influence of bakufu policy.

The daimyo castle at the core of each castle town was guarded by an outer moat and by formidable stone walls and gateways, but the town itself was generally surrounded by farm land and lacked gates and walls. Most castle towns were located along major thoroughfares, and the villages (including fishing and mountain villages) surrounding them were administered as the local daimyo's territory. The castle town functioned not only as a regional administrative center but also as the convergence point for goods, services, and finance, and as the focus of local industry. Farmers brought their produce and handicrafts to the castle town to exchange for goods they needed, primarily for special items used on ceremonial occasions. Daily necessities such as clothing and straw sandals, and basic foodstuffs such as *miso* and soy sauce they made themselves.

Villages consisted primarily of farmers, the only exception usually being the village blacksmith. Houses in both castle towns and countryside were durable structures made of wood, constructed to last for two to three generations. Housebuilding was a communal project, everyone working under the guidance of one or two carpenters. While a carpenter might sometimes be hired from the town, there was usually at least one semi-professional carpenter in the village, and many villagers had at least some knowledge of construction. Timber for the project was cut from nearby village forests, and roofs were thatched with reed grown on village land.

Farmers accounted for more than 80 percent of the total population. Every farmer's household was registered by the village, which functioned as an important social unit. While the houses in some villages were scattered about, most were clustered in a single residential area surrounded by fields. Irrigation rights generally were allotted by the village unit, though several villages might draw their water from the same river. Village population and arable acreage varied widely, but the statistically average village is estimated to have had about four hundred people producing roughly 400 *koku* of rice. Plains villages were generally larger than mountain villages. A plains village might count two hundred households while a mountain village numbered a mere handful. Fishing villages were scattered all along the coastline, precariously clinging to rugged shores with hills right at their back. The fishing villages had little arable land, and with a few exceptions where there was enough level land to make farming a meaningful supplement to fishing, the coastal villages, like their mountain cousins, were generally small and comparatively less wealthy.

In the Tokugawa ideal, village communities were made up of farmers who in principle had equal economic and social status. From the middle of the seventeenth century to the beginning of the eighteenth, advances in irrigation and cultivation techniques contributed to an expansion of arable land, and the plains villages grew larger, their populations increasing while wasteland was converted into new fields. Villages with names ending in *shinden*, meaning "new field," generally trace their origins to this period. The growth of the plains villages, excepting those that had been in existence since the Nara and Heian periods and which had no room to expand, peaked in the latter half of the Tokugawa period.

Village hamlets were laid out willy-nilly without any basic plan or vision. They lacked the kind of village plaza one often sees in other societies, in which residents might gather for an evening for conversation and companionship. Each village had an *ujigami*, or local deity, but it was usually enshrined in a wooded hill on the village outskirts. Not every village had a Buddhist temple, and those with one did not necessarily have it in a central location. Roads were not blocked out in grids, but wound their way to houses built according to a given situation, wherever their occupants thought was the most advantageous. The choicest spots were occupied by the houses of earlier residents, and every village had several old houses around which the others clustered. The newer the house, the more likely it was to be in a topographically inferior position, often vulnerable to flooding, for example. This basic setting of the village remains fairly intact to this day, visible evidence of the Tokugawa roots of Japanese village organization.

While rapid progress was made in land reclamation, extension of irrigation networks, and diffusion of improved agricultural technology, these measures could not keep up with the steadily growing population. The population problem was dealt with on the village level. Villages limited the number of households they would allow within their boundaries and increasingly discriminated among existing households, with older ones gaining priority access to the village's limited resources. Sharper distinctions emerged between earlier settlers and those who came later, as well as those who left their parents' houses to establish new branch households. In due course, a clear distinction was made between the households of wealthier owner-farmers called *honbyakushō* and their poorer cousins commonly known as *mizunomi*.

Commonly the terms *honbyakushō* and *mizunomi* are used to distinguish between those households or *ie* that owned farmland and those that did not. A more important distinction was that the former was an official member of the village, was registered in the local survey record, was required to pay annual land taxes, was responsible for furnishing a proper quantum of corvée labor, and was obligated to share in the administrative duties of the village.

2. The Institution of the *Ie*

The *ie*, or household, was the basic unit of social organization in the village, as it was in samurai and merchant communities. Indeed, the same unit was found in all kinds of occupational groups throughout Japan. The institution of the *ie* goes back much further historically, but the Tokugawa economy and polity were clearly key factors in confirming it as the basic social unit among the common people.

Once an *ie* was established, continuity was a major concern of its members, and it was passed on from one married couple to the next through successive generations. Since a household could only be succeeded by one son (usually the eldest), the remaining sons (and daughters) were eventually required to leave. If there was no son, a daughter's husband would be adopted into the household, and the couple would eventually inherit the household. When there were no children at all, a son or daughter would be adopted to carry on the household with his or her spouse. A variation on this arrangement was to adopt an already married young couple. Kinship ties to the head of the household or his wife were not an indispensable factor in adopting a successor, the candidate's suitability for carrying on the household name being considered more important.

These adoption practices make it clear that a household's existence depended not so much on actual kinship as on the principle of succession from one married couple to the next. Of course, when there was a son, he would normally be the first choice, but among merchant households in particular, a son deemed unsuitable to carry on the family business might well be sent out to establish his own home, while a longtime and faithful worker might be chosen as the successor and adopted into the household through his marriage to a daughter. Thus the *ie* might better be classified as an ongoing enterprise rather than a family.

The emergence of the *ie* as the basic social unit of the rural community suggests that the agricultural activities of the farming household had become firmly established enough by that time to require an organizational structure ensuring continuity. The economic stability of each household depended on the cultivation of a given amount of land, and by the Tokugawa period it was possible for a household to carry on independent production. Among historians of Japan, it has long been held that the conjugal family unit emerged during the Tokugawa period. Yet from the view of social anthropology, the elementary family unit of husband, wife, and offspring is a universal unit unrelated to a society's level of development, mode of production, or economic structure. Undoubtedly, conjugal families had actually existed among Japanese peasants from a much earlier time, but due to the economic developments of the Tokugawa period the concept of the *ie* gained widespread acceptance, functioning more as a farming enterprise than as a conjugal unit.

As noted above, the concept of the *ie* was, itself, of hoary vintage.

No records show Japan ever to have had the type of joint family found in India and China, in which brothers continue to live in their natal home even after they marry and beget children. Rather, among nobles and high-ranking samurai it is the *ie*, as a unit of continuity from one generation to the next, that can be traced back to before the medieval period.

However, ancestral records suggest that widespread adoption of the *ie* system by the peasantry did not occur until the Tokugawa period. In Japan, unlike in China, only the ancestors of those currently living in a house are enshrined in the household altar, so a household's origin can often be dated by its oldest ancestral tablet. Because the tablets in even the most venerable farming households seldom go back further than the first half of the eighteenth century, it can be surmised that the concept of the *ie* took root among the peasantry from about that time.

During the medieval centuries, powerful local families and major landholders had, as in other societies, a number of poor workers serving under them. There are numerous examples of these workers living at their lord's residence. Later, in the Tokugawa period, economic development made it possible for the majority of the farming population to establish their own *ie*, but there were still poor families without land or tenant rights who could not even keep their family units intact, much less found a household to last through successive generations. It was not uncommon at this level for family members to scatter as servants to different households, though the more fortunate might be hired as family units by their employing households. In all likelihood such practices were much more common in earlier centuries.

The security of a peasant household depended very much on its economic fortunes, and even when an *ie* was established, it still might disappear due to poor management or bad luck. The economy of most of these households was based on the yield from specified parcels of land, however, and by successfully cultivating such land year after year, it was possible for them to carry on independent production. The emergence of the *ie* as the basic social unit of Tokugawa rural community thus suggests that, in contrast to the medieval period, the agricultural foundation for individual farming households had become firmly established.

In general, *ie* were most extensively established and their continuity most highly valued among those of the higher stratum, and least nurtured by those of the low stratum. However, given the proper economic conditions, households employing the principles and structure of the *ie* could be found throughout the country, a fact of major importance to the nature of the Japanese family today.

The *ie* was thus not a concept formed in the Tokugawa period, but something that had existed from ancient times. Early modern economic developments simply created the conditions necessary for *ie* to become established within all social strata on a nationwide scale.

Tokugawa government policy, which sought to settle peasants permanently in stable villages, fitted very well with the established family pattern, helping to consolidate the *ie*'s standing as the basic unit of society. Subsequently, in the Meiji period, the institution of the *ie* was formalized by law (in the process incorporating the ideology behind the household codes of samurai). Today, the concept of the *ie* continues to exist as a traditional value, even though the household is no longer regarded as an enterprise. While less valued as an institution among the general populace, the *ie* remains important in families operating businesses or handing down special occupations from father to son. Within farming villages in more productive regions, the household continues to function as a management unit, the *ie* remaining firmly entrenched as the basic social unit.

In principle, an *ie* consisted of one couple per generation, and non-succeeding members had to leave their natal households upon marriage. Two or more married sons might live under the same roof for a time, but this was strictly a temporary measure until the younger sons without succession rights established their own *ie*. In such households, a clear distinction was made between the successor to the head of the household and his siblings.

In Tokugawa farm families, what was the fate of the children who did not inherit the household? Daughters left the house at marriage, and the system decreed that younger sons move out and establish their own *ie*. To make this possible, they had to be provided with livelihoods, and one method was to create a branch house. Upon his marriage, the son received a portion of land from his father. He cultivated this land, living with his wife and children in a new house built in the same village. This, however, was not a common practice after the seventeenth century, for only the wealthier households had sufficient land and other wherewithal to create such branch houses and because village approval was also required.

Another method was to have the son adopted into his wife's family. The high mortality rate throughout the Tokugawa period and on through the 1930s made this a not uncommon practice among members of the same and neighboring villages. Indeed, in many villages even today nearly one-third of the households are headed by adopted sons-in-law. The adoption of a son-in-law is treated in the same manner as the marriage of a daughter, and the two households are considered to be linked in the same kind of matrimonial alliance. Because he takes the place of a natal son, the adopted son-in-law is given all the rights and privileges of an heir apparent. But should he divorce his wife, he must leave her household, just as a woman is driven out of her husband's home upon divorce. In the Tokugawa period, younger sons were most often adopted into other households in this manner.

A third means of guaranteeing an extra son's livelihood was to have him become a servant in another household. In this case, employment was most often sought in a nearby town rather than in the same or a neighboring village. It was common to become an apprentice in a merchant house, gradually working one's way up to become the master's right-hand man and finally to establish one's own shop with the employer's blessing and assistance. In any single town, there were always large numbers of youths from nearby farming villages who were apprenticed to the town's merchants and artisans. It was also a common practice for *ie* of the town to adopt sons-in-law from surrounding farming, mountain, and fishing villages. There was thus a steady influx of younger sons from rural areas into towns, despite the sharp formal distinction maintained between the two.

It is noteworthy that the large numbers of school teachers trained since the Meiji period, when schools were built throughout the country, were for the most part such younger sons. Moreover, the people who migrated to large metropolitan centers like Tokyo to pursue the wide assortment of occupations generated by industrialization were very often younger sons with no *ie* to inherit. In this sense, the institution of the *ie* contributed to the development of cities and smoothed the process of modernization.

Urban merchant and artisan families followed the same customs

as their country counterparts. Rather than sharing in the operation
of a family business after marriage, younger sons usually established their own branches. While they maintained close contact
with their natal house and often formed a tightly knit group operating in the same business line, their *ie* were regarded as separate
entities. As noted earlier, such branch households could be headed
by a trusted former employee as well as by a son.

Indeed, in these merchant houses there was little qualitative difference in household status between those related to the household
head and those from outside the immediate family. Younger sons
were assigned a status considerably lower than that of the eldest son
and heir apparent, and as far as the *ie*'s management went, they
ranked on a par with other employees. Apprentices hired from outside usually began serving around the age of twelve, and a valued
employee would remain with the *ie* for roughly thirty years before
being granted permission to set up his own branch house and business. After such long terms of service, such men commonly were
regarded as part of the family. It becomes easier to understand this
custom when one realizes that the Japanese word *kazoku*, meaning
"family," is a relatively new term, the more traditionally used term
being the expression *ie no mono*, meaning "member of the household."

Samurai *ie* operated similarly. However, because government
policy strictly limited the number of samurai households, it was
especially difficult for these *ie* to establish branches. Extra sons
therefore had more difficulty forming their own households, and
many remained in their natal household in the unpromising status
of *heyazumi*, one who is permitted to occupy a room.

In the *ie* system, property belonged to the household, not to its
head. The lord granted the stipend of the samurai to the *ie* rather
than the individual. In merchant households, family fortunes were
regarded as the property of the *ie*, and in farming households as
well, all property and rights accruing to the *ie* belonged solely to the
ie, and in principle the household head could not make free use of
them. In both merchant and farming households, property was considered indivisible, and the assets of the *ie* were never divided up. A
farmer's bestowal of land and house upon a second or third son and
a merchant's provision of a separate shop for his younger son or
faithful servant were viewed as the providing of aid to start a new

family rather than as a formal sharing of *ie* property to the non-succeeding members of the family.

The *ie* system existed, in short, to safeguard house and property, perceived as an indivisible unit, through the generations. This made a succession system essential and gave rise to the principle of succession from the married couple of one generation to that of the next.

3. The Village Community

Organized around the basic unit of the *ie* with its principle of trans-generational continuity, the village community enjoyed a high degree of stability. As long as individual households did not create offshoots, the number of households in the village remained the same. Households lacking a succeeding son or a daughter could preserve their existence by adopting a married couple to succeed to the household. And it was nearly impossible for outsiders to move into a village and build a new house because, as noted earlier, villages had attained their maximum populations by the latter half of the Tokugawa period and had become highly exclusive.

Villages throughout the country shared a common internal structure, the most prominent features of which were tightly knit neighborhood groups and well-defined social distinctions. The neighborhood group consisted of the several households near an older house of a village. While this group often consisted of a founding house and its branches, in many instances it was composed solely of those surrounding households that had been neighbors for several generations. In villages where a strong neighborhood group already existed, households established after the group's formation were often excluded even though they might be in physical proximity. The composition of the neighborhood group could be extremely complex, depending as it did upon the historical fact of residency as well as geographical location.

The neighborhood group was an important unit of village organization, providing a mechanism for cooperation that was essential to farming life. A typical function of the group, for example, was to put on funerals. While these neighborhood groups were referred to by various local terms in different regions, in many places they were called *kumi*. Their sizes depended on the size and history of the village and could range from seven or eight households to more than thirty. Every *kumi* had a head who acted as representative of the subgroup within the village community. The Tokugawa bakufu created a system of *gonin-gumi* (five-member *kumi*) as a tool for maintaining order in villages and towns, but where the neighborhood group was already entrenched, the *gonin-gumi* merely served as a formal endorsement of an organizational system that already existed.

In addition to their division into neighborhood groups, the *ie* of a village were differentiated, as noted earlier, into those with and without land, the categories of *honbyakushō* and *mizunomi*. These villagewide distinctions were not merely economic, however, but constituted basic status differences.

The distinctions affected one's access to essential resources. Most importantly, the water supply and drainage systems required for paddy cultivation were controlled by the village unit and regarded as communal property. Water distribution became a major social problem as available supplies came to be fully utilized by the early eighteenth century, and the *honbyakushō*, who participated in village administration and determined the holders of village office, had authority over this precious resource.

Ownership of farmland and kinship ties, however, were not enough to make a person a *honbyakushō*. The number of *honbyakushō* that could exist at any one time in a village was limited by a system of shares, or *kabu*. Each share belonged to an *ie*, not its individual members, but it could be bought and sold. Younger sons born into a *honbyakushō* household would not become *honbyakushō* themselves, even though they were bequeathed land and a house of their own by their father, unless they could acquire a *honbyakushō kabu*. Any household that did not have a *honbyakushō* share of its own was subordinate to one that did. It was barred from participating in village meetings and therefore had no say in the management of village affairs.

Whether *honbyakushō* or otherwise, however, every household in a village was ranked. Among *honbyakushō*, those whose household names appeared throughout the history of the village enjoyed an especially high status so long as they did not suffer severe setbacks. Village administrators were most often selected from among such households. Other households ranked below them, creating a readily perceivable status order within the village. A household's status was an important consideration when choosing marriage partners for one's offspring, especially since there was no particular prohibition against the marriage of paternal or maternal cousins, unlike in China where there was a strong social taboo against marriage between those with the same surname, i.e., patrilineal descent group.

In addition to being ranked socially, households were listed in village registers by their actual income. This practice, which remained in effect in most villages until fairly recently, appears to have stemmed from the Tokugawa policy of dividing among the village households responsibility for paying the annual taxes that were levied against the village as a unit. While this register listing did not always correspond exactly to the village social order, it highlighted the importance of rank in the community. Admittedly, the young men's association, which was found in villages throughout the country, was a village grouping based on age rather than *ie* status, but in communities where the household-based hierarchy was entrenched, this group had only a modest function.

All these forms of organization and ranking existed within the individual village. This kind of ranking by status was possible only in a closed community, hence organizational ties did not exist among neighboring villages, no matter how close they might be. Neither the neighborhood groups nor the top-ranking *ie* of one village had joint solidarity with their counterparts in another. Not even the young men's association of one village cooperated with that of another. In fact, they were often at odds with each other.

In most cases, a village's organization was self-contained. Water rights accrued in principle to the village unit, villagers' farmland was scattered in the immediate vicinity of their hamlet, and the forested hills and mountains that were the source of fertilizer and timber were considered to be the communal property of all village residents. From these characteristics it can be surmised that nearly all of a villager's social and economic activities were confined to the village. And, as has already been noted, with intensified pressure on the resource base in the latter half of the Tokugawa period, villages became highly exclusive, closing themselves off to outsiders (a trend that continued well into the twentieth century), which only served to make them all the more cohesive and isolated. Each village had its own rules and established its own regulations pertaining to community life and production. Marriage partners were for the most part chosen from within the village, and proposed marriages with someone from another village very often met with strong opposition from the young men's association.

With the advent of the Meiji period, many neighboring villages that had been autonomous in the Tokugawa period were consolidated into larger administrative "villages." This process has been repeated several times right up to the present, but villagers have continued to use the older arrangements of the highly independent village community with its own internal management, production systems, and clearcut social groups. By "village," Japanese generally mean the older, Tokugawa-period village, not the administratively formed village, and this is also the village community (*sonraku kyōdōtai*) referred to by historians and economists.

Yet the villages of other wet-rice cultivating countries, such as China, India, and the countries of southeast Asia, are not isolated in the same way as Japan's. Several villages might be interconnected by strong kinship ties or owe allegiance to a single large landholder. Major landholders from different villages might maintain close bonds while certain residents of one village might enjoy greater interaction with those of other villages than with their own village neighbors. Water rights were not necessarily defined by the village unit, a part of one village and that of another forming a single water cooperative, for example. The kind of status ranking among households seen in Japan is either given less significance or does not exist at all in countries lacking an *ie*-like system.

The *ie* system, its ranking of households, and the isolation of the village community are distinctive characteristics of Japanese society that were established in the Tokugawa period, particularly its latter half. These structural elements of communal life were also present in the communities of merchants, artisans, and samurai. Among merchants, the basic community was that organized around main households involved in the same line of business, while among the samurai, communities were vassal bands centered on their lord's household. The concept of *kabu* also existed in the merchant and samurai status groups. Merchant guilds were referred to as *kabunakama*, or shareholders of the same stock, and as in farming villages, the number of shares in a guild was limited. Merchants in a trade who lacked *kabu* could not belong to the guild. A similar system was in force among samurai with associations based, for example, on *gokenin-kabu* (shares belonging to direct vassals of the shogun) and *gōshi-kabu* (shares belonging to rural samurai). As has been noted earlier, samurai households were assigned stipends and prohibited from increasing their numbers.

The fact that shares were the property of the *ie* rather than the individual is important. Because of this, one person, the head of the *ie*, represented his household to the outside world, and his social function was based on his position, not on any individual qualifications he might have. For example, the Japanese village did not have assemblies of all adult males of the community, as is commonly seen in other societies. Instead, it was a rule that village meetings were to be attended by the household head, or by his successor if he was not available. If the household head had died and his successor was not yet of age, the household was represented by his widow.

The custom of one representative for each household became so entrenched that it is still followed in all farming villages and remains a strong undercurrent throughout Japanese society. I believe this has been a factor hindering the wife from playing a more significant role in society. Japanese society does not resist the active participation of women in its activities so much as it has difficulty seeing any need for women to become involved when their husbands are already taking part. A wife or widow is only expected to take part when her husband is ill or has died. The high value placed on the *ie* as an independent unit is also implicit in the general presumption that a widow will not revert to dependence upon the house of her birth or her brothers. From this perspective, it seems more appropriate to speak of the *ie* or household having priority in Japanese society than to categorize this pattern as a form of sexual discrimination.

4. Characteristics of the Samurai Community and the Emergence of a Vigorous Popular Culture

Living on stipends and without land of their own, samurai had only the most fragile of economic foundations. Though their social status was high, they did not enjoy an equivalent wealth, unlike the contemporary upper classes of Europe, India, and China. In these other societies, the upper classes were the elite and intelligentsia of their societies and hence the bearers of higher culture, where clerics occupied the highest positions, priests and monks in churches and monasteries had a long tradition of learning, but there was no similar trend within Japan's clergy, who had in any case been relegated to only a minor societal role by the Tokugawa period.

Bureaucratic officials, rather than clerics, were the traditional upper stratum in East Asia, and China and Korea, like Japan, lacked a tradition of academic guidance from religious communities. However, the scholar gentry, or *shenshi* of Ming and Ch'ing China and *yangban* of Yi-dynasty Korea, were also the scholars of their respective social orders. In contrast, while Tokugawa samurai might be able bureaucrats and administrators, they did not have the wherewithal to undertake scholastic and cultural pursuits or to act as patrons of learning and the arts.

Tokugawa samurai were a hereditary office-holding status group whereas the *shenshi* of China derived from various sectors of society, including merchants and farmers, and, in principle, could attain official positions only by passing civil service examinations. In Korea, the term *yangban* (literally "two orders") originated in the Koryŏ dynasty when officialdom was formally divided into civil and military categories. By the Yi dynasty, *yangban* were a single office-holding elite who dominated government. Later in the dynasty, not only the official who passed the civil service examination but also all members of his family and his patrilineal descendants were permitted to acquire *yangban* status. This naturally gave rise to a steady increase in their numbers. By some counts, the percentage of Korea's population that was of *yangban* status, which had been 8.3 percent in 1690, had mushroomed to an incredible 65.5 percent by 1858.

This situation in Korea contrasted sharply with that of Japan, where there was little fluctuation in the samurai population because a samurai household could only be inherited by the eldest son. Indeed, statistics compiled at the end of the Tokugawa period reveal that samurai still constituted only about 6 percent of the total population. Another difference between the two societies is that Korea did adopt the Chinese examination system whereas Japan did not. Still, the *yangban* had a near monopoly on the civil service examinations, and the competition among them for bureaucratic positions was never as fierce as it was in China. Even more so the examination system could not be applied in Japan, where it might upset the firmly entrenched hierarchy of the *ie*.

The *shenshi* of China normally attained positions by passing the civil service examinations, so they generally were well educated in the classics and constituted an intellectual class in which the term "bureaucrat" was synonymous with "scholar." In Korea, there were said to be three regular ways to become a *yangban*: by rendering meritorious service to the country, passing the civil service examinations, or excelling in scholarly pursuits. Scholarship was nearly as important as the ability to pass the examinations, and in fact, many *yangban* became well-known scholars without ever taking a position in the government.

In China and Korea, scholarship was thus a prerequisite of the upper status group. In Japan, while some samurai were famous as learned men, scholarship was not in and of itself an absolute requirement for them, among whom there simply was no strong tradition of letters. Confucianism was esteemed by the samurai for its ethical guidelines, but as a status group the samurai had little scholarly impact upon society. To make another comparison, in China and Korea military officials ranked considerably lower than those in the civil service, while in Japan the very terms *bushi* and *buke* convey military service into which civil service was incorporated. The failure of samurai to play a significant scholarly role in Tokugawa life may be one of the reasons why, in contrast to some other societies, pure scholarship has had difficulty finding a niche of importance in Japan.

On the other hand, because there was no specific social stratum assuming responsibility for the furtherance of scholarship, the arts, and culture in general, it was left to the common people to provide the driving force for their development. This is why Japan has such a strong tradition of popular culture. Ironically, the hereditary separation of samurai and peasants limited the economic power of the samurai elite while at the same time it unleashed the energies of the common people.

Tokugawa culture is said to be a culture of the townsmen. Edo, Kyoto, and Osaka were the primary centers of the cultural activity, but the wealth of the merchant class helped develop culture among both townspeople and, to some extent, farmers. In the visual arts, the theater, and in all aspects of dress, diet, and home, popular culture shows a remarkable degree of sophistication. Unlike the splendor and gorgeousness of the cultural elite of other societies, the popular culture of the Tokugawa period developed a delicate aesthetic marked by maximum expression with minimum resources that is the distinguishing characteristic of Japanese culture.

The breadth of commoner organization ensured that popular culture would be quickly disseminated. One feature of this breadth was the lack of boundaries between professionals and amateurs. In principle, for example, the performing arts were not the exclusive property of a professional elite but were open to any and all who might wish to participate. Members of the public had their favorites among professionals, who were readily available to their fans and patrons. There were many figures in every field of endeavor who cannot be clearly defined as professional or amateur. This situation served to raise the level of sophistication among common people, as indicated by the widespread enjoyment of the tea ceremony, flower arrangement, and other cultural pursuits. While the masters who taught these pursuits might be regarded as professionals, commoners pursued their interests for pleasure as much as for professional reasons. There were so many stages of development between amateur and top-level professional that distinguishing between the two is quite impossible. Among the masters there was usually greater interest in seeing who could collect the most pupils than in vying with each other for professional supremacy.

Rather than a professional realm within each field of cultural activity, there were segments of professionals who originated in particular masters and who in turn took on apprentices to form groups that were loosely associated through their masters. In this society, which frowned upon changing masters in mid-apprenticeship, the strong vertical relationship of master and pupil tended to isolate the group and re-enforce cohesion among its members, making it difficult for professionals of different schools and styles to associate, even though they might be working in the same field. This tradition makes it difficult for Japanese even today to form professional societies or accurately judge professional skills not only in traditional fields but also in the modern arts and music that have been adopted from Western culture. This is one clear-cut example of Tokugawa cultural norms remaining in force to this day.

Knowing these qualities of the Tokugawa period makes it easier to understand modern Japan's high literacy rate. Intellectual activity was not the exclusive privilege of an upper sector of the society. Most samurai, who were relatively well educated, were compelled to live in the castle towns, so it was necessary for village officials, who had to maintain various records of village activities and prepare reports for their local lords, to be able to read and write on their own. Many of these village records still exist, and they are written in an excellent hand, an indication of the high level of calligraphy found even among farmers. The *terakoya*, or local school that commonly operated in village temples, are well known, but there also were private schools in homes noted for their learning, in which reading and writing were taught to village youths.

If Tokugawa Japan had had an educated elite that monopolized all intellectual activity, as in many other pre-industrial societies, the common people would probably never have developed an interest in the written word. Had such an elite existed in Japan's rural districts, it would certainly have developed an exclusive lifestyle and community of its own that would have distanced it from the peasants and discouraged the common populace from mimicking its style or attempting to learn how to read and write. It is precisely because such an elite never developed in Japan that the common people were stimulated to develop a vigorous popular culture.

That the Tokugawa rural populace was not divided into landowners and laborers was of similar consequence. Tillers of the land were for the most part independent farmers, though in the latter half of the period a distinction between owner-farmers and tenant-farmers emerged. Some farmers were both owners and tenants, and even the poorest tenant farmer was very often involved in the management of his fields. Those who worked strictly as laborers were the exception rather than the rule as in other countries, and whether owner or tenant, the Japanese farmer had a vested interest in agriculture and its development. This also served to heighten the sophistication of the farming population at large.

Among merchants and artisans, too, there was no sharp distinction such as that maintained between guild masters and others in

Europe. A faithful apprentice could look forward to the day when his master would help him establish his own household. The close relationship of novice and master was a major incentive to development.

In conclusion, the Tokugawa social system encouraged those on the bottom to strive to better themselves and thereby raised the general level of sophistication of the masses. The policy of national education instituted after the Meiji period is usually cited to explain Japan's modern development, but a more important consideration, I believe, was the superior quality and high level of consciousness of the Tokugawa peasants, merchants, and artisans—the proposition, in other words, that they were an extremely well-trained people.

(Translation by Susan Murata)

Historical Dates: A Chronology

(Only periods, eras, shogun, and historical events mentioned in the text are included.)

Yayoi	300 B.C.–A.D. 300
Nara	710–84
Heian	794–1185
Kamakura	1185–1333
Muromachi	1334–1567
(Warring States	1467–1567)
Tokugawa	1568–1867
Meiji	1867–1911

Year periods (nengo)

Kan'ei	1624–43
Keian	1648–51
Meireki	1655–57
Genroku	1688–1703
Kyōhō	1716–35
Kampo	1741–43
Enkyo	1744–47
Kansei	1789–1800
Bunka	1804–17
Bunsei	1818–29
Tempo	1830–43

Shogun

Oda Nobunaga	1567–1582
Toyotomi Hideyoshi	1582–98

Tokugawa

1st Ieyasu	1603–5
2nd Hidetada	1605–23
3rd Iemitsu	1623–51
4th Ietsuna	1651–80
5th Tsunayoshi	1680–1709
6th Ienobu	1709–12
7th Ietsugu	1712–16
8th Yoshimune	1716–45
9th Ieshige	1745–60
10th Ieharu	1760–86
11th Ienari	1787–1837

Keian Proclamation	1649
Meireki Fire	1657
Kyōhō Reforms	1716–87
Tanuma era	1767–87
Kansei Reforms	1787–93
Tempo Reforms	1841–43

Time scale: 500 B.C. — A.D. 500 — 1000 — 1500 — 1600 — 1700 — 1800 — 1900

An Equivalency Chart

for Measures and Currency Mentioned in the Text

Capacity		Metric System	U.S. System
shō		1.80 liters	1.63 quarts
koku	100 *shō*	180.39 liters	5.11 bushels
Length			
ken		1.81 meters	5.96 feet
ri		3.92 kilometers	2.44 miles
Area			
chō		0.99 hectare	

Currency*

Gold			
shu			
bu	4 *shu*		
ryō	4 *bu* = 16 *shu*		
Silver (weight measures)			
momme		3.75 grams	0.13 oz.
kan	1000 *momme*	3.75 kilograms	8.2 lbs.
Zeni coins			
mon			
kan	1000 mon		

*Gold, silver, and *zeni* were three independent units of currency. The bakufu established the following as desirable exchange rates:

one *ryō* = 50 *momme* (silver)

one *ryō* = 4000 *mon* (*zeni*).

After the Genroku period, one *ryō* equaled 60 *momme* of silver. The price of one *koku* of rice was one *ryō*.

Contributors

Tatsurō AKAI, Professor at Nara University of Education, is a specialist in the history of Tokugawa Painting.

Masakatsu GUNJI, a specialist in kabuki, is Professor Emeritus of Waseda University and Trustee of the National Theatre of Japan.

Hidenobu JINNAI is Professor of Architectural History at Hosei University.

Katsuhisa MORIYA, Professor of Social and Cultural History at Mukogawa Women's University, is a member of the Kyoto prefectural and municipal councils for the protection of cultural properties.

Satoru NAKAMURA, Professor of Economics at Kyoto University, is a specialist in industrial history.

Chie NAKANE, Professor Emeritus of University of Tokyo, is a social anthropologist specializing in Asian societies.

Shinzaburō ŌISHI, a specialist in the social, political, and economic history of the Tokugawa period, is Professor at Gakushuin University and Director of the Tokugawa Institute for the History of Forestry.

Yōtarō SAKUDŌ, Professor Emeritus of Osaka University, is Professor of Japanese Economic History at Kinki University.

Tsuneo SATŌ, a specialist in agricultural history, is Associate Professor at Tsukuba University.

Conrad TOTMAN is Professor of History at Yale University.

Index

actors: critiques of, 196, 199–200, 202; employment of, 195–96, 203; "ghetto" system for, 194; ranking system among, 195, 200–201; social status of, 194, 203

Adams, William (Miura Anjin), 26, 29

administrative structure, 28–31, 35

adoption practices, 217, 220

agricultural development, 62–73, 230

agricultural production, commercial, 72–75, 84

agricultural technology, 66–73, 213

agricultural tools, 67, 69–70

agricultural treatises (*nōsho*), 75–80

Akechi Mitsuhide, 12, 14

alternate attendance system (*sankin kōtai*), 23–24, 85, 102, 142

Andō Shigenaga, 29

Arai Hakuseki, 33

Arima Harunobu, 27

Arima Ujinori, 33

art exhibitions: contemporary (*shoga-kai*), 175–76; of temple treasures (*kai-chō*), 176–77

Ashikaga shogunate, 11–12, 16

bakuhan taisei. See political structure

banking, 152, 153

Besshi Copper Mine, 155, 156

book lenders, 117, 189

brokers (*nakagai*), 148, 205

Buddhism, 12, 99, 114, 215

budget examination office (*kanjō gimmi-yaku*), 35

buke sho-hatto (laws pertaining to the military houses), 23

bushi. See samurai

cadastral surveys, 14, 24, 38–39, 43

cash crops, 72–74

castle towns, 38, 85, 104, 124, 147, 148–49, 165, 214

censorship, 182, 183

census-taking, 39–40

Chaya Shirōjirō, 28–29, 150

checkpoints (*sekisho*), 13

China, 82, 83, 226–27

chōnin. See townspeople

Christianity, 12, 25–26, 27–28, 40

cities, three major, 97–103, 105, 165. *See also* Edo; Kyoto; Osaka

classes, segregation of social, 4–5, 17, 38, 72, 165, 213–14, 228

commerce, development of, 13, 14, 44, 82, 85–86, 95, 148, 165

commercial distribution system, 75, 83, 84, 85, 91

communications, 59–62, 105–13

community resources, 47–49

Confucianism, 228

copper smelting, 154, 155

cottage industry, 87–88, 90

cotton industries and trade, 73, 81, 82–83, 86–91, 93–96

councillors: great (*tairō*), 29: junior (*wakadoshiyori*), 29; senior (*rōjū*) 29, 32–33, 35; senior fiscal affairs (*katte-gakari rōjū*), 32, 33, 34

currencies, domain-issued, 148

currency, introduction of, 14

daimyo: constable (*shugo*), 11–12; Edo estates of, 103, 142–43; *fudai*, 22, 32; loans to, 151–52, 153; place of in political structure, 22–24, 105

235